WATERFALL HIKES IN THE CANADIAN ROCKIES VOLUME 1

STEVE TERSMETTE

WATERFALL *in the Canadian Rockies* HIKES

BANFF · KANANASKIS · CROWSNEST · WATERTON · YOHO · BC ROCKIES

Volume One

RMB

First Edition, Reprint 2025

For information on purchasing bulk quantities of this book, or to obtain media excerpts or invite the author to speak at an event, please visit rmbooks.com and select the "Contact" tab.

RMB | Rocky Mountain Books Ltd.
rmbooks.com
@rm_books
facebook.com/rmbooks

Cataloguing data available from Library and Archives Canada
ISBN 9781771606165 (softcover)
ISBN 9781771606172 (electronic)

All photographs are by Steve Tersmette unless otherwise noted.

Printed and bound in China

We would like to also take this opportunity to acknowledge the Traditional Territories upon which we live and work. In Calgary, Alberta, we acknowledge the Niitsítapi (Blackfoot) and the people of the Treaty 7 region in Southern Alberta, which includes the Siksika, the Piikuni, the Kainai, the Tsuut'ina and the Stoney Nakoda First Nations, including Chiniki, Bearpaw, and Wesley First Nations. The City of Calgary is also home to Métis Nation of Alberta, Region III. In Victoria, British Columbia, we acknowledge the Traditional Territories of the Lkwungen (Esquimalt, and Songhees), Malahat, Pacheedaht, Scia'new, T'Sou-ke and W̱SÁNEĆ (Pauquachin, Tsartlip, Tsawout, Tseycum) peoples.

We acknowledge the financial support of the Government of Canada through the Canada Book Fund and the Canada Council for the Arts, and of the province of British Columbia through the British Columbia Arts Council and the Book Publishing Tax Credit.

DISCLAIMER

The actions described in this book may be considered inherently dangerous activities. Individuals undertake these activities at their own risk. The information put forth in this guide has been collected from a variety of sources and is not guaranteed to be completely accurate or reliable. Many conditions and some information may change owing to weather and numerous other factors beyond the control of the authors and publishers. Individuals or groups must determine the risks, use their own judgment, and take full responsibility for their actions. Do not depend on any information found in this book for your own personal safety. Your safety depends on your own good judgment based on your skills, education, and experience.

It is up to the users of this guidebook to acquire the necessary skills for safe experiences and to exercise caution in potentially hazardous areas. The authors and publishers of this guide accept no responsibility for your actions or the results that occur from another's actions, choices, or judgments. If you have any doubt as to your safety or your ability to attempt anything described in this guidebook, do not attempt it.

Contents

	Foreword	7
	Introduction	9
CHAPTER 1	Banff National Park – Banff to Lake Louise	21
CHAPTER 2	Kananaskis Country	45
CHAPTER 3	Southern Rockies and Crowsnest Pass	121
CHAPTER 4	Waterton Lakes National Park	147
CHAPTER 5	British Columbia Rockies	167
CHAPTER 6	Yoho National Park to Golden	201
CHAPTER 7	More To Explore	241
	Author's Picks	243
	Endnotes	245
	References	247
	Online Resources	249
	Park Visitor Centres	249
	Index of Waterfalls	251

Diving, jumping,
or kayaking into
the pools or creek
below Sutherland
Falls is extremely
dangerous.
Most people are
hurt.
You assume all
liability for your
actions should
you attempt it.
BRITISH
COLUMBIA

Foreword

My love for hiking began in 2005 when I first moved to the Rockies from eastern Canada. The mountains inspired a "go big or go home" attitude in me, and a desire to push my physical limits as a way of exploring both farther and higher. Then, nine years ago my husband and I started a family. This required a considerable amount of adapting, and objectives in the outdoors became much simpler (primarily: get out the front door). Then there's a phase every family goes through when kids are too big to carry but too little to walk very far. It was around this time in my life as a parent that I began to seek out shorter hikes we could actually *enjoy*. It was a major bonus if there was a "reward" along the way, like a waterfall.

This all goes to say that I could have used this book when I first became a parent. Yet, as chance would have it, *Waterfall Hikes in the Canadian Rockies* is arriving on my doorstep just as my youngest daughter is ready to hike on her own two feet.

The author of this book, Steve Tersmette, first entered my orbit back in 2016 when he applied to be an ambassador for a Rockies-based media company I had co-founded. It quickly became apparent that he was as reliable for compiling local event information for me as he was with peddling copies of the *Canadian Rockies Annual* – tasks he did for five years without missing a beat. Steve also wrote a feature article for the magazine, which from his first pitch to final publication was a process drawn out over several years. Through all of my interactions with him, I was struck by his sense of commitment, passion and professionalism. It's those qualities in Steve that I know make him the perfect writer for a book that requires attention to detail, and a "guide" who is in it for the long haul. In browsing the list of hikes included in this book it's clear he has left no trail-accessible waterfall unexplored.

What readers hold in their hands is a unique contribution to the library of guidebooks created for the Canadian Rockies. This mountain range is known for world-class hiking and scenery that makes the hard work worth the climbing. But not all hikers have the time, ability or desire to reach these loftier views. Yet, where there are mountains there are also waterfalls – wonders of nature often found closer to the valley bottom. They are some of the region's most stunning – and refreshing – features. Waterfalls are the perfect objective for families, hikers with less fitness or mobility, visitors on a quick timeline and photographers looking for artistic inspiration.

Waterfall Hikes in the Canadian Rockies is one I'll be keeping handy, not only at this stage of my life but as my kids grow up as well. Because no waterfall stays the same, even from one day to the next, certainly not from season to season. These are hikes you can do again and again. It's always a privilege to have the opportunity to marvel at such a powerful and ever-changing force in the mountain landscape.

—Meghan J. Ward, outdoor, travel and adventure author

Introduction

I was that kid: face pressed against the back window of the family van searching for roadside cascades as we made our way west for an annual summer camping trip. Every single little stream that poured out of the mountains gave rise to a backseat celebration before we reset our eyes, hoping to catch another fleeting glimpse of the next waterfall. Not much has changed. I am still that kid, although now, as the driver, it is slightly more dangerous to be on the lookout for waterfalls while negotiating the busy motorways that snake their way through Canada's mountain ranges.

The captivating force that attracts people to waterfalls is nothing less than magical. From long silvery threads, to small hypnotic cascades delicately bubbling over rocks and tree limbs, to the deafening roar of a swollen river rocketing over a cliff, people go to great lengths to seek out these natural wonders. Waterfalls provide an escape, a solace for the mind while soothing the soul. And, they are pretty things to photograph.

The purpose of this book is to provide a simple, family-friendly hiking guide as an aid in locating and accessing the spectacular waterfalls in the southern Canadian Rockies. This comprehensive guide details nearly one hundred waterfalls in the Alberta and BC Rockies encompassing an area north of the United States border to Lake Louise and includes the iconic national and provincial parks that straddle the Continental Divide.

After completion of the first instalment in this series, *Waterfall Hikes in Southern British Columbia*, my wife and children operated under the assumption that they would receive a respite from the relentless hiking and waterfall exploration. They were terribly mistaken! Thank you to my far better half, Katie and our kids, Hanna and Jasper, for both their enthusiasm and patience while we continued to set our sights on the numerous hikes that peppered the Canadian Rockies.

I owe a debt of gratitude to Adam Sawyer (Professional Gentleman of Leisure) for inspiring me to get writing and for the idea of creating these guidebooks. Thanks to my good friend Robin and sister-in-law Tawny for reading and rereading draft after draft of both this edition and its predecessor. To my parents for instilling in me a deep-seated and insatiable love for the mountains, hiking and the outdoors. To my many adventuring partners over the years who continue to fuel my passion and whose own accomplishments never cease to amaze. To Meghan Ward for giving me a shot and for enthusiastically writing the foreword for this book. And finally, to Don Gorman and the team at Rocky Mountain Books for their support for this project. Their guidance, professionalism and flexibility have been critical for bringing these books to fruition. Thank you!

The Covid-19 pandemic added a litany of challenges in putting this book together, becoming a moving target with travel restrictions and closures. I owe my dear ol' dad a big high-five for helping out with the research and trail descriptions in the Kananaskis area. His motivation and availability were invaluable.

Writing this book has not only kept our family hiking and exploring together but also filled a very obvious void in the guidebook genre: kid-friendly exploration. Oh, and did I mention it's about waterfalls?!

Using this guidebook

This book provides a comprehensive, simple and family-friendly hiking guide that will assist readers in locating and accessing the many spectacular waterfalls in the Canadian Rockies. While every measure has been taken to ensure accurate driving and hiking directions, even the most competent of writers have mashed buttons on their keyboard at some point. If you find an error, please inform the author and publisher so that potential future printings can be updated.

Are there more waterfalls to explore? Yes, but for an assortment of reasons, many were omitted. First and foremost, I wanted to produce a responsible and ethical guide that did not encourage off-trail use, especially in the national and provincial parks. For safety's sake, a number of hikes were omitted due to excessive bushwhacking or unsafe river crossings. Lastly, I did not want to promote hikes where the access might be infringing on private property. I hope you as the user will employ these same ethics and standards in your travels. So let's get to it!

Trail difficulty ratings

You'll find a variety of trails described here, from five-minute walks from your car door to destinations that may require a night out in a tent. Difficulty ratings are highly subjective and depend on the reader's experience, comfort and fitness level. The hikes are rated with families in mind, including younger children that can walk a hiking trail on their own. My kids were eight and ten years old during the construction of this guidebook and therefore serve as the measuring stick for hike durations and difficulty. Read trail descriptions carefully to assess whether a particular hike may or may not be within your wheelhouse. The reader is responsible for assessing their own capabilities and conditions to ensure they are selecting hikes suited to their skill level.

Trail difficulty can vary depending on conditions, time of day, season, weather, precipitation and temperature. Hike at your own risk and make smart decisions based on your skill level and experience. Even hiking on well-used trails has its hazards such as roots, rocks and mud. Another thing to keep in mind is that waterfalls tend to get things pretty wet. Spray can travel for dozens of metres, making the area around waterfalls slippery and dangerous, even with good footwear. The author and publisher assume no responsibility for your decisions in the outdoors.

- EASY Less than half a day. One-way distance of less than 4 km or 1.5 hours on well-defined and well-marked trails with relatively minor elevation gains.
- MODERATE A half-day to a full-day hike. One-way distance between 4 km and 8 km or 2–3 hours with modest elevation gains or undulating terrain. May include shorter hikes with sustained steep or narrow sections as well as shallow creek crossings.
- DIFFICULT Requires a long day or an overnight trip. Potential challenges may include difficult-to-follow trails, creek crossings, sturdy elevation gain or steep terrain. Pay careful attention to trail descriptions.

Hiking times and distances provided are one-way

Getting there

While many trails are readily accessible from a highway, some areas, especially in British Columbia, are accessible only by forestry service roads (FSRs). Some forestry roads are well-maintained for industrial or recreational interests, while others fall into disrepair or go years without the benefit of maintenance. Access difficulty is described for a two wheel drive vehicle. If a four wheel drive vehicle is recommended or required, it is noted in the driving directions and classified as difficult.

- EASY Access and parking via a paved road.
- MODERATE Access and parking via well-maintained FSR or other unpaved road. No concerns with use of a two wheel drive vehicle.
- DIFFICULT Access via unmaintained backcountry roads. Four-wheel drive may be recommended or even necessary. Pay close attention to driving directions and noted hazards.

It should be stated that our two family vehicles had minor discrepancies in their odometer readings between waypoints. This may result in slight variances in the actual distance versus the information provided. As much as possible, a landmark or reference is provided with each distance to ensure access, directions and descriptions are as accurate as possible.

SAFETY ON RESOURCE ROADS

Forestry Service Roads are typically one- or two-lane gravel roads built for industrial purposes and used to access natural resources in remote areas. They are used primarily by vehicles engaged in forestry, mining, oil and gas or agriculture operations. In addition to industrial access, resource roads are used by the general public and commercial operators, such as backcountry skiing or hunting businesses, lodges or accommodations. FSRs serve as crucial links for rural communities and access to recreational opportunities.

As they are not built or maintained to the same standards as public highways, resource roads can be rough with narrow gravel surfaces. There may be roadside brush limiting visibility, soft shoulders, more curves, tighter curves and much steeper road grades than encountered on public highways. These roads do not necessarily have signs or barriers identifying all hazards or dangers. Common dangers include large industrial vehicles; high traffic volume; poor visibility due to brush, alignment, dust, fog or smoke; passing or being passed on narrow roads; changing road surface conditions; weather; wildlife and so forth. A radio is recommended on resource roads that are actively being using for forestry or mining. It is also a good idea to drive with your headlights on to improve your own visibility.

Resource road users must drive with an abundance of caution at all times!

Waterfall safety

Waterfalls are incredibly beautiful but can be incredibly dangerous. In this age of smart phones, social media and the selfie, more and more people are taking risks to get The Shot. Most of these safety tips should be common sense, but you know what they say about common sense!

1. Stay on established trails. Deviating from trails not only destroys vegetation but undeveloped terrain can be highly unstable. Hiking off trail may put others below you at risk, as soil or rocks can be knocked loose.
1. Don't swim or cross creeks above waterfalls. One wrong step or a strong current can take you from the top of a waterfall to the bottom in a split second. Some locations have designated viewing areas or fencing to restrict access to dangerous or unstable areas. These fences, guards and railings are in place for your safety.
1. Don't. Jump. Off. Waterfalls. Period. There are so many factors to consider including water depth, currents and rocks or debris below the surface. Pools can change year to year, even season to season, with runoff carrying rocks, logs and debris downstream. Water levels change seasonally and can also be affected by rainfall. Never assume a pool is safe. People have died at some of the waterfalls in this very book. Again: do not jump off waterfalls.
1. Avoid rocks and climbing at the base of waterfalls. Spray and mist from waterfalls make rocks and trails slippery, especially near the pools at the base of falls.
1. Watch for streamflow advisories (usually posted during spring runoff). Water can rise up over established trails or creek crossings. The higher volume in the spring creates fast-moving water, debris flows and bank erosion. Streamflow can increase as much as 15 times the normal volume, especially during periods of rapid melting, after rainstorms and high runoff.
1. Wear appropriate footwear. A good pair of hiking shoes or light hiking boots are a must for most routes. Trails may be slippery, especially as you approach waterfalls. If you need to cross a creek, best to have a pair of water shoes or a full-coverage sandal that can be secured to your foot at the top and back (read: flip flops are not appropriate footwear).

Hiking with kids

One of the biggest hurdles we faced as new parents was to find a variety of short, easy hikes to take our kids on. Most of the hiking guides currently in publication describe breathtaking vistas, shimmering mountain lakes and, without a doubt, some of the highest value scenery in the world. Many are lengthy day hikes. Some involve backcountry camping. Most include substantial elevation gain. Like many parents we transitioned from baby wraps to kid carriers to hand holding or to simply carrying kids in our arms. Some days were hugely successful while others were nothing short of torturous. The one thing we craved was to have more options to transition our kids off of our backs and onto their feet.

As a father of two I can say my biggest fault was expecting too much from my kids at too young an age. Fortunately, I did not completely break them. So, having learned the lesson myself, the most important wisdom I can pass along is this: be patient. When patience fails, however, here are a few tips to keep kids keen on hiking.

1. Make sure they're comfortable. It might mean bringing an extra jacket, pants, toques, mitts, socks, hats and undies. If a child isn't comfortable, don't expect them to hike with you.
2. Arm yourself with games to play such as I Spy, 20 Questions, riddles or just plain old silly facts and useless information. If a child isn't interested, don't expect them to hike with you.
3. Bring snacks and take breaks. Yes, I agree that being asked to take a break five minutes from the car is annoying and I'll leave it up to you to decide how reasonable the stop-for-a-snack request is, but if a child is hungry, don't expect them to hike with you.
4. Pick hikes that are within your kids' ability and comfort level. While carefully pushing my own children in an effort to help them grow, I will never advocate for doing something unsafe. There is also a discernible difference between comfort and safety. If a child feels unsafe, don't expect them to hike with you.
5. Take a camera. No, not for you. For the kids. Taking photos gives kids a sense of purpose and achievement. They can see the results immediately; it gives them a task and keeps their interest up. Celebrate the little victories whether it's as simple as taking a good photo or completing an easy hike. If a child doesn't feel like they've accomplished something, don't expect them to hike to with you.
6. Bring candy.

My children asked if they could provide some commentary from their perspective as well. So, in no particular order:

1. "Just because an adult thinks they're right, doesn't mean they're right. Didn't you bring a map?"
2. "We're lost, aren't we."
3. "Ummmm, dad ... kids don't really like bushwhacking."
4. "If we ask 'Are we there yet?,' just say we're close."
5. Bring candy.

PHOTO BY HANNA TERSMETTE

Leave No Trace

If you're like me, finding garbage in the backcountry puts me in a bad mood. And it's not just the garbage. I despise braided trails and shortcuts on switchbacks. I shudder when I happen upon random fire rings, and cairns without purpose. The Leave No Trace principles are critical in preserving the outdoor experience, and it is never too early to familiarize yourself with backcountry etiquette. If you consider yourself a pro in this regard, pass your knowledge along to teach the next generation of trail stewards!

THE SEVEN PRINCIPLES OF LEAVE NO TRACE

1. Plan ahead and prepare
2. Travel and camp on durable surfaces
3. Dispose of waste properly
4. Leave what you find
5. Minimize campfire impacts
6. Respect wildlife
7. Be considerate of other visitors

For more information visit leavenotrace.ca.

It is important to note that dogs must be leashed when hiking in all national and provincial parks. If your furry friends are tagging along for the hike, keep them leashed and under control at all times, and pick up after them (including disposing of the bag afterwards).

Wildlife

What would a guidebook be without speaking about wildlife? Let's face it, this is their backyard and we are guests, so give wildlife a wide berth. You can encounter all sorts of woodland creatures at any time and without warning, including everything from ground squirrels and deer to porcupines, rattlesnakes, foxes and bears. While the discussion about an animal such as a chipmunk is limited mostly to "don't feed the chipmunks," the pep talk on an apex predator such as a grizzly bear is a slightly different chat. It is also one that warrants precious space on paper.

Bears

While bears generally tend to avoid people, encounters do happen. The best preparation is knowledge: knowing how to avoid an encounter and knowing what to do in case of an encounter. Avoiding one altogether is the best idea. Take precautions such as travelling in larger groups, making lots of noise and keeping dogs on leash. Watch for fresh markings such as scat, tracks, overturned rocks and torn up logs. If you come across a dead animal, leave the area and report the carcass to a conservation officer or Parks staff. Carry bear spray, keep it easily accessible and know how to use it.

If you do encounter a bear, stay calm and have your bear spray ready to use. Speak to the bear in a firm voice. Make yourself appear as large as possible and back away slowly. Stay together in your group and pick up small children. If you're carrying a backpack, leave it on. Either wait for the bear to move on, give it a wide berth or slowly back away and leave the area. Report encounters to a conservation officer or Parks staff.

If the bear escalates its behaviour and charges, be prepared and use your bear spray. If the bear attacks and makes contact, play dead by lying on your stomach with your hands over the back of your neck. However, if the attack continues for more than two minutes, fight back. We recommend reading other resources on bear safety. The more knowledge you have about bear behaviour, avoiding encounters and using bear spray, the better prepared you will be in bear country. Parks Canada and WildSafeBC both have excellent information available for free (see the Online Resources list at the back of the book).

As a wise co-captain of the Waterton Shoreline Cruise Company once said: "Make some noise. This is their home. The least we can do is ring the doorbell to let them know we're here."

Mosquitos

Mossies, bloodsuckers, vampires ... merchants of death!! In addition to being hugely annoying, these insects can make being in the outdoors aggravating in certain locations. Even at elevations where their very presence may be confusing, they are looking for a meal and will certainly find you. If you're outdoors in the Canadian Rockies, you are in mosquito country. Even if you personally feel you can tough it out, for the sake of your children, bring bug spray.

ADDITIONAL NOTES ON WILDLIFE

The primary objective when it comes to wildlife conflicts while recreating outdoors is to reduce the opportunities for encounters altogether. The best thing you can do is arm yourself with knowledge. Know what types of wildlife you can expect to come across and how to deal with a direct encounter. Be vigilant with food and garbage. Animals that are fed become habituated to human interactions and the chances of conflicts with animals become much higher.

Logistics and planning

It's important to note that the majority of these hikes are located within a national park of Canada or in Alberta's Kananaskis Country, where a pass is required to stop, park and utilize parks infrastructure. Passes can be purchased at park gates at the entry points to Jasper, Banff, Yoho, Kootenay and Waterton national parks. They are also available at visitor centres and through some online outlets.

Frontcountry camping locations generally offer a limited number of first-come, first-served sites, although reservations are highly recommended to avoid disappointment. Backcountry camping requires a permit and reservations in all national parks and most provincial parks, usually obtained at the time of booking. Random camping is generally not permitted unless on Crown land, with some exceptions in provincial wildland areas.

For park pass, camping and reservation information, contact the appropriate powers that be. We have compiled a useful list of contacts and resources in the back of this guidebook.

Hiking seasons

Many trails in this book are accessible year-round and each season brings with it a unique beauty as well as a different set of conditions and hazards.

In the springtime, especially later in the season, streams will become swollen with runoff from the melting snowpack. Spring is generally the rainy season in western Canada as well which can cause unexpected surges water levels. Expect damp, muddy or even snow-covered trails. With swift streamflow and high water levels, creek crossings can be dangerous or even impossible. Stay back from banks as fast moving water can cause them to erode and potentially slough without warning. It is advisable to pack warm layers and extra socks.

In the summertime, the streams begin to return to their normal rate of flow. The summer months bring hot temperatures and insects. Pack plenty of water, even on short hikes. Remember your sunscreen and bug repellent.

Autumn is a beautiful time to tackle waterfalls hikes. The change in season brings a rich pallet of colour to the scene, in addition to cooler and insect-free days. These days also shorter and can cool off quickly. Frost may be present on trails early in the day and snow is a common occurrence, even in September. Daytime temperatures can still get quite hot. Remember to pack layers, an extra jacket and even a headlamp, especially if you're starting a hike later in the day.

Winter brings the most dramatic change to the landscape. Many waterfalls will partially freeze while others will ice over completely. When hiking in the wintertime it is critically important to wear warm clothes, even on sunny days, as hypothermia can set in quickly. Wear a toque and warm gloves; an extra pair is a great idea. Expect trails to be snowbound and slippery. Hiking poles and micro-spikes for footwear are strongly recommended. For longer day hikes you may want to consider packing a warm drink in a thermos. When hiking in the winter it is also important to consider the avalanche risk in some locations. If you are in doubt as to whether or not a route is safe or do not have the appropriate training, it would be best to avoid the area altogether.

A quick note on waterfall names

For the most part, the names of waterfalls given are their official name as recognized on mapping sources such as Natural Resources Canada, National or Provincial Parks Maps, or a published name as per other literature and guides. If there is no official or recognized name to reference, the name of the watercourse is referenced as well as a notation that this is an unofficial name. Some waterfalls have been christened with a variety of names that may be used locally rather than officially. To avoid confusion, where waterfalls have been referred to by more than one name, their alias will be listed in the description.

Credits

All photographs are by the author except where noted otherwise.

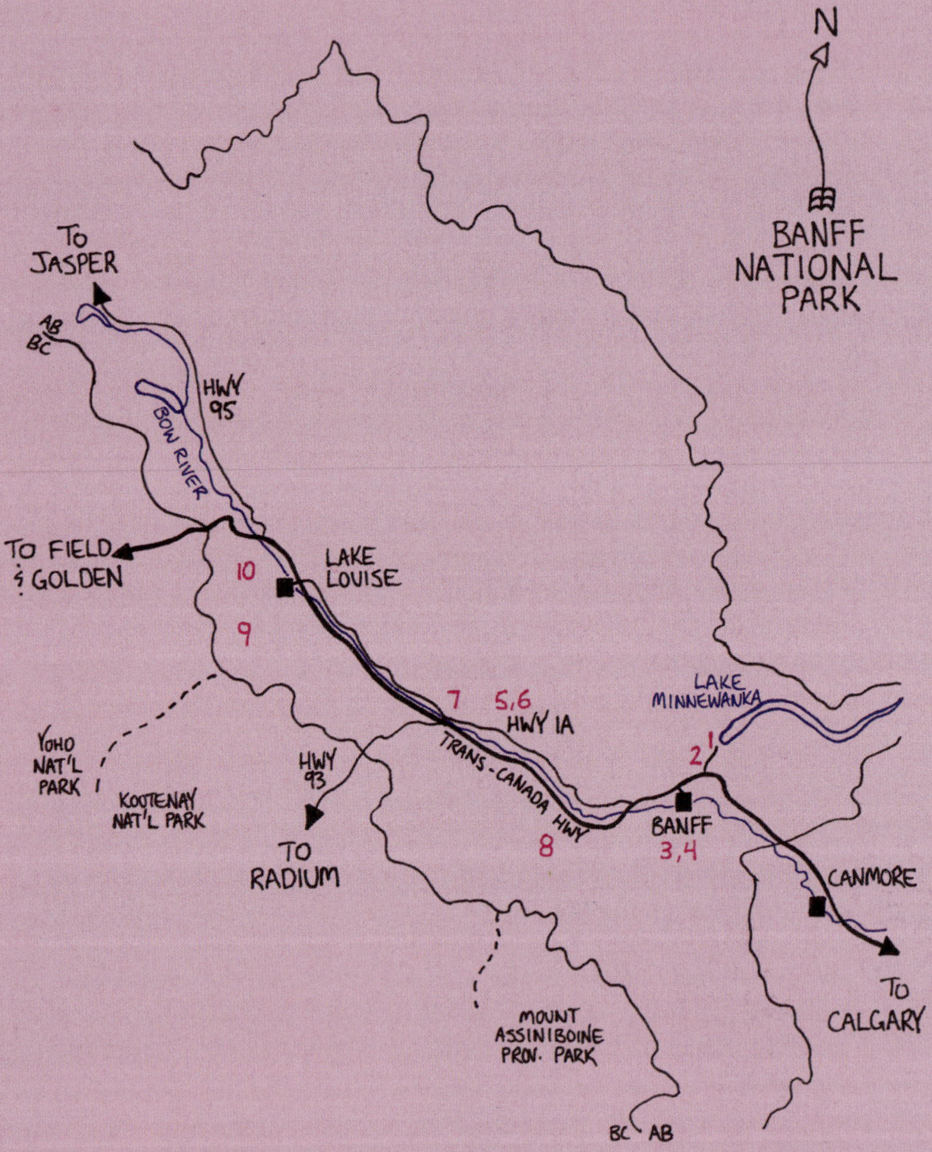
N
BANFF NATIONAL PARK
TO JASPER
AB
BC
HWY 95
BOW RIVER
TO FIELD & GOLDEN
10
LAKE LOUISE
9
7
5,6
HWY 1A
LAKE MINNEWANKA
1
2
YOHO NAT'L PARK
KOOTENAY NAT'L PARK
HWY 93
TO RADIUM
TRANS-CANADA HWY
8
BANFF
3,4
CANMORE
TO CALGARY
MOUNT ASSINIBOINE PROV. PARK
BC AB

CHAPTER 1

Banff National Park – Banff to Lake Louise

Banff National Park was the first established in this fine country and is the crown jewel of the Canadian National Parks system. The town of Banff is to Canada as Venice is to Italy or Santorini is to Greece: picturesque beyond compare and a natural attraction for visitors. In fact, the town was created solely with tourism in mind: with access to some of the most spectacular mountain scenery in the entire solar system, it is not difficult to see why people from around the galaxy flock to see these towering peaks, dazzling glaciers and sparkling lakes of Canada's flagship national park.

Waterfalls are in great abundance here as towering walls of stone rise from the valley floors, many being capped with glaciers and snowfields that feed streams and creeks year-round. Here you'll find some of the most accessible hiking in the country, with numerous trailheads located along the Trans-Canada Highway. This makes Banff an ideal venue for families with small children or time constraints to take in the many amazing short hikes with little effort or organization required.

Banff National Park can be accessed from five directions:

1. The southeast via the Trans-Canada Highway from Calgary and Canmore
2. The west via Highway 93S from Radium and Kootenay National Park
3. The northwest via the Trans-Canada Highway from Golden, Field and Yoho National Park
4. The north via Highway 93N from Jasper and Jasper National Park
5. The east via Highway 11 from Red Deer and Nordegg

All vehicles stopping in the national park are required to display a park pass, which can be purchased at the park gates, visitor centres and some online sites. Most frontcountry and many backcountry campsites require reservations. All backcountry campsites require permits as well as the vehicle pass.

Visit pc.gc.ca/en/pn-np/ab/banff;
Banff: 403-762-1550 Lake Louise: 403-522-3833

1. *Tessa Falls*

LOCATION: Banff National Park
DRIVING DIFFICULTY: EASY
HIKING DIFFICULTY: EASY
HIKING DISTANCE: 700 m
HIKING TIME: 25 min.

"Hidden treasures" and "Banff National Park" are generally not grouped together in phrases or descriptions. Yes, Banff has an abundance of treasure but very little of it is hidden. Tessa Falls, though, has somehow managed to avoid earning a reputation as a "must see" within a region full of "must sees." This is a beautiful spot with easy access but is relatively unknown amidst the wealth of spectacular, yet crowded, hiking destinations.

Driving directions

From the town of Banff, drive east on the Trans-Canada Highway for 3 km to the Lake Minnewanka / Banff Avenue interchange. Exit the highway, looping beneath the overpass, and follow signs for the Lake Minnewanka Scenic Drive. Continue for 5 km to a small, unsigned parking area on the right, 1 km before the main Lake Minnewanka parking lot.

Hiking directions

From the parking area, walk over the berm to pick up a lightly used trail and follow it for 600 m to the south. A short, steep descent then leads to the Cascade River. Once near the river, head to the right for a short distance and Tessa Falls will be visible across the waterway.

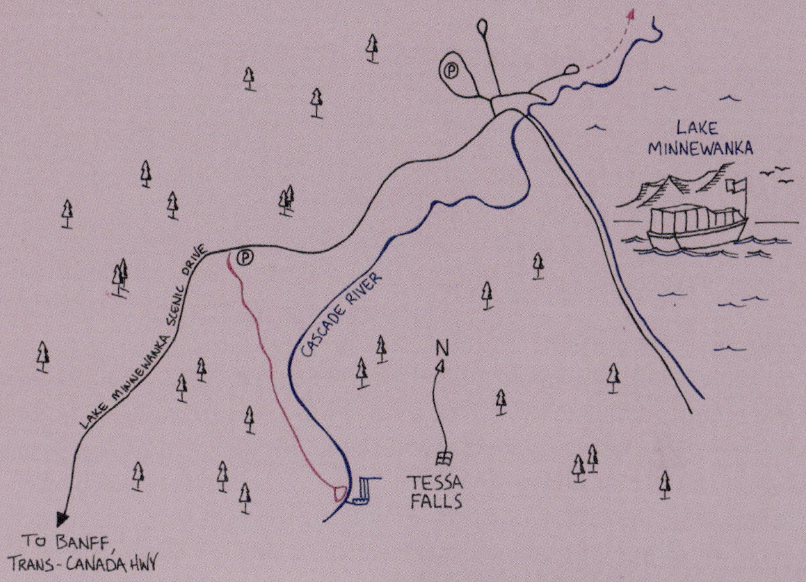

More to explore: Lake Minnewanka

Lake Minnewanka is a very popular day-use area year-round with many activities located at the lake. There is a picnic area with cooking shelter and even a café. If you don't have your own canoe, kayak or paddleboard those are available to rent at the docks. There are hiking trails leaving the parking area in all directions including to Stewart Canyon, Devil's Gap and Two Jack Lake. This is also prime real estate for wintertime activities such as snowshoeing, cross country skiing and even ice skating if your timing is right.

2. Cascade Falls

LOCATION: Banff National Park
DRIVING DIFFICULTY: EASY
HIKING DIFFICULTY: EASY
HIKING DISTANCE: 500 m
HIKING TIME: 15 min.

Shortly after crossing through the park gate, the hulking mass of Cascade Mountain quickly fills the windshield. On the lower flanks of the mountain is one of the most recognizable waterfalls in the Rockies and one that every visitor will remember from their first trip to Banff. In the summer, a silvery thread of water slips down the mountainside to the valley bottom. In winter, the falls are a delicate tassel of ice clinging to the massif. Regardless of the season, the view is captivating. Now stop rubbernecking, stay in your lane and remember that the speed limit is 90 km/h.

Driving directions

From the town of Banff, drive east on the Trans-Canada Highway for 3 km to the Lake Minnewanka / Banff Avenue interchange. Exit the highway, looping beneath the overpass, and follow signs for the Lake Minnewanka Scenic Drive. Drive 500 m to a parking area on the left below Cascade Falls. Alternatively, you can park in the Cascade Ponds picnic area on the right-hand side of the road.

Hiking directions

From the parking area along the roadway, follow a well-used trail which ascends steadily to the base of Cascade Falls. The short trail gains 100 metres over its 500-metre distance. Avoid venturing beyond the base of the falls. Numerous parties have attempted to scramble higher and found themselves cliffed out and subsequently stranded in steep terrain. Many rescues have taken place here as over-ambitious visitors have climbed beyond the end of trail.

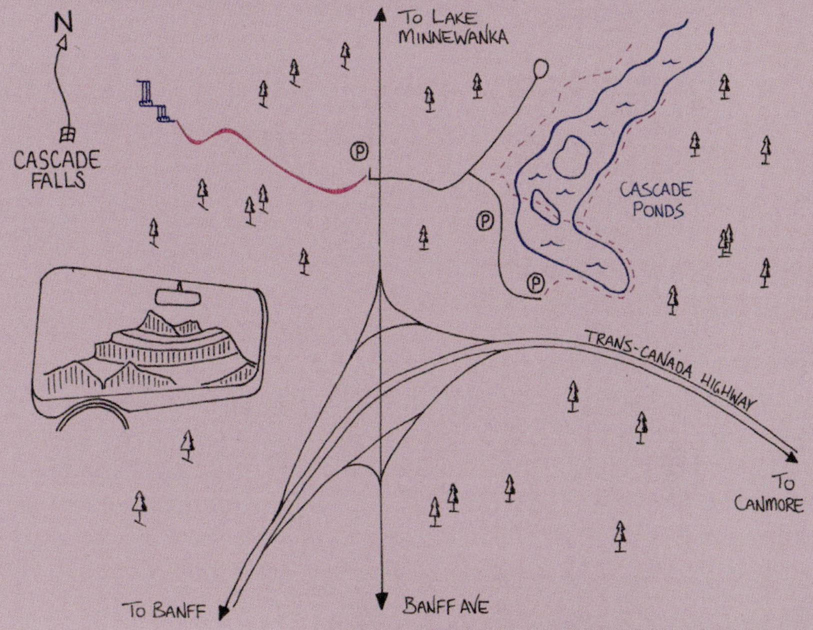

Pack your picnic blanket

The Cascade Ponds picnic area is a beautiful and serene spot to break out some snacks and refuel before continuing on your adventures. Other options for a nearby pit stop are Lake Minnewanka, Two Jack Lake and Johnson Lake, all accessed via the Lake Minnewanka scenic drive.

3. Bow Falls

LOCATION: Banff National Park
DRIVING DIFFICULTY: EASY
HIKING DIFFICULTY: EASY
HIKING DISTANCE: 1.2 km
HIKING TIME: 20–30 min.

From the shadow of the country's most iconic accommodation – the Banff Springs Hotel – it's a casual stroll to the equally recognizable Bow Falls. This is the perfect short walk if the weather prevents you from venturing higher. It is also an ideal outing to work off some calories after dinner on Banff Avenue. We recommend the bison burger and a pint of the Black Pilsner at the Banff Ave Brewing Company, but you'll find that waterfalls go well with most dining options.

Driving directions

In the town of Banff, follow Banff Avenue to its south end, where it crosses over the Bow River. Once across the bridge, turn left onto Spray Avenue. A short distance farther, turn left onto River Avenue and follow signs for the Bow Falls Viewpoint parking area.

PHOTO BY WALTER TERSMETTE

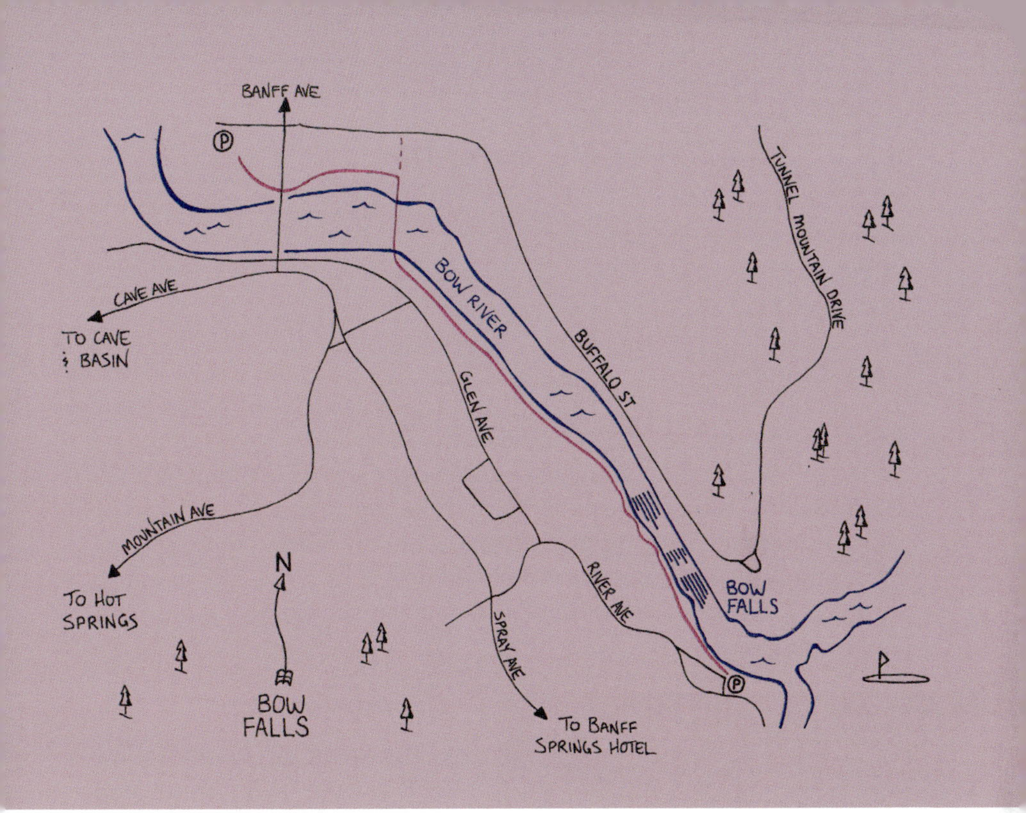

Hiking directions

Follow a broad pathway back along the Bow River. Stop when you reach the falls. Short ... sweet ... waterfall found!

Banff Springs Hotel

Dubbed the "Castle in the Rockies," the original version of this landmark hotel was completed in 1888 and quickly gained international appreciation. In the decades that followed, the building was expanded several times to keep up with the increased demand from wealthy visitors. The hotel's history was also marred by setbacks that included fires and an extended closure during the Second World War. In 1984 it was declared a UNESCO World Heritage Site, and on its one 100th anniversary it became a National Historic Site. The hotel remains, to this day, the epitome of luxury and one of the cornerstones of tourism in Banff National Park.[1]

4. Sundance Canyon

LOCATION: Banff National Park
DRIVING DIFFICULTY: EASY
HIKING DIFFICULTY: EASY
HIKING DISTANCE: 3.7 km
HIKING TIME: 1.5 h

When the mother-unit steps in and says, "Sundance Canyon must be added to your book or you will be disowned," one is inclined to obey. Admittedly, I initially overlooked this hike as not being worthy of inclusion until the threat of banishment from my family convinced me otherwise. I was beyond pleasantly surprised by what this hike has to offer. So, as per the mother-unit, you too should go explore Sundance Canyon.

Driving directions

In the town of Banff, follow Banff Avenue to its south end, where it crosses over the Bow River. Once across the bridge, turn right onto Cave Avenue. Follow the road to its end at the Cave and Basin National Historic Site and a large parking area. It is recommended to arrive before 9:30 a.m. to secure a parking spot and start the hike before the mid-day crowds arrive.

Hiking directions

From the parking area, follow a paved pathway past the Cave and Basin buildings. Continue south for 2.5 km toward a signed junction at the mouth

PHOTO BY WALTER TERSMETTE

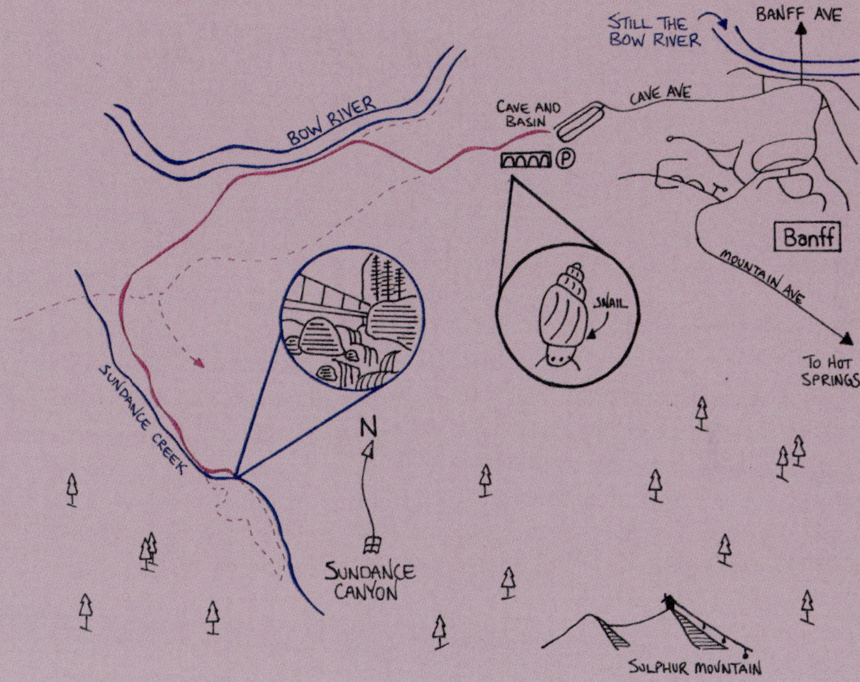

of a small canyon. Bikes are permitted to this point. From here a trail ascends gently up the canyon. There are steps in place where the trail steepens, and bridges for the creek crossings. The cascades are below the uppermost bridge, 3.7 km from the parking area.

From this point you can return the way you came, or extend the hike with a 1.6 km loop beyond the upper bridge.

The Cave and Basin and a threatened gastropod

After discovery by Canadian Pacific Railway construction workers in 1883, the Cave and Basin hot springs were developed with a nearby swimming pool and bathhouse. In 1885 the area was designated as Canada's first national park, a reserve created around the site of the springs. While the springs and pools are closed to the public, they can be viewed as part of tours and interpretive walks through the Cave and Basin National Historic Site. These springs are also home to the Banff Springs snail, an endangered species found nowhere else in the world.[2]

5. Johnston Canyon Lower Falls

LOCATION: Banff National Park
DRIVING DIFFICULTY: EASY
HIKING DIFFICULTY: EASY
HIKING DISTANCE: 1.2 km
HIKING TIME: 25 min.

Nowhere in the Canadian Rockies is the popularity of our national parks more evident than at Johnston Canyon. This short, scenic hike winds its way up a narrow canyon to a series of waterfalls and is bombarded by the relentless and year-round onslaught of local and international visitors. Its reputation is well-deserved, though, and becomes obvious within minutes of leaving the parking area. This hike truly delivers world-class views from start to finish, so it's only fitting that you enjoy it with the whole world.

Driving directions

From Banff, drive west on the Trans-Canada Highway for 6 km to a signed junction for the Bow Valley Parkway (Highway 1A). Exit here and drive north for 17 km to the signed parking areas for Johnston Canyon. During the summers of 2020 and 2021, the Bow Valley Parkway was closed to vehicular traffic with the exception of tour buses, so many people accessed the area by bicycle. As always, check for closures before heading out.

Alternatively, Johnston Canyon can be accessed from Castle Junction if you're coming from the west. Due to the reduced speeds on the Bow Valley Parkway, this is also a slightly quicker route from Banff. Exit via the off-ramp to Highway 93 and turn right. Follow for an additional kilometre to the Castle Mountain gas station and the Bow Valley Parkway (Highway 1A). Turn right onto the Parkway and follow it for 6.3 km to the signed parking areas for Johnston Canyon.

Hiking directions

From the parking area, cross the creek and follow the wide, well-signed pathway. The trail starts beside the Johnston Canyon Resort and follows the left-hand side of the creek for 1.2 km to a junction at the Lower Falls where you can view from either the overlook, the bridge or through a small cave.

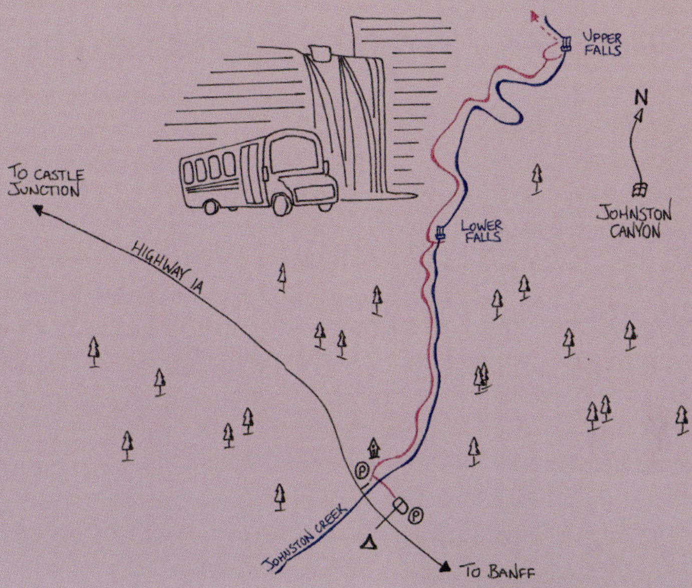

The early bird gets the worm

The popularity of Johnston Canyon makes it a busy place all year round and every day of the week. If you would prefer some semblance of privacy, it is recommended to arrive early in the day or wait until the evening. Like many trailheads throughout the park, the parking area and trail fill up very quickly. Midday visitors will likely find themselves walking single file along the bridges and catwalks. Best to brush up on your "pardon me" and "excuse me" before tackling this trail. Alternatively, bells can be purchased at most (if not all) cycling shops nationwide.

6. Johnston Canyon Upper Falls

LOCATION: Banff National Park
DRIVING DIFFICULTY: EASY
HIKING DIFFICULTY: EASY
HIKING DISTANCE: 2.5 km
HIKING TIME: 45–60 min.

The Lower Falls are a common turnaround point for many visitors, especially those with younger children. While the spectacular Lower Falls are absolutely deserving of the fanfare, don't stop here (unless your younger, angrier and hungrier children dictate the turnaround). The Upper Falls are equally impressive with multiple vantage points. Along the way you'll pass a number of smaller waterfalls for a total of seven, count 'em, seven waterfalls!

Driving directions

From Banff, drive west on the Trans-Canada Highway for 6 km to a signed junction for the Bow Valley Parkway (Highway 1A). Exit here and drive north for 17 km to the signed parking areas for Johnston Canyon. During the summers of 2020 and 2021, the Bow Valley Parkway was closed to vehicular traffic with the exception of tour buses, so many people accessed the area by bicycle. As always, check for closures before heading out.

Alternatively, Johnston Canyon can be accessed from Castle Junction if you're coming from the west. Due to the reduced speeds on the Bow Valley Parkway, this is also a slightly quicker route from Banff. Exit via the off-ramp to Highway 93 and turn right. Follow for an additional kilometre to the Castle Mountain gas station and the Bow Valley Parkway (Highway 1A). Turn right onto the Parkway and follow it for 6.3 km to the signed parking areas for Johnston Canyon.

Hiking directions

From the parking area, cross the creek and follow the masses. The trail starts beside the Johnston Canyon Resort. The well-used pathway follows the left side of the creek for 1.2 km to a junction at the lower falls. From here the trail gains elevation gently over the next kilometre, where short detours give you the option to view the Upper Falls from a catwalk near their base or from an overlook at the top.

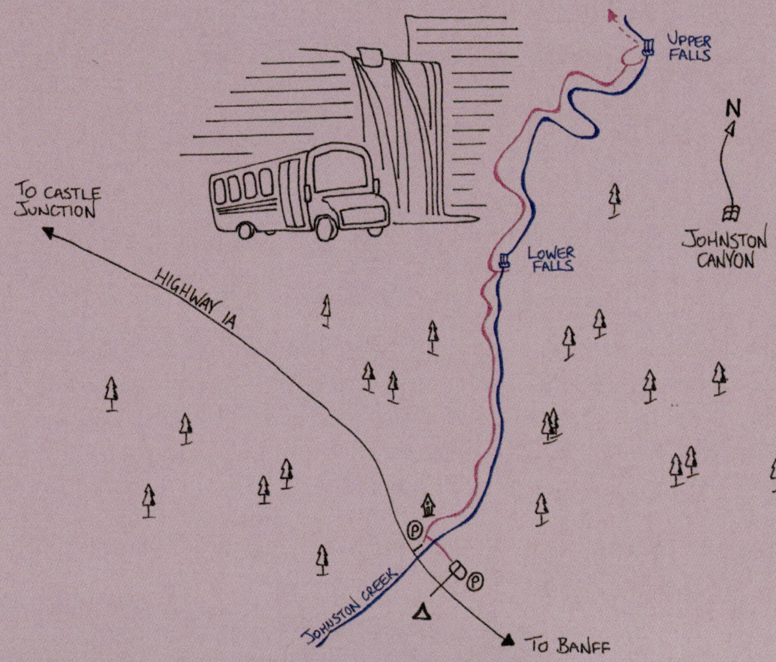

More to explore: the Ink Pots

For a longer outing and an extended day hike, you can shed the crowds substantially by continuing an additional 3.0 km to the Ink Pots, another classic Canadian Rockies scene. The Ink Pots are five shallow pools characterized by their vibrant shades of green and blue. From the Upper Falls the trail gains some additional elevation before levelling off in a meadow.

7. Silverton Falls

LOCATION: Banff National Park
DRIVING DIFFICULTY: EASY
HIKING DIFFICULTY: EASY
HIKING DISTANCE: 700 m
HIKING TIME: 15 min.

Silverton Falls is a short and sweet hike close to the highway and makes a great addition to an outing if you have already stopped at Johnston Canyon or other small hikes around Banff. It is also a quick detour for those hiking to and from Rockbound Lake, perched high amongst the fortress-like walls of Castle Mountain.

Driving directions

From Banff, drive west on the Trans-Canada Highway for 30 km to Castle Junction. Exit via the off-ramp to Highway 93 and stay right. Follow for an additional kilometre to the Bow Valley Parkway (Highway 1A). Turn right, onto the Parkway, follow it for 100 m and then turn left into the parking area signed for Rockbound Lake.

Hiking directions

From the parking area, start up the wide pathway for the Rockbound Lake hike. After a couple hundred metres, keep to your right at a junction signed for Silverton Falls. The trail will begin to switchback shortly after and gain gentle elevation before arriving at small viewing area looking directly at the falls. Use caution on the final 200 metres and at the viewpoint, as the slope below the trail drops off very steeply.

A nugget of history: the Silver City mine

In 1882 John Healy staked a claim near the base of Castle Mountain to extract copper ore from the site. The original name, Copper Mine, was replaced by Silver City, and the following year, just as the Canadian Pacific Railway reached the site, so did the prospectors. At one

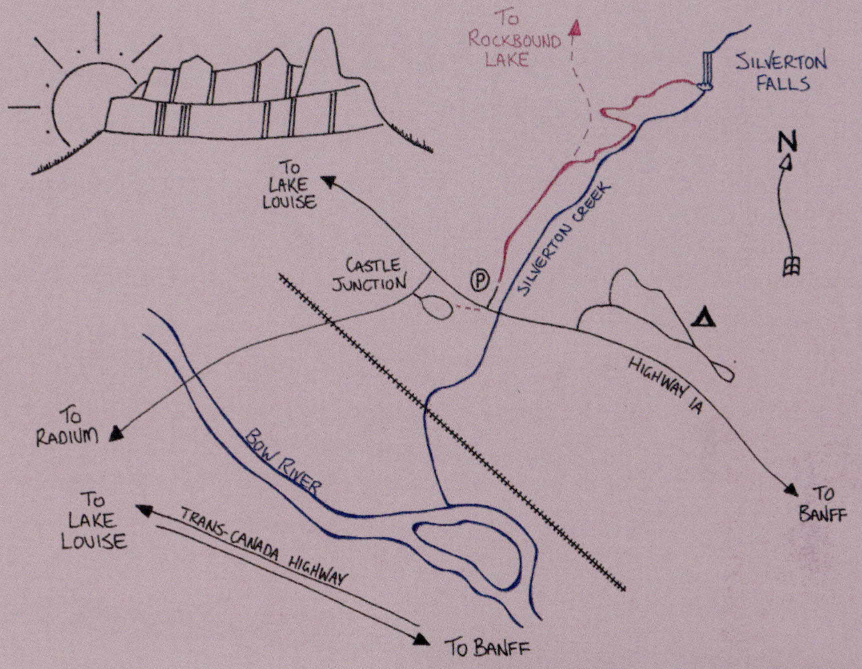

point there were five active mines and over 3,000 residents. However, by the end of 1885, due to rumours of fraud, the town of Silverton was vacated as quickly as it sprang up. Over the next three years, many of the buildings were removed and relocated.[3]

8. Wolverine Creek Waterfall (unofficial)

LOCATION: Banff National Park
DRIVING DIFFICULTY: EASY
HIKING DIFFICULTY: MODERATE
HIKING DISTANCE: 5.2 km
HIKING TIME: 2–2.5 h

The hike to Bourgeau Lake and Harvey Pass is a popular full-day hike that is close to both Banff and the highway. While the scenery high in the alpine is what draws people to this trail, there is a waterfall on Wolverine Creek that makes for a solid half-day outing if that is all that time permits or if undesirable weather keeps you in the valley.

Driving directions

From the town of Banff and the overpass to the Norquay ski hill, drive west on the Trans-Canada Highway for 11.5 km. Look for a sign reading "*Bourgeau 2 km*," drive the 2 km farther, then turn left at an unsigned crossing of the forested median (turning lane). Afterwards

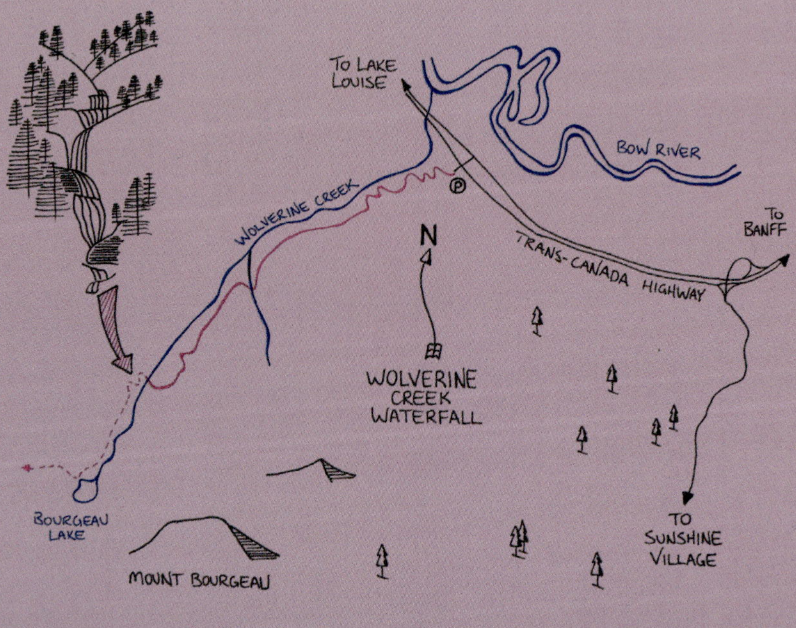

you'll be required to cross the eastbound lanes of the busy highway. Drive up the short road to the parking area for the Bourgeau Lake trail.

A safer option is to drive eastbound on the Trans-Canada for 18.5 km from Castle Junction. Here the turnoff for the Bourgeau parking area is well signed and there's ample space to exit from the highway.

Hiking directions

From the parking area, follow the Bourgeau Lake trail for 5.2 km. The trail starts through a gate beside the outhouse near a kiosk with maps and trail information. The wide pathway immediately begins to gain gentle elevation for the first two kilometres through a series of switchbacks. Cross a bridge over a small stream at 3.2 km. Continue along Wolverine Creek for two more kilometres to where a series of large cascades plummet through the forest below Bourgeau Lake.

More to explore: Bourgeau Lake

Bourgeau Lake, Harvey Pass and Mount Bourgeau are the main attractions here. Beyond the waterfall on Wolverine Creek, the trail gains elevation steadily over the next 2.3 km to the shores of Bourgeau Lake (7.5 km from trailhead). To this point you will have climbed more than 700 metres. Another 2.2 km and an additional 300 m of elevation gain leads to Harvey Pass (9.7 km) and spectacular views of the surrounding peaks. For a truly long day, and if suffering is your thing, continue the climb from Harvey Pass to the summit of Mount Bourgeau!

PHOTO BY WALTER TERSMETTE

9. The Giant Steps

LOCATION: Banff National Park
DRIVING DIFFICULTY: EASY
HIKING DIFFICULTY: MODERATE (overnight recommended)
HIKING DISTANCE: 10.0 km
HIKING TIME: 3–4 h

In the shade cast by some of the highest peaks in the Canadian Rockies, the Giant Steps is only one small offering in Paradise Valley. Due to its length, Paradise Valley only attracts a fraction of the hikers that flock to other nearby destinations such as Larch Valley at Moraine Lake or the Lake Agnes Teahouse at Lake Louise. Don't let its length deter you: this is a spectacular hike that can be done in a long day or as a very manageable overnight trip, with plenty of jaw-dropping sights along the way.

Driving directions

From the Lake Louise townsite, follow Lake Louise Drive as it winds above town towards the lake. After 2 km, turn left onto Moraine Lake Road (signed) and follow it for 2.5 km to the Paradise Creek parking area and trailhead on the right.

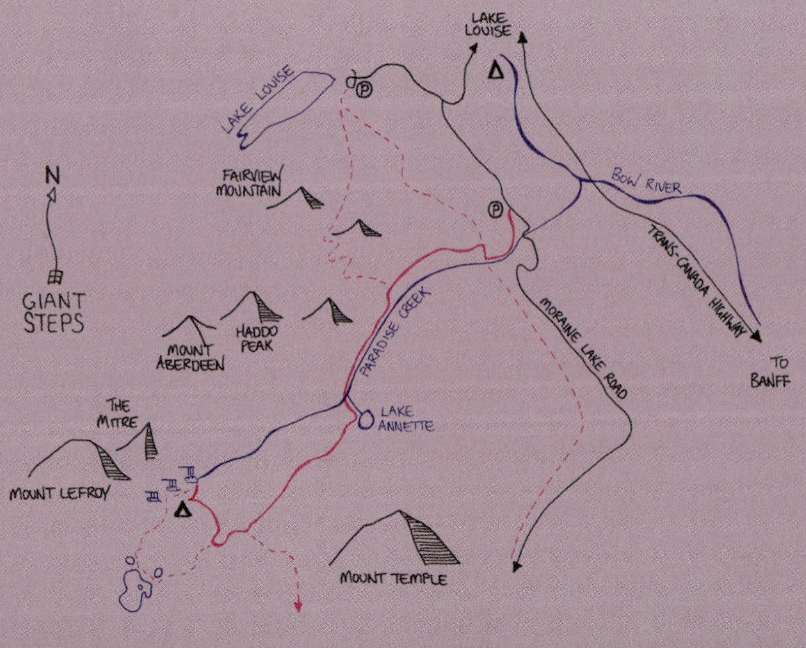

Hiking directions

From the parking area, follow the signed Paradise Valley trail for 10 km to the Giant Steps. The trip gains a relatively casual 385 m as you weave through the valley with Mount Temple soaring overhead. The main path is well signed along the way and easy to follow. Here are the key waypoints:

0.0 km – Trailhead
1.0 km – Stay right (junction with Moraine Lake Trail)
1.3 km – Stay left (junction with Moraine Lake Trail)
3.3 km – Bridge over Paradise Creek
3.9 km – Bridge over Paradise Creek
4.2 km – Stay straight (junction for Saddleback Pass and Sheol Valley)
5.0 km – Stay straight (signage where original Paradise Creek trail is being reclaimed – no access)
5.1 km – Bridge over Paradise Creek
5.7 km – Lake Annette
8.5 km – Stay right (junction for Sentinel Pass)
9.8 km – Stay right (junction for Paradise Valley Campground)
10.0 km – Giant Steps

Logistics

While the Paradise Valley trail can be completed as a long day hike, with children it is recommended this trip be an overnight outing. The Paradise Valley backcountry campground (Banff National Park campground Pa10) has ten campsites which can be reserved through the Banff National Park reservation system, either online at reservation.pc.gc.ca or by calling 1-877-RESERVE (1-877-737-3783). Ensure you are up to speed on current trail restrictions and closures at all times. Depending on the level of bear activity, travel on this trail may be restricted to groups of four or more.

10. Bridal Veil Falls

LOCATION: Banff National Park: Lake Louise
DRIVING DIFFICULTY: EASY
HIKING DIFFICULTY: EASY
HIKING DISTANCE: 3.0 km
HIKING TIME: 1.5 h

If you tell anyone you're going to check out Bridal Veil Falls at Lake Louise, you may be met with raised eyebrows. On the other hand, mention the Lake Agnes Teahouse and the recognition will be far more evident. This small waterfall can be spotted above Mirror Lake en route to Lake Agnes and is simply a bonus to the many vistas that Lake Louise is famous for.

Driving directions

From the Lake Louise townsite, follow Lake Louise Drive for about 4 km to the parking area near the lake. This parking lot is busy and generally fills up early in the day. A shuttle service is available from the Lake Louise overflow and shuttle parking area, located a couple kilometres east of town off the Trans-Canada Highway.

Hiking directions

From the parking area, follow the shoreline trail counter-clockwise around the lake. You'll be looking for, on your right, the Lake Agnes Trail and Teahouse (signed). The busy and well-used pathway switchbacks through the trees as it climbs above the turquoise waters of Lake Louise. It is 3.0 km to Mirror Lake, where Bridal Veil Falls can be seen cascading through the trees under the Lake Agnes Teahouse and the Big Beehive. From here it is an additional 800 m to Lake Agnes.

More to explore: Lake Louise

Let's face it, you likely didn't come all this way, risking life and limb to secure a parking spot at Lake Louise, just to catch a glimpse of this waterfall. The trail network around this world-famous attraction is extensive and features numerous short and long day hikes. If you have a parking spot, don't squander it! Make the most of your fortunes by linking up or extending the hike to include Lake Agnes and the Big Beehive, or by connecting to the Plain of Six Glaciers trail.

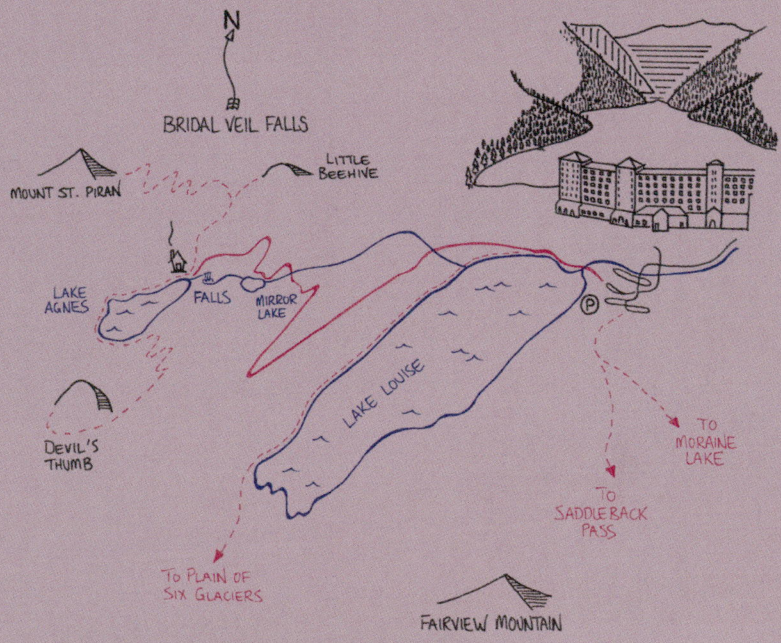

PHOTO: WALTER TERSMETTE

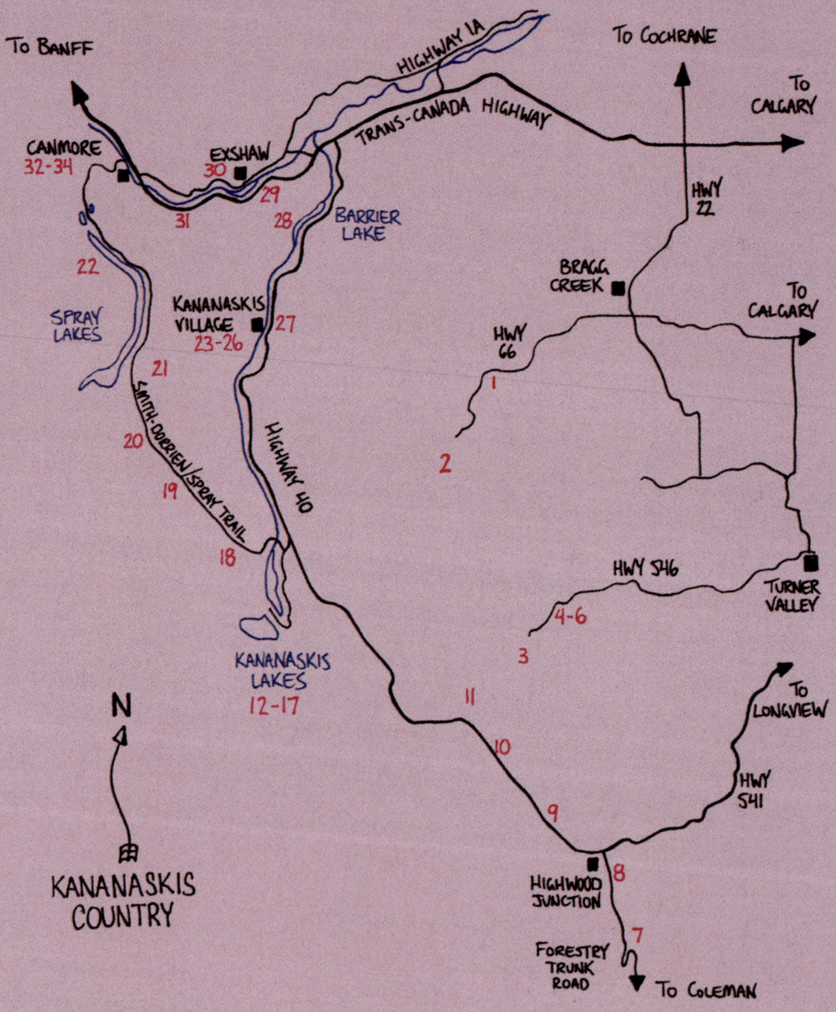
To Banff
Canmore
32-34
Exshaw
30
29
31
28
Highway 1A
Trans-Canada Highway
To Cochrane
To Calgary
Hwy 22
Barrier Lake
22
Spray Lakes
Kananaskis Village
23-26
27
21
20
19
18
Smith-Dorrien/Spray Trail
Highway 40
Bragg Creek
To Calgary
Hwy 66
1
2
Hwy 546
Turner Valley
4-6
3
Kananaskis Lakes
12-17
11
10
9
8
7
N
Kananaskis Country
To Longview
Hwy 541
Highwood Junction
Forestry Trunk Road
To Coleman

CHAPTER 2

Kananaskis Country

Back in the day, Kananaskis had traditionally flown under the radar of many people: an obvious yet uncelebrated junction on the Trans-Canada Highway that saw tourists and locals alike breeze right on by, their sights set on Banff and Jasper national parks. As interest in outdoor recreation soared, along with Calgary's population, the small parking lots along Highway 40 started to fill with much more regularity as people explored the offerings in their very own backyard. And what a backyard it is!

K-Country has all the hallmarks of its federally managed counterparts, including high-value scenery, lofty peaks, shimmering lakes, alpine meadows and waterfalls aplenty. While most southern Alberta habitués remember Kananaskis as an off-the-beaten-path mountain playground, the parks have had to adjust to the increase in popularity. The great thing is that there are dozens upon dozens of trails that disperse hikers quickly.

In June 2021, Alberta Parks introduced a permit system similar to Parks Canada's where visitors can purchase day-use or annual passes to register their vehicles. The price of admission is more than fair to explore the countless trails that weave throughout the valley.

Kananaskis Country is easily reached west of Calgary from the Trans-Canada via Highway 40 near Canmore, Highway 541 near Longview from Highway 22 or the Spray Lakes Trail from right in Canmore. These routes afford access to the three parks that make up Kananaskis Country: Peter Lougheed, Bow Valley and Spray Valley provincial parks, in addition to numerous provincial recreation areas that line its eastern boundary.

Note: Highway 40 from Highwood Junction to Kananaskis Lakes Trail is closed from December 1 to June 14 each year. At over 2200 m above sea level, this is the highest paved roadway in the country. It also receives large volumes of snow and cuts through avalanche terrain, making it impractical to maintain during the winter months.

For more information, contact the Kananaskis Provincial Park visitor centre at is.gd/pn3rtG; 403-678-0760.

1. Elbow Falls

LOCATION: Elbow Falls Provincial Recreation Area, Bragg Creek, AB
DRIVING DIFFICULTY: EASY
HIKING DIFFICULTY: EASY
HIKING DISTANCE: 250 m (depending on how close you can park)
HIKING TIME: 5 min.

The only thing near Calgary that rivals the popularity of Elbow Falls is giant pandas at the zoo and maybe a Calgary Flames playoff run. While the river and falls were drastically altered by the 2013 flood, one thing that hasn't changed is its animal-like magnetism. With their location close to town, near the road, and with picnic tables at hand, Elbow Falls maintains its status as a great place to get outside. Most people will pair a visit here with another nearby hike. It is recommended that you visit early in the day or later in the evening to avoid the party animals.

Driving directions

From the junction of Highways 22 and 66/758 near Bragg Creek, drive west on Highway 66 for 19 km to a large parking lot and picnic area on the left signed for Elbow Falls.

Hiking directions

The falls are located just beyond the far end of the parking lot. Wide pathways leave the parking area from numerous points and wind their way through the trees and along the Elbow River to a series of viewpoints beside and above Elbow Falls.

Are you getting shorter or am I getting taller?

Prior to 2013, Elbow Falls was nearly 5 metres high. During the flood event of 2013, a large volume of rock and gravel was carried down the rivers and streams over a prolonged period that saw creeks and rivers flowing well over their banks. In addition to depositing huge amounts of rock at the base of the falls and downstream, the swollen Elbow River also swept away the picnic tables, benches and pathways. When the water receded, Elbow Falls was reduced to less than half its original height.

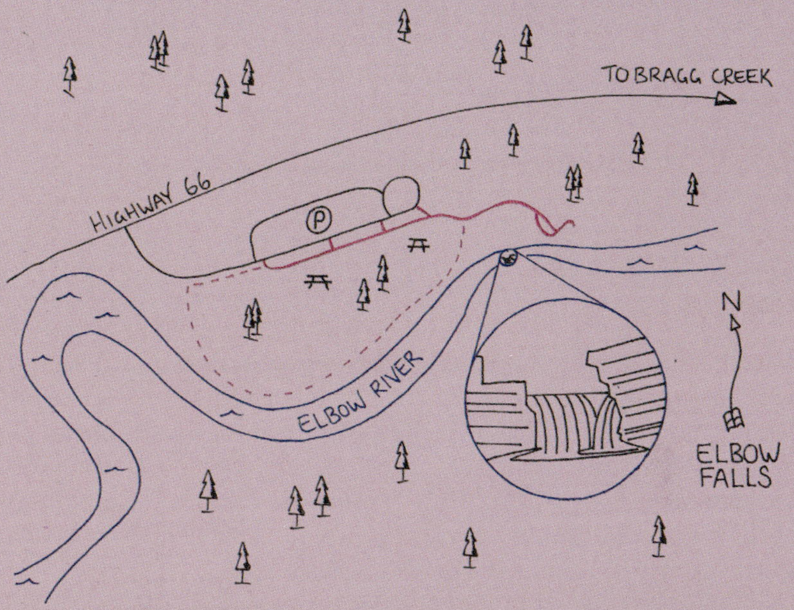
TO BRAGG CREEK
HIGHWAY 66
ELBOW RIVER
N
ELBOW FALLS

2. Cornwall Creek Falls

LOCATION: Little Elbow Provincial Recreation Area, Bragg Creek, AB
DRIVING DIFFICULTY: EASY
HIKING DIFFICULTY: MODERATE
HIKING DISTANCE: 8.3 km
HIKING TIME: 3–3.5 h

If you close your eyes and imagine the perfect waterfall, what does it look like? Is it a picturesque creek flowing through a forest below towering mountaintops? Does it slide over the lip of a wall of bedrock before plunging into a turquoise pool below? Okay, now open your eyes, step to the side and let those cyclists pass before you get hit. A lengthy but casual saunter on the Big Elbow trail will bring you to a waterfall pretty much like the one you just imagined.

Driving directions

From the junction of Highways 22 and 66/758 near Bragg Creek, drive west on Highway 66 for 28 km to an intersection for the Little Elbow Provincial Recreation Area (left) and the Powderface parking area (straight). Turn left and go an additional 1.5 km to the Little Elbow trailhead parking area.

Hiking directions

From the parking lot, follow the wide Little Elbow trail west along the Elbow River for 500 m to a large bridge. Once across, stay to the left on the main trail for 200 m until it turns into a gravel road. Follow the road to the right. You are now on the Big Elbow trail (trail kiosk). Stay on this road for the next 6.6 km (7.3 km from the trailhead) at which point the road will bend sharply to the right and then immediately hard to the left. As the road bends back to the left, pick up a faint trail leaving the road that leads into a gravel outwash along Cornwall Creek. Late in the summer the flow decreases and the water may be running underneath the rocky streambed. From here there are two options for the last kilometre.

To reach the base of the falls, follow alongside the creek. Like many in Kananaskis, Cornwall Creek was not spared from the destruction of the 2013 flood. The path of least resistance may be determined by the water level, but you can follow either side of the creek for the first

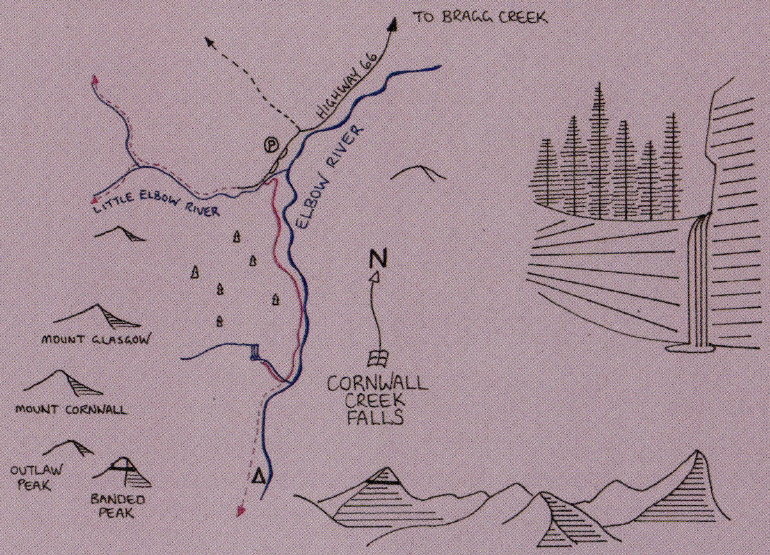

few hundred metres before you will eventually be forced to the right-hand side. A better defined trail can be picked up at this point and followed to the falls.

The other option to view the falls is on a trail that leads to Banded Peak high above. After leaving the road, cross the creek and look for a boot-beaten trail that ascends a bank above the creek bed. Follow this trail for 1 km as it steadily gains elevation from the valley bottom to a gorgeous viewpoint looking towards the falls. It is important to note that the Big Elbow trail is a mixed-use pathway for hiking, equestrian and bicycle traffic. Stick to the right side of the trail, keep your eyes and ears open and allow faster traffic to pass.

3. Junction Falls

LOCATION: Sheep River Provincial Park, Turner Valley, AB
DRIVING DIFFICULTY: EASY
HIKING DIFFICULTY: MODERATE
HIKING DISTANCE: 6.8 km
HIKING TIME: 2.5–3 h

One of the lesser known waterfalls may also one of the most enchanting in Kananaskis Country. Here, a small stream drops in three spectacular steps and flows from one turquoise pool to the next before meeting up with Junction Creek a little farther downstream. It would be only fitting if a chorus of woodland creatures started singing while you admire the setting before you. But I'll stop short of mentioning a certain brand of cartoon princesses on white horses prancing into the scene, due to copyright laws.

Driving directions

From the junction of Highways 22 and 546 in Turner Valley, drive west into Sheep River Provincial Park for 38.5 km to the end of the road. This is the picnic and day-use area for Junction Creek.

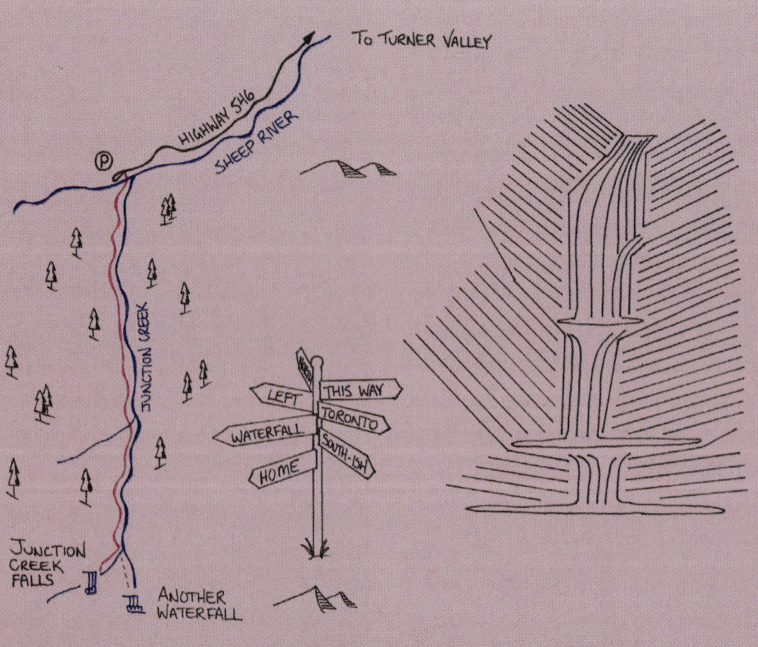

Hiking directions

The Junction Creek trail is unsigned and unmarked. From the parking area, descend to the Sheep River. Locate the confluence of the Sheep River and Junction Creek. Cross the Sheep River in slower moving water just upstream of where they meet and rejoin the trail. It is recommended to wear sturdy sandals or water shoes for the stream crossing. You can hang your footwear in a tree on the other side for the return trip.

Follow this trail for 4.0 km to where it meets a small stream feeding Junction Creek (signs for "Falls Left" and "Lake Right"). The trail to this point is frequented by equestrian traffic, resulting in a wide, muddy and rutted trail. Stay left and cross the stream on either logs or rocks. Once across, follow alongside Junction Creek for an additional 2.6 km. At this point the trail turns to the right as it approaches yet another small creek in a shallow canyon. Stay to the right of the creek and ascend the trail for 200 m. Junction Falls is tucked into an alcove and hidden from sight until the moment you arrive.

More to explore: bonus waterfall

There is a second amazing waterfall a short distance upstream on Junction Creek. From Junction Falls, retrace your steps about 100 metres back down along the creek until another trail is visible across the shallow canyon (refer to map for approximate location). Continue on this trail alongside Junction Creek for 300 m until a waterfall can be heard below you and to the left. A faint, steep trail leads down to the creek and the base of another large, picturesque cascade.

4. Sheep River Falls

LOCATION: Sheep River Provincial Park, Turner Valley, AB
DRIVING DIFFICULTY: EASY
HIKING DIFFICULTY: EASY
HIKING DISTANCE: 200 m
HIKING TIME: mere minutes

Sheep River Falls is a popular day trip from the nearby towns of Turner Valley, Black Diamond and Okotoks as well as south Calgary. The river itself is well regarded as a fine fishing destination, while Sheep River Provincial Park offers numerous day-use trails and picnic areas.

Driving directions

From the junction of Highways 22 and 546 in Turner Valley, drive west for 35.5 km into Sheep River Provincial Park. Turned left into a parking area signed for Sheep River Falls.

Hiking directions

From the parking area, all trails lead down to the river. To reach the falls, follow a wide pathway back to the east. Cross a minor stream using a small wooden bridge and continue to rocky slabs overlooking the two tiers of Sheep River Falls.

Place names

Many toponyms in this part of the Rockies are derived from words or historical references used by the Blackfoot First Nations. *Eetookiap* is their word for this river, which means "sheep." The name of the nearby town of Okotoks comes from *oohkotok*, meaning "rock," a reference to the glacial erratic called the "Big Rock," near the town. Another Alberta town bearing an Indigenous name is Ponoka, from the Blackfoot word for "elk."

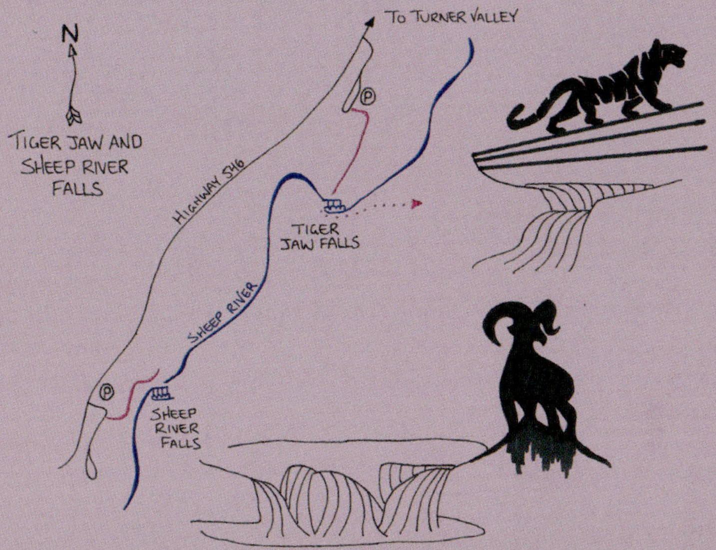
N
TIGER JAW AND SHEEP RIVER FALLS
TO TURNER VALLEY
HIGHWAY 546
SHEEP RIVER
TIGER JAW FALLS
SHEEP RIVER FALLS
P
P

5. Tiger Jaw Falls

LOCATION: Sheep River Provincial Park, Turner Valley, AB
DRIVING DIFFICULTY: EASY
HIKING DIFFICULTY: EASY
HIKING DISTANCE: 300 m
HIKING TIME: 5 min.

Tiger Jaw is a small waterfall on the Sheep River that flows under a recently reconstructed bridge. During runoff the falls may be inundated by a torrent of rushing water, rendering them indistinguishable as a waterfall.

Driving directions

From the junction of Highways 22 and 546 in Turner Valley, drive west for 34.5 km into Sheep River Provincial Park. Turned left into a parking lot signed for Indian Oils.

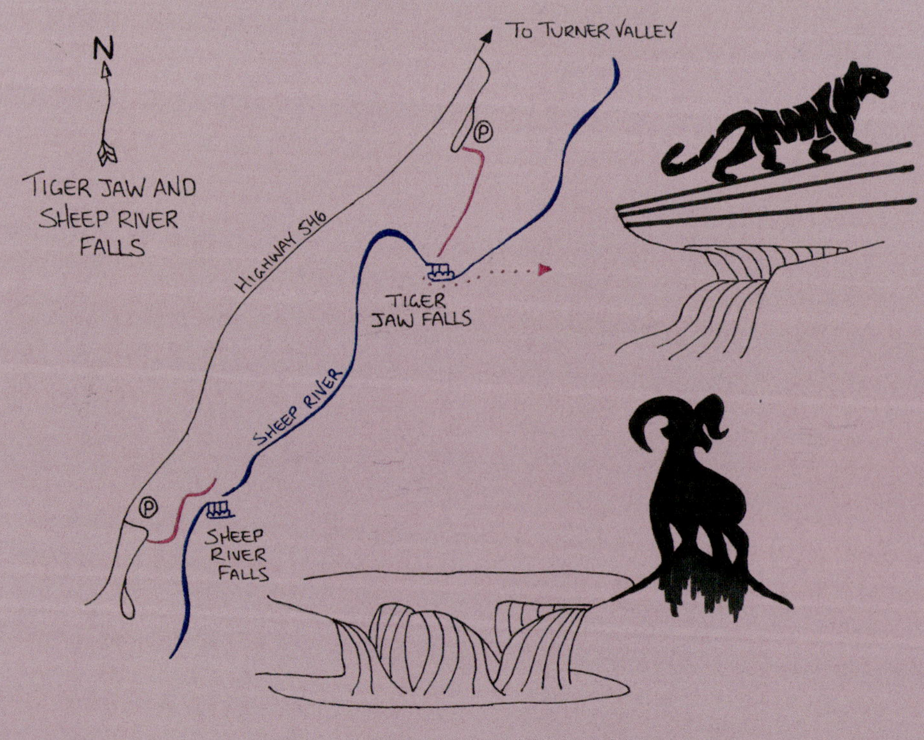

Hiking directions

From the west side of the parking area, pick up one of a few trails heading into the trees. These trails descend and connect with an old road. Head to the right upon reaching the road, then cross a bridge over the Sheep River, with Tiger Jaw Falls below.

Flooding on the Sheep River

While the river provides a lifeline for communities downstream, including drinking water, fishing, transportation and logging, its flooding over the years has claimed lives while causing extensive property damage. The most recent and likely the most notable flooding, in 2013, reshaped the landscape throughout the southern Canadian Rockies, yet other floods, in 2005, 1932, 1915 and 1902, destroyed critical infrastructure, bridges and roadways as well as the homes of residents near the river.[4]

6. Dyson Falls

LOCATION: Sheep River Provincial Park, Turner Valley, AB
DRIVING DIFFICULTY: EASY
HIKING DIFFICULTY: EASY
HIKING DISTANCE: 4.4 km
HIKING TIME: 1.5–2 h

This small, hidden gem of a waterfall is off the radar of the provincial parks trail network but has seen a recent boost in popularity due to its inclusion on many smart-phone trail apps. While most people circulate around the waterfalls along the Sheep River, the crowd thins rapidly if you make a break for Dyson Falls. The backdrop is a peaceful meadow with only the sound of the waterfall itself to break the silence.

Driving directions

From the junction of Highways 22 and 546 in Turner Valley, drive west for 34.5 km into Sheep River Provincial Park. Turned left into a parking area signed for Indian Oils.

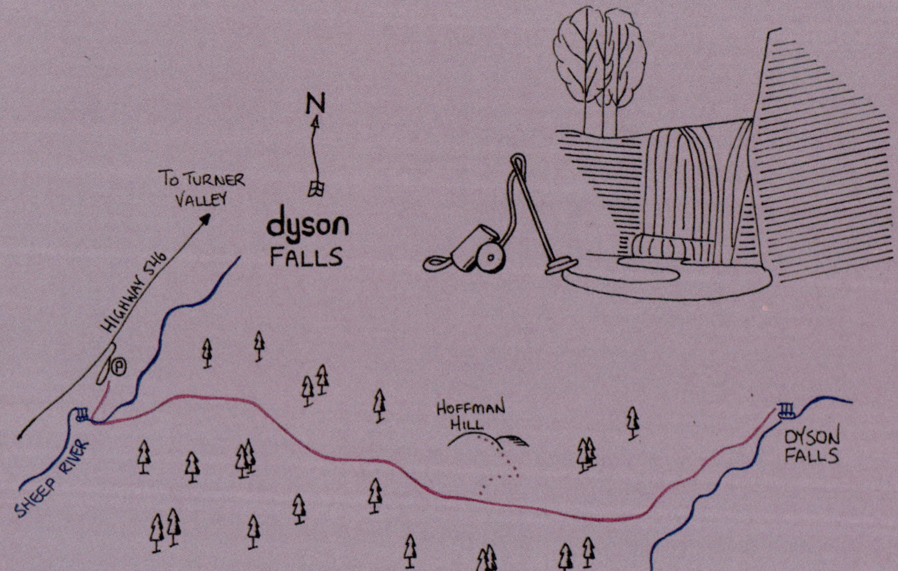

Hiking directions

From the west side of the parking area, pick up any one of a few trails heading into the trees. These trails descend and connect with an old road. Upon reaching the road, head to your right and cross a bridge over the Sheep River with Tiger Jaw Falls below. Once across, turn left and continue along the road for the next 4 km, which climbs gently but steadily before levelling off in a small meadow. The route then descends slightly to a clearing. Here the creek becomes briefly visible before it plummets over a short cliff. For the best views of the waterfall, stay to the left of the creek and continue to a rocky outcropping that offers a nice look at it from above. It is also possible to scramble down a short but steep slope to the pool at the base of the falls.

7. Hercules Falls and Titan Falls

LOCATION: Cataract Creek Recreation Area, Highwood Junction, AB
DRIVING DIFFICULTY: MODERATE
HIKING DIFFICULTY: MODERATE
HIKING DISTANCE: 4.6 km
HIKING TIME: 1.5–2 h

If it's solitude you crave, these lesser known waterfalls all but guarantee it. Unless you've camped at Cataract Creek, delved into the margins of a couple local guidebooks or a friend spilled the beans, chances are that you've never even heard of them. Their more remote location outside of the provincial parks and away from the highway has kept them in relative obscurity. In late spring and early summer when Cataract Creek swells with meltwater, Hercules and Titan falls are as immense as their names suggest.

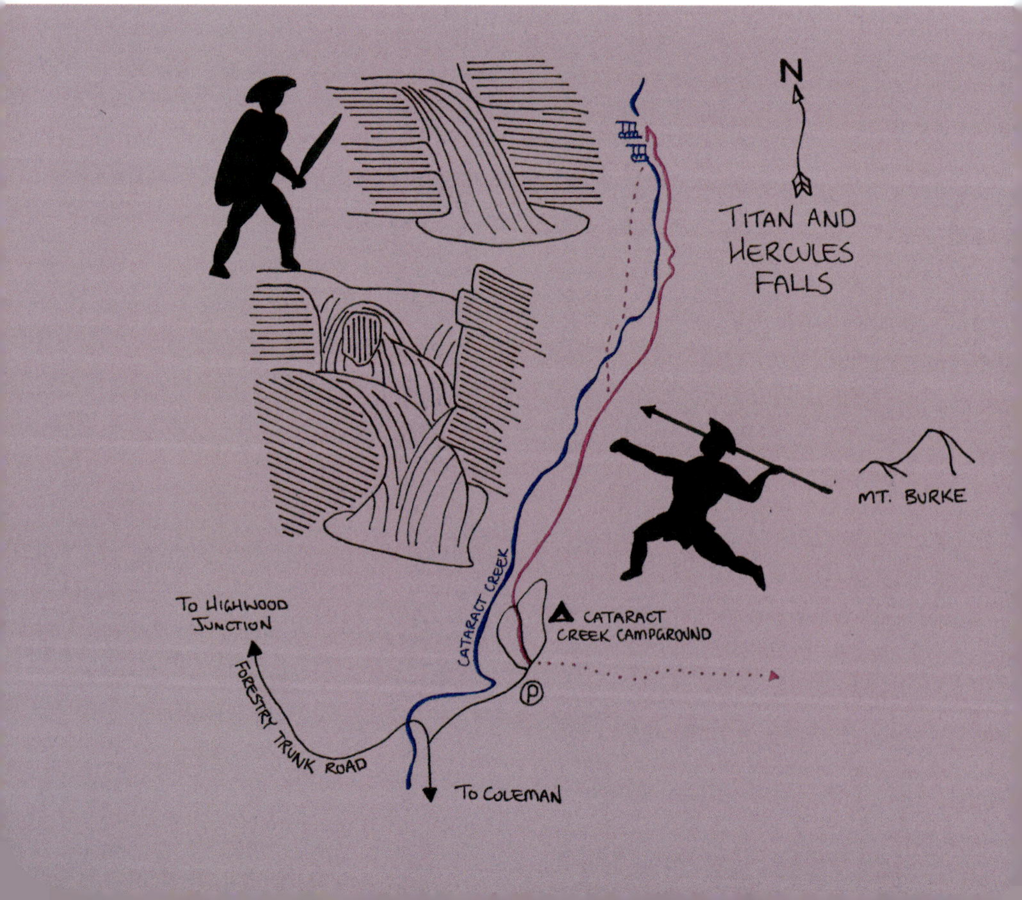

Driving directions

From Highwood Junction (the intersection of Highways 541 and 40), drive south on the forestry trunk road (signed as Highway 940) for 13.5 km to the Cataract Creek recreation area. Turn left and follow for an additional kilometre to the Cataract Creek campground. Day-use parking is on the right-hand side of the road, just before the campground entrance (parking is signed for Mount Burke).

Hiking directions

From the parking area, walk into the campground and follow Loop A down to campsite #27 (600 m). On the right side of the campsite, a trail leaves the road and drops onto a grassy bench above Cataract Creek. Follow boot-beaten trails through grass and shrubs along the right-hand side of Cataract Creek until a large gravel washout crosses the trail. At this point, the trail becomes indistinct. Look for a large cairn in the gravel outwash which marks a point where the trail re-enters the trees (2.7 km). The faint trail winds through a forested area until you reach a viewpoint of Titan Falls, the lower of the two cataracts, at 4.6 km.

If you are unable to locate the cairn, stick to the right-hand side of the creek, where other hikers have worn down faint paths. These are indistinct at times but if you stick with them, they will eventually connect with the larger, more heavily used path. Don't be discouraged if you have to push some branches and bushes aside. The falls are worth the effort and the trail is easier to pick up on the return trip.

Alternatively, some people have crossed Cataract Creek closer to the campground and followed a trail to the falls on the left-hand side of the creek. Refer to the map for rough location.

From the Titan Falls viewpoint, backtrack slightly along the trail and look for a faint trail leading towards the creek. It will approach the top of Titan Falls and then veer left where Hercules Falls, carving its path through a tight gorge, comes into view.

8. Baril Creek Falls

LOCATION: Highwood Junction, AB
DRIVING DIFFICULTY: EASY
HIKING DIFFICULTY: EASY
HIKING DISTANCE: 450 m
HIKING TIME: 10 min.

If unmarked pullouts, nondescript trailheads and questionable access to off-the-beaten-path objectives are your thing, Baril Creek Falls is the sadistic justification for inclusion in this book. Sure, you could jockey for position to photograph a far more popular location. Or you could study the confusion on other people's faces when you mention Baril Creek Falls. While few will recognize the name or location, when you start to run low on things to see and do, this is a good place to spend some time poking around.

Driving directions

From Highwood Junction (the intersection of Highways 541 and 40), drive south on the forestry trunk road (signed as Highway 940) for 3.0 km. Park in a widening on the shoulder on the east side of the road, just south of the berm over the culvert that Baril Creek runs through.

Hiking directions

From the roadside parking area, walk towards Baril Creek, following the edge of the trees. A faint trail enters the trees at a metal survey post. After a couple hundred metres in the forest, the trail descends sharply to the canyon floor at the confluence of Baril and Etherington creeks. As you reach the creeks, turn left and go back upstream along Baril to the base of a small cascade in the narrow canyon. Take care with your footing both on the descent to and along the creek, as things remain slippery long after a rainfall.

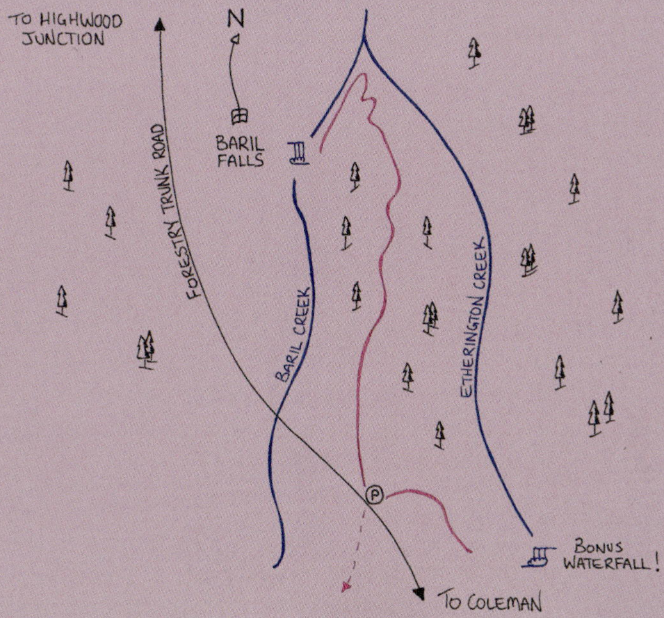

More to explore: bonus waterfall

From the parking area, walk due east into the trees (no trail) for just 100 metres to the edge of a deep gorge with Etherington Creek flowing far below. Follow the canyon rim back upstream just a short distance to where another small waterfall can been seen from high above.

9. Cat Creek Falls

LOCATION: Highwood Junction, AB
DRIVING DIFFICULTY: EASY
HIKING DIFFICULTY: EASY
HIKING DISTANCE: 1.3 km
HIKING TIME: 30 min.

Even though it is located outside the trendier quarter of K-Country, Cat Creek Falls is a short and popular hike that is worth a little extra driving time. This two-tiered waterfall is flanked by modest cliffs with a crystal clear pool at the base, making it the perfect refuge on a hot day. Seating is limited, so get your tickets early!

Driving directions

From Highwood Junction (the intersection of Highways 541 and 40), drive west on Highway 40 for 5.5 km and turn left into a parking lot signed for the Cat Creek day-use area. Drive past the first picnic site to a larger parking lot at the end of the roadway and look for the signed trailhead.

Alternatively, instead of parking in the day-use area, there is a gravel pullout on the right-hand side of Highway 40, just to the east of Cat Creek. The trail is visible ascending a grassy slope on the opposite side of the creek bed.

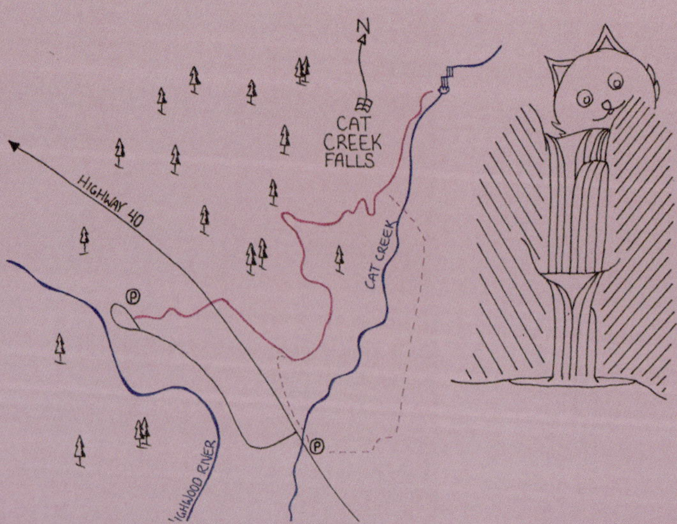

Hiking directions

From the Cat Creek day-use area, locate the trailhead signed for the Cat Creek Interpretive Trail. The well-used path ascends and then crosses the highway. Take extra care with children and be aware of traffic travelling in both directions. Once across the road the trail continues to gain elevation to a small lookout over the broad valley. It then enters a more heavily forested area and descends towards Cat Creek. Cross over the creek and back again on wooden bridges before rounding a final corner to the base of the gorgeous Cat Creek Falls.

As far as swimming holes go …

… this might be one of the best!

10. Ptarmigan Cirque Waterfalls

LOCATION: Peter Lougheed Provincial Park, AB
DRIVING DIFFICULTY: EASY
HIKING DIFFICULTY: EASY
HIKING DISTANCE: 4.5 km (loop)
HIKING TIME: 2.5–3 h (round trip)

It is a short hiking season up at Highwood Pass. With Highway 40 through the pass being closed from December 1 through June 14 and the trails often snowbound by Thanksgiving, timing is everything up here. But don't let any of that deter you from adding this hike to your to-do list! Early in the summer the cirque sheds its snow cover, liberating numerous small waterfalls which tumble down cliffs in a spectacular alpine basin.

Driving directions

From the junction of the Trans-Canada and Highway 40, drive south on Highway 40 for 67 km to a parking area on the right signed for Highwood Meadows and Ptarmigan Cirque.

Hiking directions

From the Highwood Meadows and Ptarmigan Cirque parking area, locate the signed trailhead at the north end of the parking lot. The trail starts as a serene stroll through a small meadow for 400 m before crossing the highway and beginning an ascent through gradually thinning forest. At 1.2 km, stay left at a junction. A couple hundred metres later, the trail levels off in an alpine meadow. The first waterfalls are at 2.0 km where boot-beaten paths leave the main trail for the base of the cascades. From here, continue along the loop in a clockwise direction and begin the return trip.

To extend the route a little farther, when the trail reaches its high point at the falls, another, less-used path at an unmarked junction leads to a second waterfall about 300 m farther. After returning to the main trail, continue along the loop rather than the way you came.

Ptarmigan Cirque Interpretive Trail

Alberta Parks publishes an interpretive guide for this hike that highlights many interesting facts about the cirque and its alpine environment. It contains pages of information about the flora and fauna that inhabit this high-elevation world. As much of the signage along the trail is in a state of disrepair, weathered or damaged, the interpretive trail guide can be used instead. It is available in pdf from the Alberta Parks website (is.gd/1oRPxa) and can easily be saved to your mobile device or printed.

PHOTO: WALTER TERSMETTE

11. Edworthy Falls

LOCATION: Peter Lougheed Provincial Park, AB
DRIVING DIFFICULTY: EASY
HIKING DIFFICULTY: MODERATE
HIKING DISTANCE: 4.8 km
HIKING TIME: 2 h

Starting a hike at nearly 2000 metres above sea level has its advantages, one being that you'll find yourself at treeline quite quickly. The views from Elbow Pass are vast, with the rippled limestone of the Opal Range towering above sprawling alpine meadows. Edworthy Falls is simply a cherry on top to one of the best hikes in Kananaskis Country.

Driving directions

From the junction of the Trans-Canada and Highway 40, drive south on Highway 40 for 62 km to a parking area on the left signed for Elbow Pass. Best to arrive early to secure parking in the lot, though; otherwise you'll find yourself relegated to the shoulder of the highway.

Hiking directions

From the Elbow Pass parking area, follow a decommissioned road for 1.3 km to Elbow Lake. Once at the lake, contour around its shore in a clockwise direction to the far end. Cross a bridge and continue along another decommissioned road. The old roadway occasionally has water flowing over and around it, but well-worn trails detour around any obstacles with ease. At 4.7 km, turn left into the trees (this junction was marked with a large boulder with the words "Water Fall" spray-painted on it). Another hundred metres through the trees takes you to a viewpoint of Edworthy Falls. A short, steep descent is available for those wanting to hang out at the base of the cataract.

More to explore: Piper Pass

There is a lot to see and do around Elbow Lake. Many are content to stay by the lakeshore and fish. Edworthy Falls is a great way to spend a half-day. One of the most spectacular options is the hike to Piper Pass. As signage is lacking, it is recommended to research the route ahead of time. About 400 metres past the Edworthy Falls junction, there is another junction, on the left, marked by a cairn. Descend to and cross the Elbow River and then start the long, gradual ascent to Piper Pass. From the junction it is 5.0 km one-way to the pass, about 17.5 km round-trip from Elbow Lake and nearly 20 km round-trip from the highway. A very long but very worthwhile day.

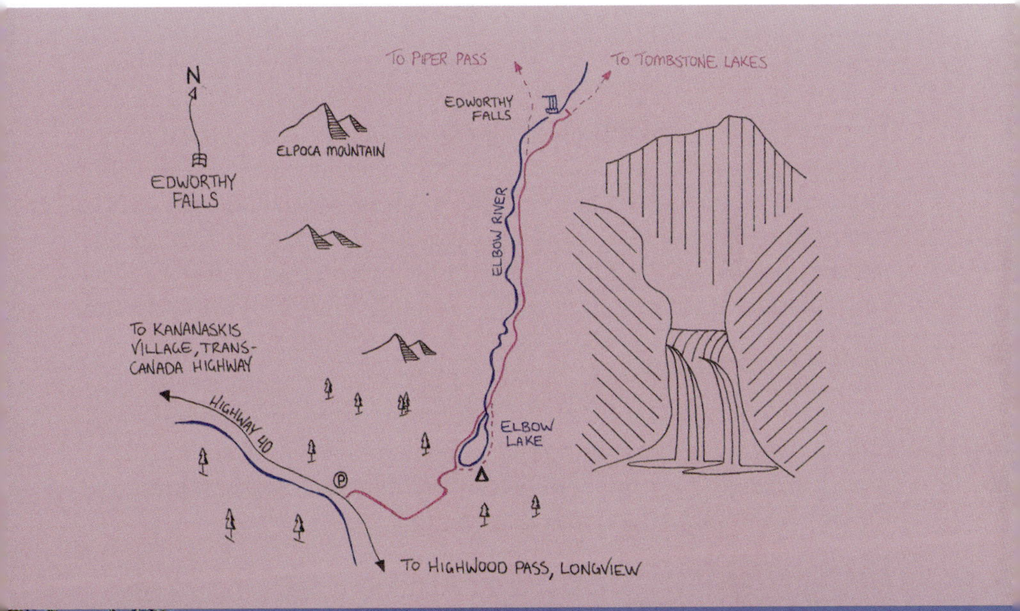

12. Sarrail Falls

LOCATION: Peter Lougheed Provincial Park, AB
DRIVING DIFFICULTY: EASY
HIKING DIFFICULTY: EASY
HIKING DISTANCE: 1.1 km
HIKING TIME: 20 min.

The short walk to Sarrail Falls is a mere drop in the lake when it comes to the trail network in, around and above the Kananaskis Lakes. The recreation opportunities are virtually endless and include day hiking, backpacking, scrambling, climbing, camping, paddling and fishing. The parking lot fills quickly during the summer months, especially on weekends, but the crowd quickly disperses around the lakeshore and beyond.

Driving directions

From the junction of the Trans-Canada and Highway 40, drive south on Highway 40 for 50 km to the intersection with Kananaskis Lakes Trail. Turn right here and follow for 12.7 km to an intersection signed for Upper Lake. Turn left and drive to the parking area.

Hiking directions

From the Upper Lakes parking, follow trailhead signage for Rawson Lake. The broad lakeshore pathway traces the entire circumference of Upper Kananaskis Lake. There is a bridge over Sarrail Creek 1.1 km from the trailhead where you get an in-your-face look at Sarrail Falls.

More to explore: Rawson Lake

Hmmm ... where to start? One classic option is to extend the hike beyond Sarrail Falls to the spectacular Rawson Lake. Just past the bridge over Sarrail Creek is a signed trail on the left which climbs steadily for another 2.7 km to the alpine lake tucked against the lofty walls of Mount Sarrail. While the trail gains 300 metres of elevation from the lakeshore pathway, the trail is well graded, well maintained and well worth the additional effort to see one of the many outstanding vistas in Kananaskis Provincial Park. If you've still got gas in the tank at this point, a difficult but spectacular route leaves Rawson Lake and climbs to Sarrail Ridge, where you can take in an aerial view of the entire Kananaskis Lakes region.

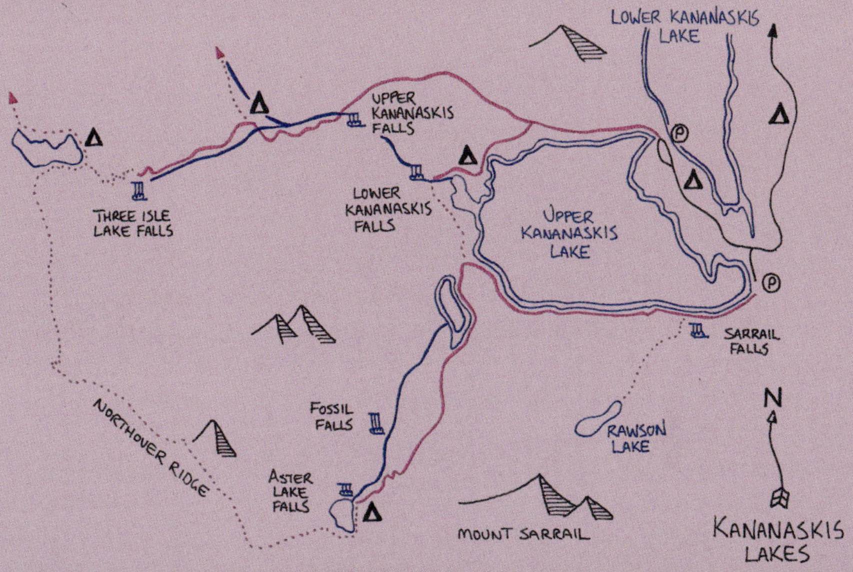
LOWER KANANASKIS LAKE
UPPER KANANASKIS FALLS
THREE ISLE LAKE FALLS
LOWER KANANASKIS FALLS
UPPER KANANASKIS LAKE
SARRAIL FALLS
FOSSIL FALLS
RAWSON LAKE
NORTHOVER RIDGE
ASTER LAKE FALLS
MOUNT SARRAIL
N
KANANASKIS LAKES

13. Fossil Falls

LOCATION: Peter Lougheed Provincial Park, AB
DRIVING DIFFICULTY: EASY
HIKING DIFFICULTY: DIFFICULT (due to elevation gain)
HIKING DISTANCE: 8.5 km
HIKING TIME: 4–5 h

Fossil Falls is an immense torrent and commands attention from a number of locations around Upper Kananaskis Lake. It thunders year-round, draining the large glacial basin above. While it can be seen and heard from kilometres away, few get close enough to appreciate how massive it actually is. Fossil Falls can be explored as a long day hike from the Upper Lakes day-use area or en route to the backcountry campsite at Aster Lake. Both are difficult but the pain will be quickly forgotten when you take in views of one of K-Country's largest waterfalls.

Driving directions

From the junction of the Trans-Canada and Highway 40, drive south on Highway 40 for 50 km to the intersection with Kananaskis Lakes Trail. Turn right here and follow for 12.7 km to an intersection signed for Upper Lake. Turn left and drive to the parking area.

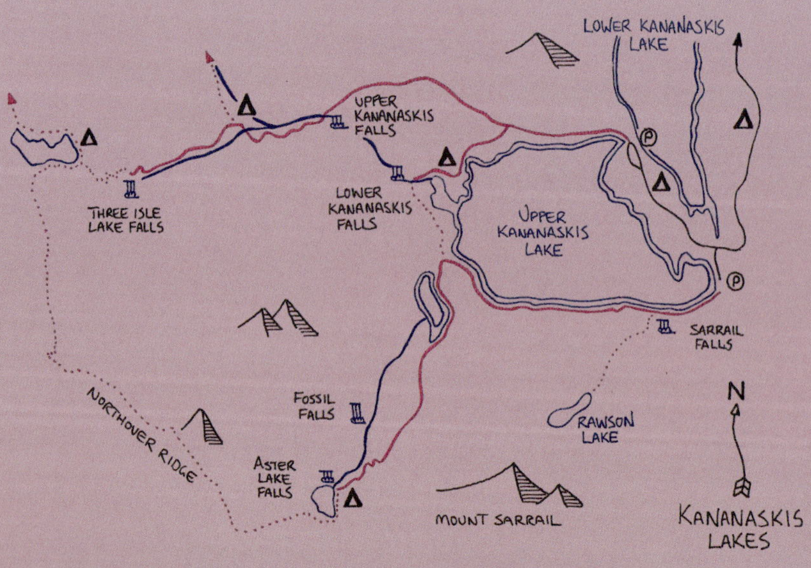

Hiking directions

From the Upper Lake parking, follow trailhead signage for Rawson Lake. The broad lakeshore pathway traces the entire circumference of Upper Kananaskis Lake. Hike the lakeshore trail for 5.4 km to a junction signed for Aster Lake. A few hundred metres past the junction is Hidden Lake, which can be skirted clockwise (early in the season, when the lake is full, you may be forced into the trees). Beyond Hidden Lake, the trail begins a steady climb towards Aster Lake, but not before the immense Fossil Falls comes into view at the 8 km mark.

From this point it is possible, although not recommended, to reach the base of the falls with some travel across steep talus slopes. Some of the best views, however, are from a little higher up the trail, where you can look down on Fossil Falls in its entirety. The falls remain visible until 8.5 km. Return the way you came or continue ahead to Aster Lake.

More to explore: Northover Ridge

Most folks heading past Fossil Falls are destined for a night out at Aster Lake along the classic Northover Ridge trip, one of the premier backpacking trips in the Rockies. While Fossil Falls is certainly a worthy objective in itself, extending the trip to include a night at the Aster Lake campground makes for an amazing overnight stay in the mountains. More-experienced hikers frequently opt to continue even farther by traversing along the Northover Ridge alpine route for a multi-day loop that returns to Upper Kananaskis Lake via Three Isle Lake.

14. Aster Lake Falls

LOCATION: Peter Lougheed Provincial Park, AB
DRIVING DIFFICULTY: EASY
HIKING DIFFICULTY: DIFFICULT (overnight recommended)
HIKING DISTANCE: 10.5 km
HIKING TIME: 5–6 h

Aster Lake Falls is a series of small cascades that drain a very picturesque alpine basin. The landscape around the lake is nearly devoid of vegetation, making for a somewhat lunar panorama. Although the spacesuits can stay on the rack at home, bringing the supplemental oxygen might be worthwhile. This hike gains more than 500 metres from Kananaskis Lakes and is sure to leave you breathless in more ways than one.

Driving directions

From the junction of the Trans-Canada and Highway 40, drive south on Highway 40 for 50 km to the intersection with Kananaskis Lakes Trail. Turn right here and follow for 12.5 km to an intersection signed for Upper Lake. Turn left and drive to the parking area.

Hiking directions

From the Upper Lake parking, follow trailhead signage for Rawson Lake. The broad lakeshore pathway traces the entire circumference of the Upper Kananaskis Lake. Hike the lakeshore trail for 5.4 km to an unmarked junction for Aster Lake. A few hundred metres past the junction is Hidden Lake, which can be skirted clockwise (early in the season, when the lake is full, you may be forced into the trees). Beyond Hidden Lake the trail begins a steady climb towards Aster Lake, but not before passing the immense Fossil Falls at kilometre 8.

Continue ascending beside Fossil Falls on a steep trail that cuts up and across the rocky slopes. A couple spots require hands-on scrambling over rocky outcroppings and ledges. Above the headwall the trail levels off for the next couple of kilometres. Just before you arrive at the Aster Lake campground, a small waterfall welcomes you into a breathtaking alpine basin. Mount Sarrail is to your left, Warrior Mountain straight ahead and Mount Northover a little farther to the right. Just beyond the campground is the spectacular Aster Lake and another small waterfall at the outflow of the lake.

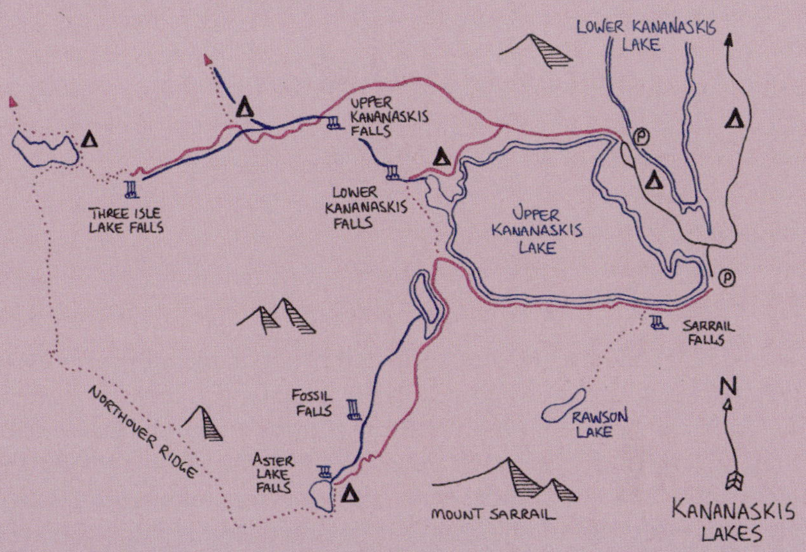
LOWER KANANASKIS LAKE
UPPER KANANASKIS FALLS
THREE ISLE LAKE FALLS
LOWER KANANASKIS FALLS
UPPER KANANASKIS LAKE
SARRAIL FALLS
FOSSIL FALLS
RAWSON LAKE
NORTHOVER RIDGE
ASTER LAKE FALLS
MOUNT SARRAIL
N
KANANASKIS LAKES

15. Lower Kananaskis Falls

LOCATION: Peter Lougheed Provincial Park, AB
DRIVING DIFFICULTY: EASY
HIKING DIFFICULTY: EASY
HIKING DISTANCE: 4.2 km
HIKING TIME: 1.5–2 h

The name game can get confusing here, so to avoid a big argument, let's go straight to the Alberta Parks map, which squarely assigns "Lower Kananaskis Falls" as the name for this waterfall. This is as official as it gets; all the online references (and there are a lot) to any other name are poppycock. Also, this is a great hike, a fact that is glaringly omitted from Alberta Parks mapping.

Driving directions

From the junction of the Trans-Canada and Highway 40, drive south on Highway 40 for 50 km to the intersection with Kananaskis Lakes Trail. Turn right here and follow for 15 km to an intersection signed for the North Interlakes day-use area. Continue to the parking area.

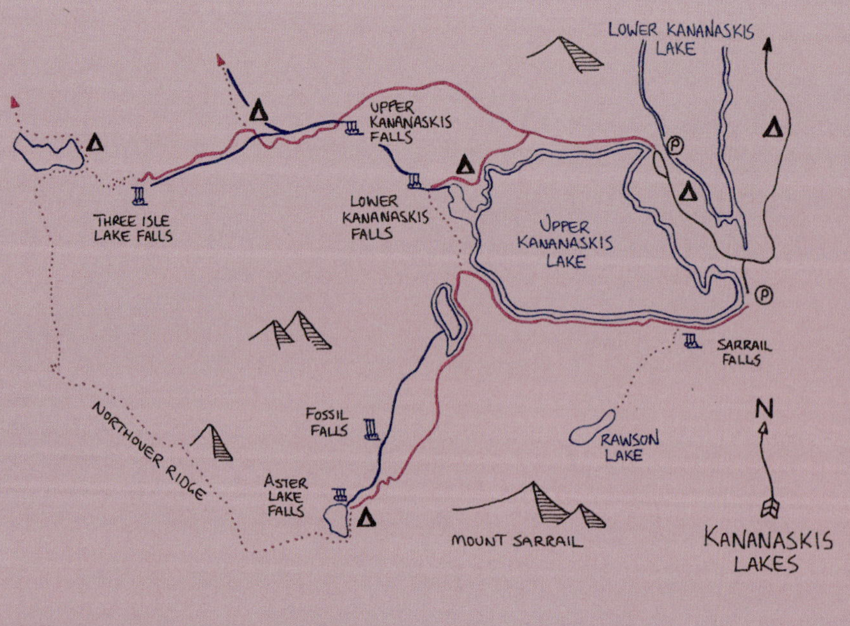

Hiking directions

From the North Interlakes day-use area, cross the dam and follow the lakeshore trail in a counter-clockwise direction. After 2.3 km, stay left at a junction signed for the Point campground. Reach the campground in an additional 1.3 km, and then stay right for the falls, which are 600 m farther.

16. *Upper Kananaskis Falls*

LOCATION: Peter Lougheed Provincial Park, AB
DRIVING DIFFICULTY: EASY
HIKING DIFFICULTY: MODERATE
HIKING DISTANCE: 5.9 km
HIKING TIME: 2–2.5 h

The hike to Upper Kananaskis Falls is an easy way to find oneself walking alone. Most hikers don't venture beyond the shoreline trail unless they have ulterior motives such as a night out at a backcountry campsite at the Forks, Turbine Canyon or Three Isle Lake. The falls themselves are a beautiful mess of turbulent water ricocheting off boulders which can be seen from a number of vantage points from along the river as well as from a bridge above the torrent.

Driving directions

From the junction of the Trans-Canada and Highway 40, drive south on Highway 40 for 50 km to the intersection with Kananaskis Lakes Trail. Turn right here and continue for 15 km to an intersection signed for the North Interlakes day-use area. Follow to the parking area.

Hiking directions

From the North Interlakes day-use area, cross the dam and follow Upper Lake Trail in a counter-clockwise direction. After 2.3 km, stay straight at a junction signed for the Point campground. Continue on the main pathway for an additional 3.6 km to Upper Kananaskis Falls.

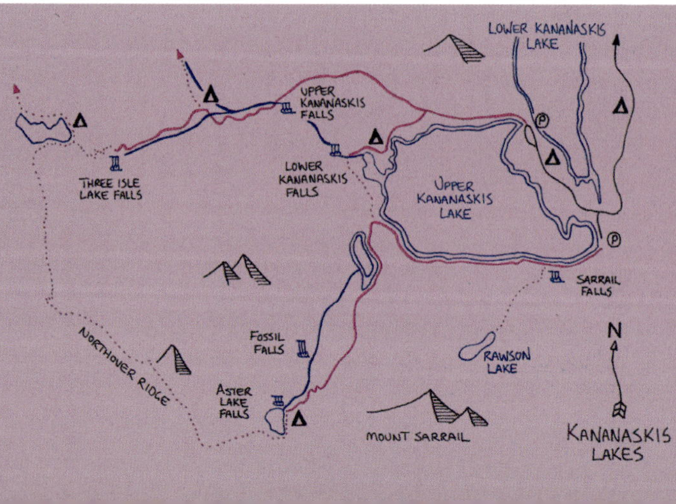

More to explore: Turbine Canyon and beyond

One of the classic backpacking offerings in Kananaskis Country is a trip to Turbine Canyon and the many amazing sights that pepper the far reaches of the Upper Kananaskis River. The Turbine Canyon campground is 15 km from the North Interlakes day-use area, and although a longer day is needed to get there, it makes for a spectacular basecamp to explore the surrounding area. Take in big views of Haig Glacier, North Kananaskis Pass, Turbine Canyon and Lawson Lake.

17. Three Isle Lake Falls

LOCATION: Peter Lougheed Provincial Park, AB
DRIVING DIFFICULTY: EASY
HIKING DIFFICULTY: DIFFICULT (due to distance)
HIKING DISTANCE: 9.0 km
HIKING TIME: 4 h

If Three Isle Lake were a bathtub in the penthouse suite of an 85-storey luxury condo, that would make Three Isle Lake Falls a busted drain pipe in the underground parkade. But since Three Isle Lake has no drain outlet, water sneaks its way down inside the limestone fortification and emerges as a waterfall nearly 250 metres below the lake. The water level slowly decreases throughout the year and gets topped up annually by melting snow from the surrounding mountains.

Note: This waterfall is not to be confused with Three Isle *Creek* Falls, a large but inaccessible cascade which is briefly visible from the trail downstream of Three Isle *Lake* Falls.

Driving directions

From the junction of the Trans-Canada and Highway 40, drive south on Highway 40 for 50 km to the intersection with Kananaskis Lakes Trail. Turn right here and follow for 15 km to an intersection signed for the North Interlakes day-use area. Continue to the parking area.

Hiking directions

From the North Interlakes day-use area, cross the dam and follow Upper Lake Trail in a counter-clockwise direction. After 2.3 km, stay straight at a junction signed for the Point campground. Continue on the main pathway, passing Upper Kananaskis Falls at 5.9 km and the Forks campground at 7.2 km. At the junction signed for Three Isle Lake, stay left and follow the trail for an additional 1.8 km to Three Isle Lake Falls at the base of a large headwall.

If you plan to camp at Three Isle Lake, you could take a sturdy and sustained ascent that continues above the falls, zigzagging up the headwall for the next 1.5 km to the backcountry campground near this high alpine lake. In total the hike to the lake gains nearly 600 metres of elevation, much of it in the final 2 km.

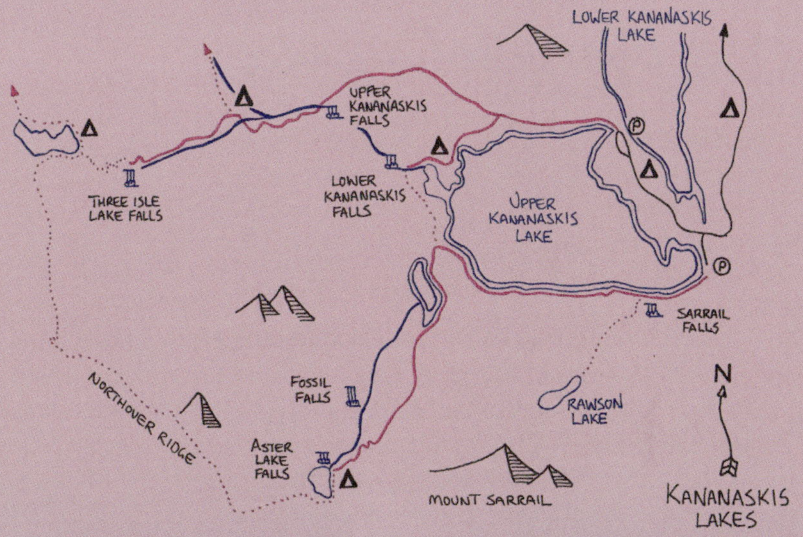

LOWER KANANASKIS LAKE
UPPER KANANASKIS FALLS
THREE ISLE LAKE FALLS
LOWER KANANASKIS FALLS
UPPER KANANASKIS LAKE
SARRAIL FALLS
FOSSIL FALLS
NORTHOVER RIDGE
RAWSON LAKE
ASTER LAKE FALLS
MOUNT SARRAIL
N
KANANASKIS LAKES

18. Warspite Cascades

LOCATION: Peter Lougheed Provincial Park, AB
DRIVING DIFFICULTY: MODERATE
HIKING DIFFICULTY: EASY
HIKING DISTANCE: 3.0 km
HIKING TIME: 1–1.5 h

This waterfall is a tall cascade, cartwheeling down a headwall below – you guessed it – Mount Warspite. The hike is better known for being a casual stroll to Black Prince Lake or a longer, more strenuous day hike to Blank Prince Cirque, but a closer look at the cascades here are a very noteworthy addition to the outing. Early in the hiking season, the water level in the lake is much higher, so skirting the lake might result in damp feet. As the water drains throughout the summer, however, getting around the lake, closer to the falls and high up into Black Prince Cirque, becomes a much drier task.

Driving directions

From the junction of the Trans-Canada and Highway 40, drive south on Highway 40 for 50 km to the intersection with Kananaskis Lakes Trail. Turn right here and follow for 2.2 km to the intersection with Spray Lakes / Smith-Dorrien Trail. From the intersection, drive a well-maintained gravel road for 8.5 km to the Mount Black Prince day-use area. Turn left, descend the roadway briefly and park.

Hiking directions

From the parking area, at a trailhead kiosk for Black Prince Lakes Interpretive Trail, hike into the trees and cross Smith-Dorrien

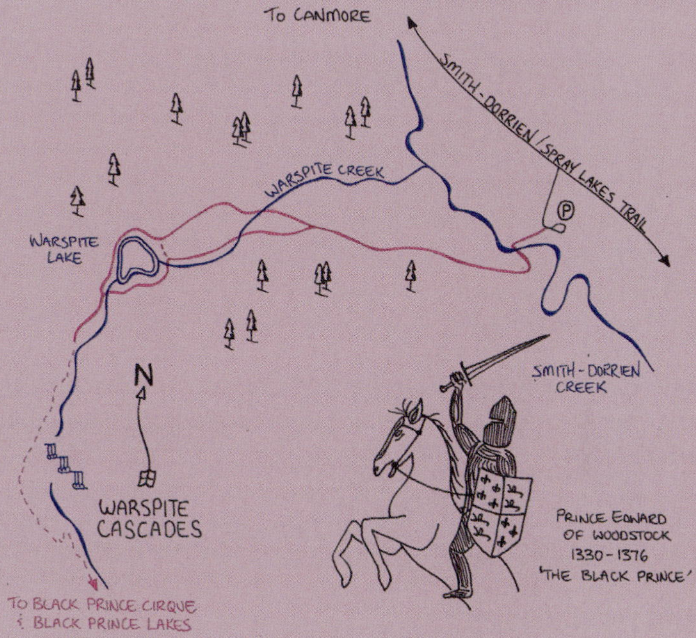

Creek. The wide pathway ascends gently but steadily over the next kilometre. At 1.4 km, stay right at a junction and continue to the lakeshore at 2.1 km. From here the Warspite Cascades can be seen tumbling down a steep, treed slope below Mount Warspite. For an up-close view, continue counter-clockwise around the lakeshore until the trail meets the creek. Stay right and follow the trail as it winds through trees and bushes before reaching a talus rock slope (cairn at 3.0 km).

More to explore: Black Prince Cirque

From the viewpoint at 3.0 km, a faint trail continues into the hanging valley above the Cascades. The trail climbs sharply on the right-hand side of the creek and into Black Prince Cirque. A short distance farther is a group of small tarns called the Black Prince Lakes. It is 5.0 km from the trailhead to this point, a strenuous but worthwhile endeavour.

Also of note, the Black Prince Cirque trail, similar to Ptarmigan Cirque, is an interpretive trail. A pamphlet available online from Alberta Parks at is.gd/oGgixa describes the natural history and human history of the trail.

19. French Creek Falls

LOCATION: Peter Lougheed Provincial Park, AB
DRIVING DIFFICULTY: MODERATE
HIKING DIFFICULTY: EASY (to first waterfall)
or MODERATE (to second, third and fourth waterfalls)
HIKING DISTANCE: 2.2 km (to first waterfall)
HIKING TIME: 1.5–2 h

If you arrive to a full parking lot here you can take comfort in knowing that nearly everyone else is headed for Burstall Pass. Hiking up French Creek by your lonesome is a reasonable expectation, save for the occasional mountaineer. The reward for being unsociable is not one, not two, not three, but four stunning waterfalls in the French Creek valley, each as striking at the last.

Driving directions

From the junction of the Trans-Canada and Highway 40, drive south on Highway 40 for 50 km to the intersection with Kananaskis Lakes Trail. Turn right here and follow for 2.2 km to the intersection with

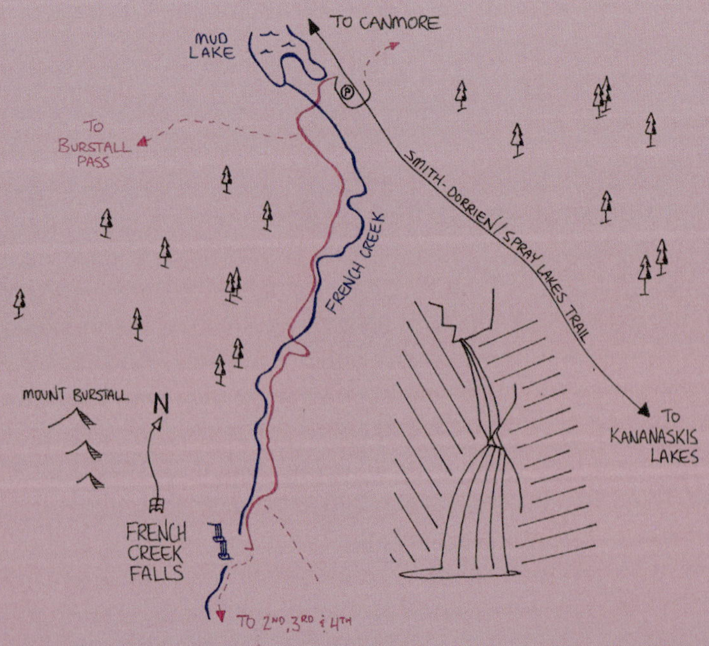

Spray Lakes / Smith-Dorrien Trail. From the intersection, drive a well-maintained gravel road for 22 km to the Burstall Pass day-use area. Turn left and follow the short road to its end.

Hiking directions

From the parking area, follow the main Burstall Pass trail only briefly. Once across the Mud Lake dam, stay left at a junction. Follow a well-used trail to the left, ignoring the much wider Burstall Pass trail bending to the right. The route to the first waterfall stays on the right-hand (west) side of French Creek and leads right to the base of the falls.

More to explore: 2nd, 3rd and 4th waterfalls

Beyond the first fall, the route is occasionally indistinct as it crosses washouts and overgrown meadows. As this trail is not heavily used or well marked, you may find yourself wandering a bit to locate it. From the first waterfall, ascend slopes next to the right-hand side of the falls and continue along French Creek looking for a reasonable place to cross the creek where you'll rejoin a more heavily used trail. The second waterfall is about a kilometre past the first and just off the trail, where several faint trails leave the main path and head for the creek. The third and fourth waterfalls are in close proximity to each other and another two kilometres farther.

PHOTO: WALTER TERSMETTE

20. Commonwealth Creek Falls

LOCATION: Peter Lougheed Provincial Park, AB
DRIVING DIFFICULTY: MODERATE
HIKING DIFFICULTY: EASY
HIKING DISTANCE: 3.2 km
HIKING TIME: 1–1.5 h

Commonwealth Creek wins the award for smallest waterfall in this guide, a title which had to be handed out eventually. It is routinely passed by hikers carrying on to the alpine basin high above for scrambling opportunities on Mount Smuts and Smutwood Peak or for those making a loop south to Burstall Pass. So, as a stand-alone hike, this one may be a little underwhelming.

Driving directions

From the junction of the Trans-Canada and Highway 40, drive south on Highway 40 for 50 km to the intersection with Kananaskis Lakes Trail. Turn right here and follow for 2.2 km to the intersection with the Spray Lakes / Smith-Dorrien Trail. From the intersection, drive a well-maintained gravel road for 26.5 km to the Mount Shark road. Turn left into the parking area and follow for 500 m to an unsigned parking area on the left. This is the Commonwealth Creek trailhead; park here.

Hiking directions

From the parking area, follow a decommissioned road for about 3 km. As the trail nears Commonwealth Creek, it narrows and begins a gentle ascent into a more heavily forested area. The waterfall is a short distance farther.

More to explore: Smutwood Peak

One of the most popular scrambles in Kananaskis Country is the route up Smutwood Peak. It is well known for its five-star views overlooking the Birdwood Lakes, Mount Birdwood and other nearby peaks. As popular as this objective has become, it is not to be taken lightly. The route is long and gains significant elevation, around 800 vertical metres. Most people will require a full day for the 18 km round trip. Plan and pack accordingly, wear sturdy shoes, layer appropriately and remember your bear spray.

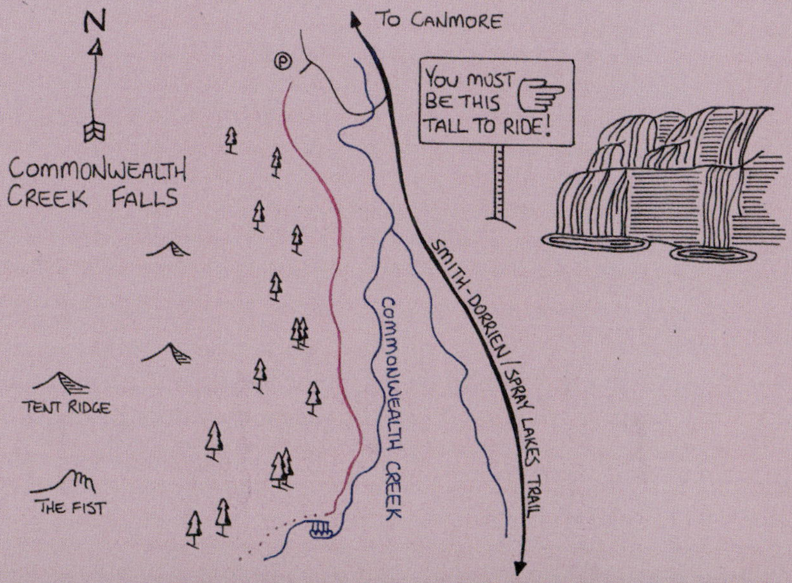

N
TO CANMORE
COMMONWEALTH CREEK FALLS
YOU MUST BE THIS TALL TO RIDE!
SMITH-DORRIEN/SPRAY LAKES TRAIL
COMMONWEALTH CREEK
TENT RIDGE
THE FIST

21. Buller Creek Falls

LOCATION: Peter Lougheed Provincial Park, AB
DRIVING DIFFICULTY: MODERATE
HIKING DIFFICULTY: MODERATE
HIKING DISTANCE: 4.8 km
HIKING TIME: 2–3 h

This small waterfall en route to Buller Pass is an unexpected surprise along a trail known more for its big alpine views. While South Buller Pass and the Buller Pass loop are certainly worthy of having a day committed to exploring them, a shorter trip to the waterfall is deserving of a visit. It is a sturdy and steady climb, even to the falls, but don't let the elevation gain get in the way of tackling this one.

Driving directions

From the junction of the Trans-Canada and Highway 40, drive south on Highway 40 for 50 km to the intersection with Kananaskis Lakes Trail. Turn right here and follow for 2.2 km to the intersection with the Spray Lakes / Smith-Dorrien Trail. From the intersection, drive a well-maintained gravel road for 30 km to the Buller day-use area. Turn left into the parking area.

Hiking directions

From the parking area, return to the main road, cross and locate the trailhead off the east shoulder of the roadway. Shortly after, there are two junctions with the High Rockies trail. Stay straight at the first intersection, ignoring the trail on the right. A few hundred metres farther it meets the High Rockies trail a second

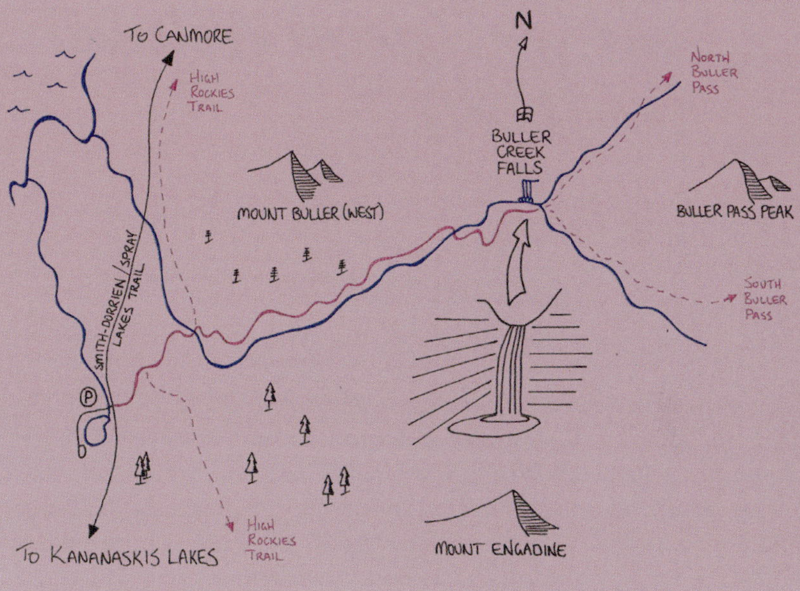

time just past a bridge over Buller Creek. Turn to the right and begin the ascent above the creek. From here, the well-used trail gains elevation steadily to a view of the waterfall: 300 metres to this point.

More to explore: South and North Buller Pass

The hike to South Buller Pass is one of the premier day hikes in the Kananaskis, although you should expect it to be a long day. The trail gains nearly 700 metres to the pass over its 6.7 km. Just remember, you'll have to cover that distance on the hike back out as well. Experienced and fit hikers can extend the day by following an alpine route that links the south and north Buller passes. This option will be a strenuous but very rewarding day out. All told, this trip will hit you up for over 900 metres of elevation gain and add 16 km to your odometer.

When tackling hikes with lots of elevation gain, it is important to note how temperatures fluctuate. All things being equal, one can anticipate that for every 100 metres of elevation gain, the temperature will drop one degree Celsius. If the forecast high is 20° at valley bottom, expect Buller Pass (for example) to be only 12 or 13°. All of a sudden that extra layer left in the car is looking pretty good. Plan accordingly!

22. Old Goat Glacier Waterfall (unofficial)

LOCATION: Peter Lougheed Provincial Park, AB
DRIVING DIFFICULTY: MODERATE
HIKING DIFFICULTY: EASY (to gravel flat and view of waterfall)
HIKING DISTANCE: 2.5 km
HIKING TIME: 1 h

If you experience chronic neck pain, the hike to Old Goat Glacier might not be for you. There is an all too natural tendency to want to look up ... waaay up. Whether it is Old Goat Mountain itself soaring high overhead or the waterfall that drains its glacial basin, everything here will divert your eyes skyward. If neck pain is preventing you from viewing waterfalls, talk about it with your family doctor.

Driving directions

From the town of Canmore, follow the Spray Lakes Road past the Nordic Centre (well signed throughout the town). Just past the Grassi Lakes parking area, the road becomes gravel. Follow the gravel Spray Lakes / Smith-Dorrien Trail (Highway 742) for 13 km to the Spray Lakes reservoir. Turn right and cross the berm to the west shore. Turn left onto Spray Lakes West Road and follow it for 1.1 km to a large unsigned parking area on the right. This is the trailhead to Old Goat Glacier.

Hiking directions

From the parking area, locate a trail ascending into the trees. After a brief ascent, the trail descends slightly to the creek and follows alongside it for 2.5 km. At this point, leave the trees and enter a large gravel flat with an immense and impressive cascade tumbling down the headwall from above. It is possible to ascend the rocky streambed for an additional 300 m to the base of the falls, or ...

More to explore: Old Goat Glacier

From the gravel flat, the Old Goat Glacier trail wanders left before beginning a steep ascent up the headwall. After cresting the headwall,

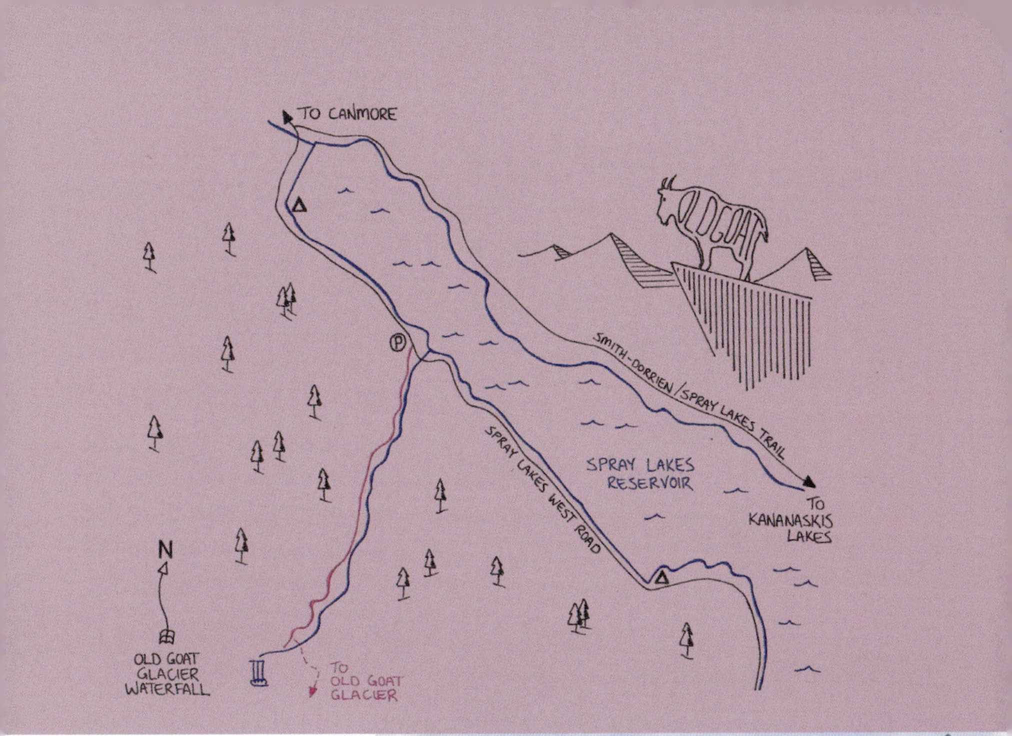

the trail continues to gain elevation steadily atop a moraine overlooking the remnants of Old Goat Glacier. The route is indistinct occasionally and is marked intermittently with cairns. It gains nearly 700 metres over its 5.0 km distance and can be very cool and windy up the basin, even on hot summer days, so don't forget that extra layer.

23. Ribbon Falls

LOCATION: Evan Thomas Provincial Recreation Area, AB
DRIVING DIFFICULTY: EASY
HIKING DIFFICULTY: DIFFICULT (due to distance)
HIKING DISTANCE: 9.3 km
HIKING TIME: 4–5 h

This is one of the classic hikes in Kananaskis Country. While often done as a longer day hike, there are backcountry campgrounds above and below the falls that allow for an easy overnight backpacking trip. The trail is deservedly popular and boasts many sights along the way, including numerous other small waterfalls and opportunities for further exploration.

Driving directions

From the junction of the Trans-Canada and Highway 40, drive south on Highway 40 for 23 km to the intersection signed for Kananaskis Village. Turn right and follow the road for 800 m to Centennial Drive. Turn right immediately onto Ribbon Creek Road and follow it to the main parking area at the end of the road.

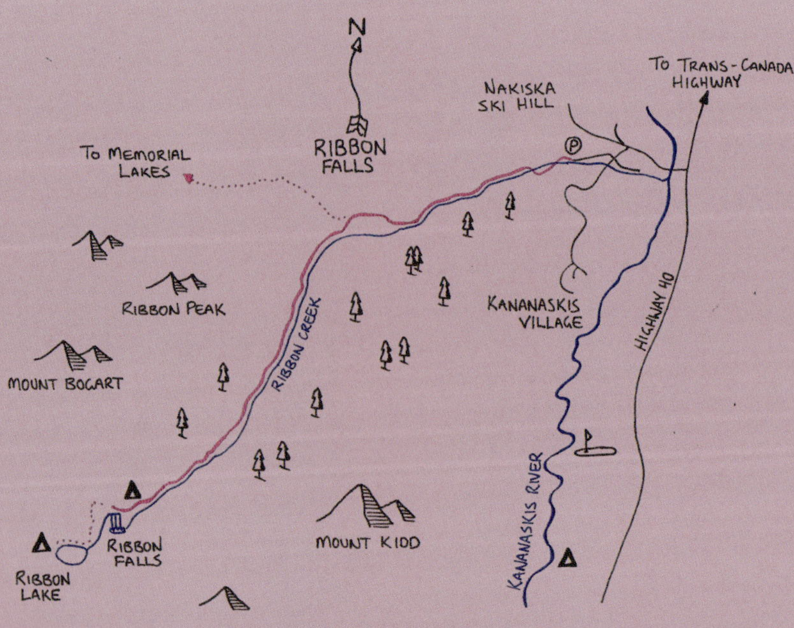

Hiking directions

From the parking area, locate the start of the trail at the far west end of the parking area. The initial trail is quite wide and well maintained, weaving back and forth over Ribbon Creek for the first two kilometres. Be aware of cyclists for the first 4.5 km. After this point the trail narrows and begins to climb gently for the rest of the way to the falls. Trail waypoints are as follows:

- 1.6 km – Junction with numerous trails; stay straight along the right-hand side of the creek.
- 2.5 km – Junction; stay right with the trail ascending gently above the creek.
- 3.5 km – Junction; turn left (signed for "Ribbon"; turn right for Memorial Lakes).
- 4.5 km – End of wide, maintained trail. You can ride a bicycle to this point and lock it up on a bike rack here.
- 5.6 km – Start of a small canyon. There is a series of waterfalls visible along the trail above the creek.
- 6.5 km – Waterfall
- 6.7 km – Waterfall
- 9.0 km – Ribbon Creek campground
- 9.3 km – Ribbon Falls

More to explore: Ribbon Lake

There is a second campground 2 km beyond Ribbon Falls, at the west end of Ribbon Lake. These next two kilometres are quite steep involving the use of chains to ascend the headwall above the waterfall. From here there are opportunities to explore South Buller or North Buller Pass as well as Guinn's Pass.

24. Troll Falls

LOCATION: Evan Thomas Provincial Recreation Area, AB
DRIVING DIFFICULTY: EASY
HIKING DIFFICULTY: EASY
HIKING DISTANCE: 1.7 km
HIKING TIME: 40 min.

Troll Falls is one of the best family-friendly hikes in K-Country, if not the entire Rockies. The trail is gentle and well maintained, making it stroller friendly and manageable for even the smallest of hikers. Kids get a kick out of the teepees along the way and are rewarded with a beautiful waterfall at the end. The falls are accessible year-round and can be combined with numerous other trails for extended outings if desired. Use extra caution on the bridge: it's not just kids that love candy at Troll Falls!

Driving directions

From the junction of the Trans-Canada and Highway 40, drive south on Highway 40 for 23 km to the intersection signed for Kananaskis Village. Turn right and follow the road for 1 km to a turnoff on the right-hand side signed for the Troll Falls trailhead.

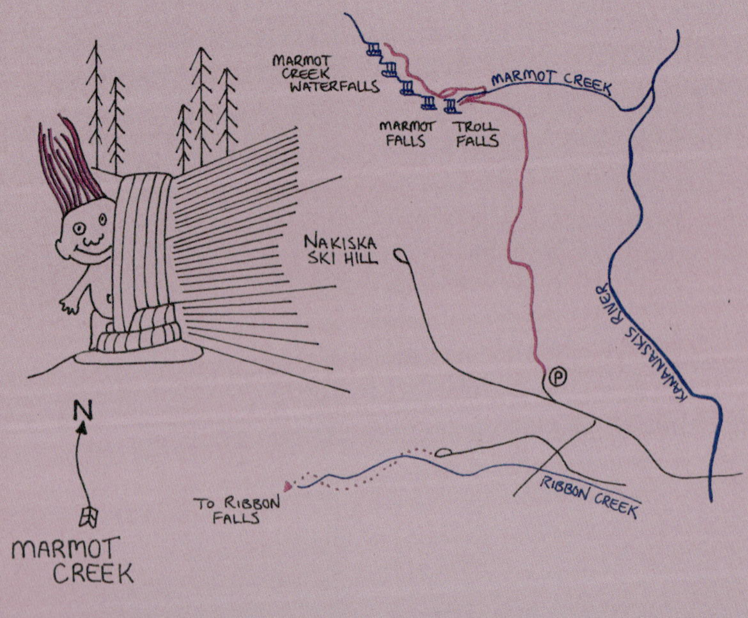

Hiking directions

From the parking area, walk past the gate on the gravel road and pick up a wide pathway beside the outhouse. The trail winds through mixed forest for 1.7 km to Troll Falls. Roads and pathways intersect the main trail on occasion, but junctions are generally signed for Troll Falls.

For the upper falls, either cross the creek just below Troll Falls or backtrack along the main trail for 200 m and follow signs for Upper Falls Route. The trail narrows as it ascends through the forest to the base of the upper falls at 2.3 km. From here you can return the way you came or proceed past the end of the maintained trail to Marmot Creek Falls.

Are there really trolls at Troll Falls??

There have been sightings ... keep your eyes peeled!

25. Marmot Falls and Upper Troll Falls

LOCATION: Evan Thomas Provincial Recreation Area, AB
DRIVING DIFFICULTY: EASY
HIKING DIFFICULTY: EASY
HIKING DISTANCE: 2.3 km
HIKING TIME: 1 h

While the namesake waterfall, Troll Falls, draws most of the attention to this hike, Marmot Falls and Upper Troll Falls are only a minimal addition along the well-maintained trail and should be included for everyone visiting this spot. Marmot is about the same size as Troll Falls, with the added bonus of a small alcove that allows you to sneak right in behind the cataract. Upper Troll is a beautiful, multi-tiered cascade that tumbles over mossy steps.

Driving directions

From the junction of the Trans-Canada and Highway 40, drive south on Highway 40 for 23 km to the intersection signed for Kananaskis

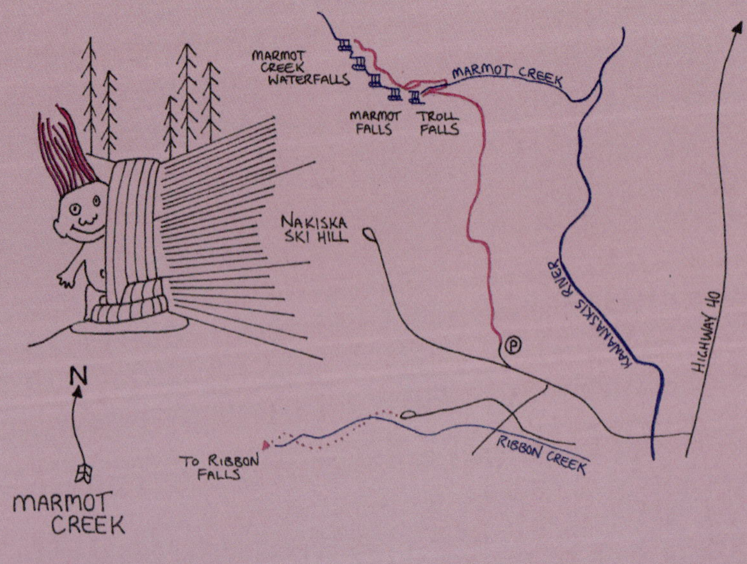

Village. Turn right and follow the road for 1 km to a turnoff on the right-hand side signed for the Troll Falls trailhead.

Hiking directions

From the parking area, walk past the gate on the gravel road and pick up a wide pathway beside the outhouse. The trail winds through mixed forest for 1.7 km to Troll Falls. Roads and pathways intersect the main trail occasionally, but junctions are generally signed for Troll Falls.

For the Upper Falls, either cross the creek just below Troll Falls or backtrack along the main trail for 200 m and follow signs for the Upper Falls route. The trail narrows as it ascends through the forest to the base of the upper falls at 2.3 km. The picturesque Marmot Falls can be viewed en route to or on the return from Upper Troll Falls: a short detour, staying along the creek, gets you there.

26. Marmot Creek Waterfalls (unofficial)

LOCATION: Evan Thomas Provincial Recreation Area, AB
DRIVING DIFFICULTY: EASY
HIKING DIFFICULTY: EASY
HIKING DISTANCE: 2.7 km
HIKING TIME: 1–1.5 h

The trail to the Marmot Creek waterfalls is the 4×4 extension to the Troll Falls trail. For the surefooted hiker, the extra effort is well worth the reward of the waterfalls just beyond. While the names may be confusing with this many waterfalls in the mix, all you need to know is there are falls and lots of them here at Marmot Creek!

Driving directions

From the junction of the Trans-Canada and Highway 40, drive south on Highway 40 for 23 km to the intersection signed for Kananaskis Village. Turn right and follow the road for 1 km to a turnoff on the right-hand side signed for the Troll Falls trailhead.

Hiking directions

From the parking area, walk past the gate on the gravel road and pick up the wide Troll Falls trail beside the outhouse. Follow this trail for 1.5 km to a junction signed for the Upper Falls route. At 2.3 km you'll come to the Upper Falls and the end of the official trail. From here a boot-beaten trail beyond the sign climbs more steeply and is often slick. Take care with your footing, especially on the edge of the canyon rim. From along the trail you can look down onto two more cataracts. The lower of these is just 200 m past Upper Troll Falls, with the uppermost one being an additional 200 m farther.

The name game

There are numerous online and other guidebook references that refer to Upper Troll Falls and the Marmot Creek waterfall by a variety of names. The only one officially named on Alberta Parks' maps is Troll Falls. Upper Troll Falls is now referenced specifically on the

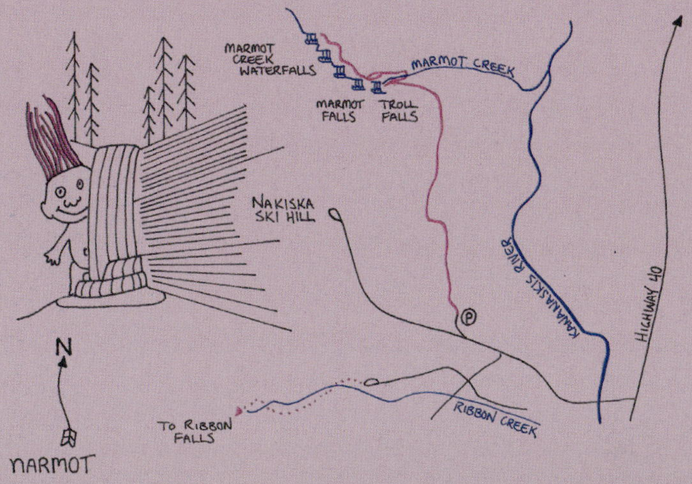

Alberta Parks website with the recently upgraded extension to the Troll Falls trail. Marmot Falls is about as official as it gets, as the name is broadly accepted even though it lacks a formal designation on available maps. The waterfalls farther up Marmot Creek also lack references on maps as well as agreement on their nicknames.

27. Kananaskis Falls (unofficial)

LOCATION: Bow Valley Wildland Provincial Park, AB
DRIVING DIFFICULTY: EASY
HIKING DIFFICULTY: EASY
HIKING DISTANCE: 1.2 km
HIKING TIME: 40 min.

To add to the earlier confusion over the names and locations of Upper and Lower Kananaskis Falls, this small cascade known locally as "Kananaskis Falls" only further muddies the waters. The trail follows alongside a small stream that drains a basin below Kananaskis Peak, so as fitting as the name may be, it's not very creative. Any suggestions?

Driving directions

From the junction of the Trans-Canada and Highway 40, drive south on Highway 40 for 22.5 km. Just before the junction for Kananaskis Village and the Nakiska ski hill, look to the left side of the highway. The ditch is an unsigned parking area that hikers use to access Wasootch Peak and Kananaskis Peak. Turn left across the northbound lane and park.

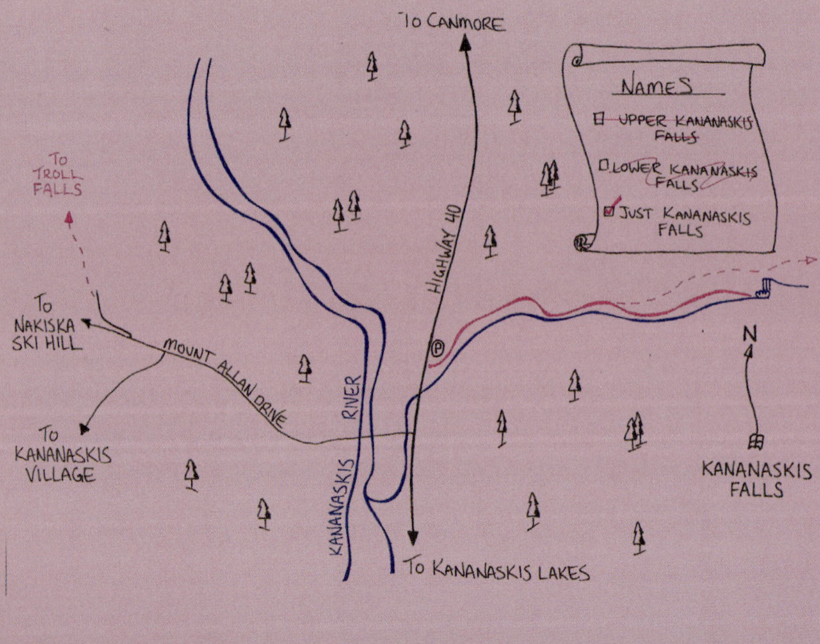

Hiking directions

From the parking area, a flagged stake marks the start of the trail. The initial 300 m of this trail is now buried under a couple feet of rock from an earlier washout of the creek. Walk up the gravel on the left-hand side of the creek channel (usually dry) for those 300 m until the trail is visible in the trees. After another 500 m there is a yellow Wildland Provincial Park Boundary sign. Just past the sign is a junction with a lightly used trail to the right. Leave the main trail here and descend to the creek. Follow along the left-hand side of the creek for another 500 m to a small waterfall plunging off a plate of bedrock.

Even though this hike is short, it gains elevation steadily: nearly 200 metres from the parking area to the falls.

More to explore: Wasootch Peak

Wasootch Peak is one of the most popular and accessible scrambles, offering big views over the Kananaskis Valley, Mount Allan and the Nakiska ski resort as well as other well-known peaks such as Mount Kidd. Don't let its popularity suck you in without knowing what you are getting into, though. The route up Wasootch gains more than 900 vertical metres over its 6 km length and should not be taken lightly. Allow for most of a day and research the route thoroughly beforehand. Although the exposure is relatively minimal, there are rocky sections which may require hands-on scrambling where a slip or fall would substantially ruin what would otherwise be considered a good time. The reward for success, however, is 360-degree views of Kananaskis Country!

28. Jewell Falls

LOCATION: Bow Valley Provincial Park, AB
DRIVING DIFFICULTY: EASY
HIKING DIFFICULTY: EASY
HIKING DISTANCE: 4.8 km
HIKING TIME: 2 h

The hike to Jewell Pass is generally visited by those tackling the Prairie View and Yates Mountain routes, with Jewell Falls being a pleasant surprise along the way. While the entire loop is certainly recommended for experienced and fit hikers, those with kids will find that a hike to Jewell Falls can round out a day quite nicely.

Driving directions

From the junction of the Trans-Canada and Highway 40, drive south on Highway 40 for 9 km to a picnic area signed for Barrier Dam. Turn right and follow the road for 600 m to a parking area for the Barrier Lake interpretive trail.

Hiking directions

From the parking area, locate the trailhead for Prairie View Trail. Follow a decommissioned utility road for 1.1 km to a junction. Stay left

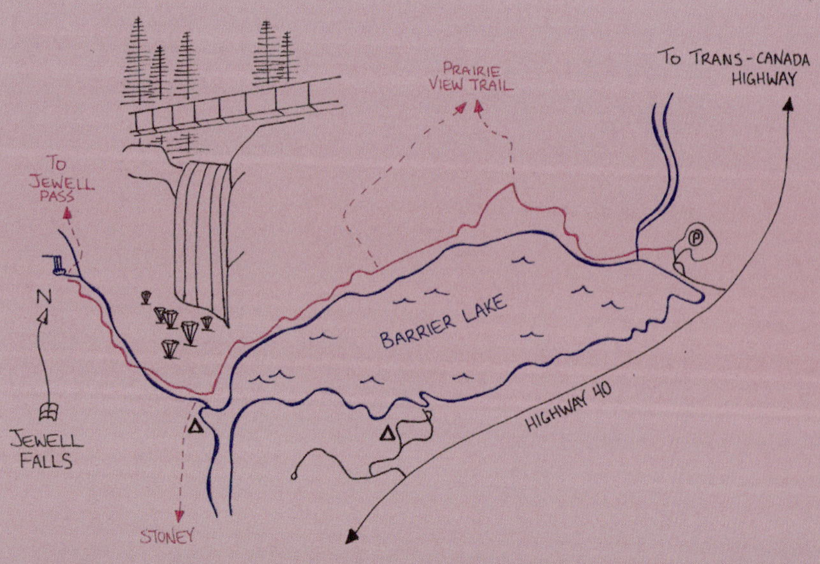

and follow the road for 3.2 km along the shoreline of Barrier Lake to another junction near the Jewell Bay campground. Turn right (signed for Jewell Pass) and follow a narrower hiking trail for 500 m to Jewell Falls.

More to explore: Jewell Pass

The Prairie View and Jewell Pass loop is a stunning hike that takes you high above the floor of Kananaskis Valley and rewards you with views of nearby peaks and Barrier Lake. The recommended route goes counter-clockwise, ascending via the Prairie View trail and returning to the lake via Jewell Pass, with a visit to Jewell Falls along the way.

PHOTO: WALTER TERSMETTE

29. Acephale Falls

LOCATION: Bow Valley Provincial Park, AB
DRIVING DIFFICULTY: EASY
HIKING DIFFICULTY: EASY
HIKING DISTANCE: 2.1 km
HIKING TIME: 45–60 min.

Do you enjoy suddenly slamming on your brakes on a busy highway, jerking the steering wheel abruptly and coming to rapid stop in a ditch in a less than controlled fashion? Don't let the rapid exit from the Trans-Canada Highway take away from what the hike to Acephale Falls has to offer. This short stroll to a secluded waterfall is sure to calm the nerves.

Driving directions

Note: Access to Acephale Falls is via the eastbound lanes of the Trans-Canada Highway ONLY.

From Canmore, drive east on the Trans-Canada for 16 km to the Lac des Arcs junction, continuing past the overpass for 2.8 km to an unmarked trailhead off the right-hand shoulder of the highway. This is the trailhead for the Quaite Valley trail. Use extreme caution when exiting and entering the highway.

If driving westbound from Calgary, take Exit 105 for Lac des Arcs. Turn left at the top of the overpass, cross over the Trans-Canada, then head back eastbound for the 2.8 km.

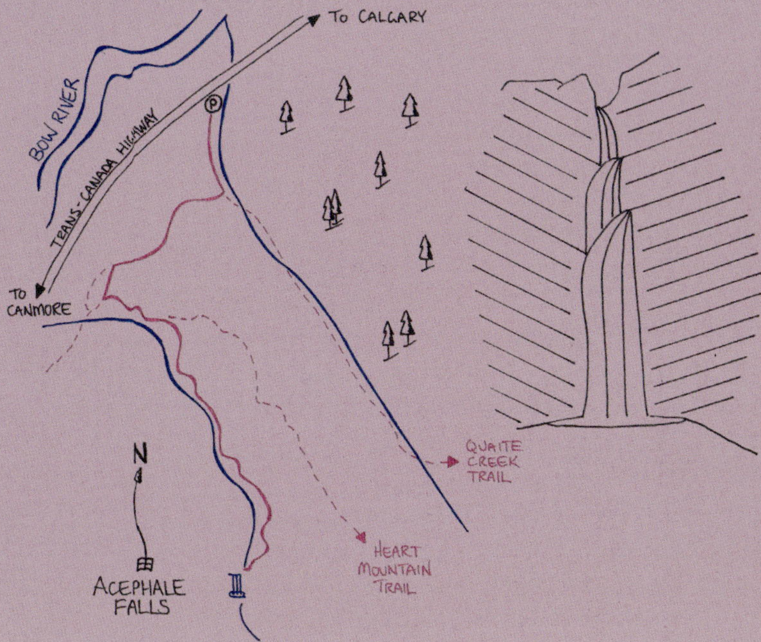

Hiking directions

From the parking area, head west on a decommissioned road for 300 m. Look for a path on the right; there is a sign with a trail map. Follow this for 500 m to a powerline cut. Turn left and follow a trail below the powerline for about 150 m. Keep your eyes peeled for a small sign in the trees on the left for Heart Mountain Trail. Enter the trees and follow this for 200 m to a fork in the trail with another small wooden sign for Heart Mountain Trail. Stay to the right and follow for an additional kilometre, where Acephale Falls will be visible just off the trail on the right-hand side.

More to explore: Heart Creek

Another popular hike nearby is Heart Creek, accessed from a trailhead near the Lac des Arcs overpass. This trail ventures deep into Heart Creek Canyon, where it hops back and forth over the creek on wooden bridges. It is 2.4 km from the trailhead to the end of the trail near the back of the canyon. Even with kids, Acephale Falls and Heart Creek can be combined into a great day of hiking.

30. Grotto Falls

LOCATION: Exshaw, AB
DRIVING DIFFICULTY: EASY
HIKING DIFFICULTY: EASY
HIKING DISTANCE: 2.0 km
HIKING TIME: 45–60 min.

Grotto Canyon is a fabulous excursion deep into the limestone underbelly of the Rockies' front range mountains. It is popular with hikers and climbers alike and is accessible nearly year-round.

Driving directions

From the town of Canmore, drive east on Highway 1A for 11 km to the signed Grotto Pond day-use and picnic area on the left. This is a fabulous lunch spot, complete with tables and outhouse facilities, and features a short stroll around the small lake.

Alternatively, if travelling from the east, leave the Trans-Canada Highway at Exit 114 (Highway 1X, signed for Exshaw and Seebe). Follow for 4 km to Highway 1A and turn left. Drive west on Highway 1A for 11 km to the Grotto Pond picnic area on the right.

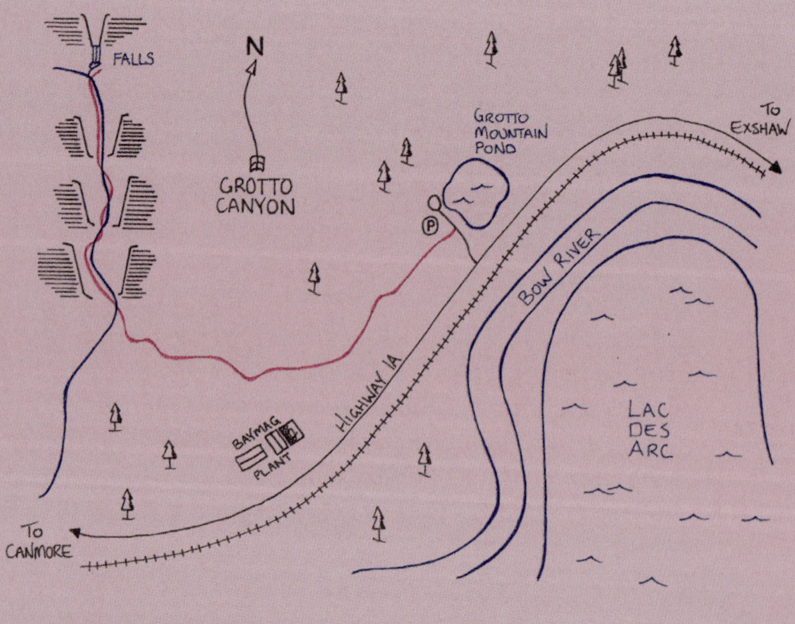

Hiking directions

From the Grotto Mountain picnic area, follow a wide pathway for 1 km to the mouth of a narrow canyon. Walk along the canyon floor for an additional kilometre to a large cliff face and a fork in the gorge. The waterfall is another hundred metres to the right. Take particular care scrambling up to the base of the falls, as the rock is polished and very slippery.

During periods of high stream flow you may be prevented from hiking the canyon floor. It is possible to follow trails in the trees above the canyon for some portions of the route, but at the peak of runoff or after a significant rain, the canyon could be inaccessible altogether.

Grotto Canyon in winter

The frigid winter months might be the most picturesque way to experience Grotto Canyon. As water seeps from the limestone walls it freezes into curtains and pillars of ice. It is understandably popular with ice climbers for this reason, but its sheer beauty can be appreciated by everyone. Donning a set of micro-spikes, crampons or some other traction device for your boots is recommended for any winter hike, to manage the ice and even hard-packed snow.

31. Spray Falls

LOCATION: Dead Man's Flats, AB
DRIVING DIFFICULTY: EASY
HIKING DIFFICULTY: EASY
HIKING DISTANCE: 600 m
HIKING TIME: 15 min.

Spray Falls is a short, sweet and simple hike out of view and off the radar of most. Many people at the trailhead have their sights set on Mount Collembola and Mount Allan as well as Wind Ridge and Skogan Pass, leaving you, the distinguished reader, a waterfall (hopefully) all to yourself.

Driving directions

From the town of Canmore, drive east on the Trans-Canada Highway for about 8 km. Take Exit 98, signed for Dead Man's Flats. Exit off the highway and stay right, onto George Biggy Sr. Road. Follow a good gravel road for 1.5 km to its end. Banff Gate Mountain Resort is on the left and the Pigeon Mountain day-use area and trailhead are on the right. Park in the day-use parking area.

Hiking directions

From the Pigeon Mountain day-use parking, walk back down the gravel road for about 300 m, past a powerline cut. Just beyond the powerlines, look for a trail on the left-hand side of the road that descends into the trees (marked with a wooden stake and flagging tape). Follow a lightly used trail through the trees towards Pigeon Creek. Spray Falls will become visible shortly after. Clamber over deadfall and descend to the creek.

Private property

As you drive (slowly) past the quarry on George Biggy Sr. Road, keep your eyes peeled for Lower Spray Falls pouring out of the forest across the Thunderstone rock quarry. Unfortunately, this is the best view of this waterfall you will get. The quarry is private property, and any would-be access to the falls would also be trespassing. There are a couple other waterfalls that have been excluded from this guidebook for similar reasons.

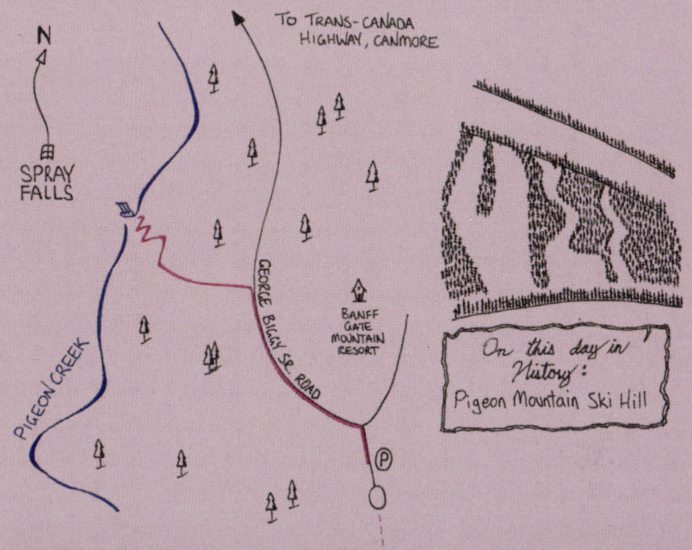
N
SPRAY FALLS
TO TRANS-CANADA HIGHWAY, CANMORE
GEORGE BIGGY SR. ROAD
BANFF GATE MOUNTAIN RESORT
PIGEON CREEK
P
On this day in History:
Pigeon Mountain Ski Hill

32. Three Sisters Creek Waterfalls

LOCATION: Canmore, AB
DRIVING DIFFICULTY: EASY
HIKING DIFFICULTY: EASY
HIKING DISTANCE: 2.0 km
HIKING TIME: 45 min.

Below the summits of Canmore's skyline attraction, the Three Sisters, awaits an amazing, family-friendly jaunt to a pair of small waterfalls on a creek by the same name. The lower of the two falls tumbles through the remnants of an old dam, while the upper falls is a larger and equally picturesque cascade sliding over rock slabs in the creek.

Driving directions

From the town of Canmore, drive east on the Trans-Canada Highway to Exit 93, signed for Three Sisters Parkway. Leave the highway and stay to the right on the Parkway. Ahead at the four-way stop, proceed straight on Three Sisters Boulevard to the end of the road at Hubman Landing. Park opposite the houses, taking care not to block the access and parking of residents.

Hiking directions

From the available parking along Hubman Landing, locate the gate at the end of Three Sisters Boulevard. Walk 200 m up the road beyond the gate, alongside an old fence. At a junction with the Canmore Highline trail, marked with blue stakes, head to the right on the Highline trail. Follow this for just over 1 km to a bridge over Three Sisters Creek. After crossing the creek, look for a less-used trail on the left. Follow alongside the creek for an additional 200 m to a small waterfall. To get to the second waterfall, cross the creek below the first. Continue along the left-hand side of the creek for an additional 400 m to the upper cascade.

Please note that Canmore Highline Trail is a very popular mountain biking and mixed-use route. Keep your eyes and ears open and stay to the side of the trail to allow cyclists to pass.

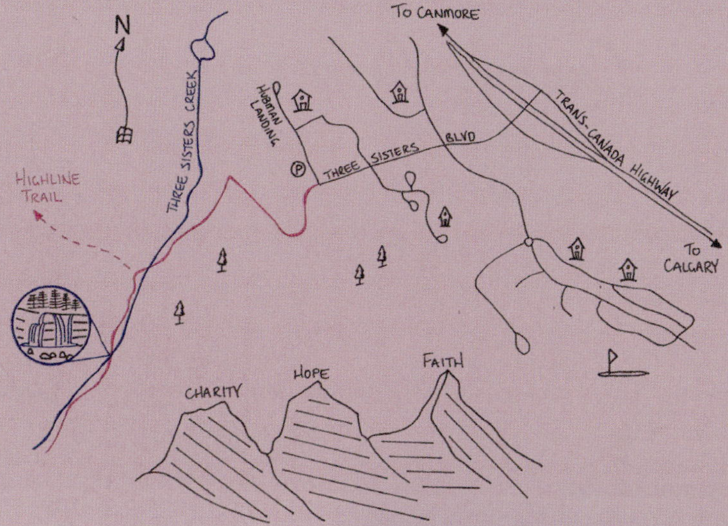

Picture perfect

The Three Sisters may be the most iconic and photographed scene in and around Canmore, easily recognized from any angle. These peaks are an attraction for visitors from far and wide and a reliable muse for local artists at any time of the year. A couple of the best vantage points are from near Policeman's Creek and from the bridge over the Bow River near the boat launch. If you're really talented you can even get a postcard-worthy photo by rolling down the passenger window of your car and snapping a quick one as you fly by doing 110 km/h on the Trans-Canada.

PHOTO: WALTER TERSMETTE

33. Canmore Creek Falls

LOCATION: Canmore, AB
DRIVING DIFFICULTY: EASY
HIKING DIFFICULTY: EASY
HIKING DISTANCE: 400 m
HIKING TIME: 15 min.

Canmore Creek Falls is a short, sweet and relatively hidden hike that makes for a great addition to a day exploring the town of Canmore. The shady trail is also a welcome refuge from the summer heat.

Driving directions

From pretty much anywhere in Canmore, follow signage for the Canmore Nordic Centre. You'll find yourself on Three Sisters Drive, along which you are looking for a turn onto Spray Lakes Road. Follow for 900 m to the Quarry Lake Park day-use area on your left.

Hiking directions

From the Quarry Lake parking, cross Spray Lakes Road and locate a well-used trail descending from the roadway. Once on the trail, stay to the left and below the road for 100 m, crossing Canmore Creek along the way. Once across the creek, head to the right and walk another 100 m until the upper waterfall comes into view.

Continue descending along the pathway for another 200 m, then down a set of wooden stairs, where the lower

PHOTO: WALTER TERSMETTE

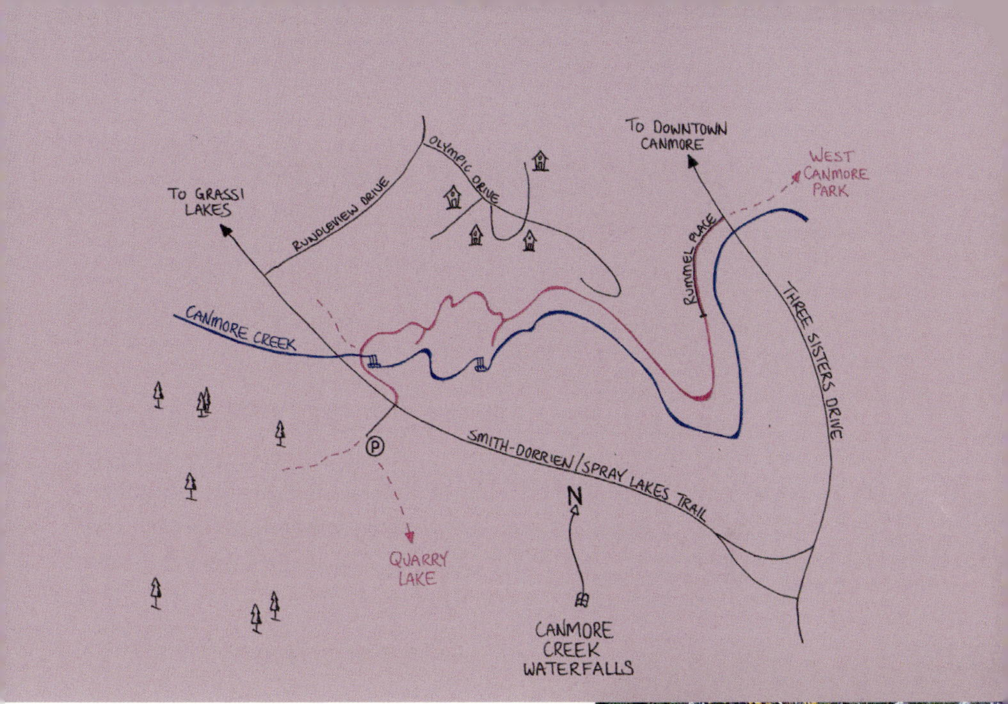

waterfall comes into view shortly after. Return the way you came or continue down the trail along the creek for a slightly longer stroll.

Alternative access

A second option for this hike is to park at the Canmore public boat launch off Rundle Drive near the bridge over the Bow River. From here, walk 500 m on a wide pathway alongside the river to West Canmore Park. Exit the park to the west behind some houses, cross Three Sisters Drive and walk up Rummel Place. As Rummel Place bends hard to the right, pick up a hiking trail that enters the forest, with Canmore Creek on the left. Continue for another hundred metres to the lower falls (1.3 km from parking), then another 200 m to the upper falls (1.5 km from parking).

PHOTO: WALTER TERSMETTE

34. Grassi Lakes Waterfall

LOCATION: Canmore, AB
DRIVING DIFFICULTY: EASY
HIKING DIFFICULTY: EASY
HIKING DISTANCE: 1.5 km
HIKING TIME: 30–40 min.

The Grassi Lakes area is well known as one of the main hubs for outdoor recreation in Canmore. It attracts everyone from hikers to bikers to climbers to paddlers as well as photographers and people that just want to lounge around in the fresh air. The short waterfall hike is just one way you can spend your time here.

Driving directions

From pretty much anywhere in Canmore, follow signage for the Canmore Nordic Centre. You'll find yourself on Three Sisters Drive, along which you are looking for a turn onto Spray Lakes Road. Follow Spray Lakes Road for 1 km past the turnoff to the Nordic Centre. Drive a bit farther and turn left into the Grassi Lakes day-use area. Parking is 300 m farther along this road. There is also an overflow parking area alongside Spray Lakes Road, near the turnoff.

Hiking directions

From the Grassi Lakes day-use area, locate a large trailhead kiosk for Grassi Lakes. A large pathway enters the trees, which is followed for 100 m to a junction. Stay left and continue for another 1.4 km to a viewpoint of the waterfall. It is possible to continue along the trail and

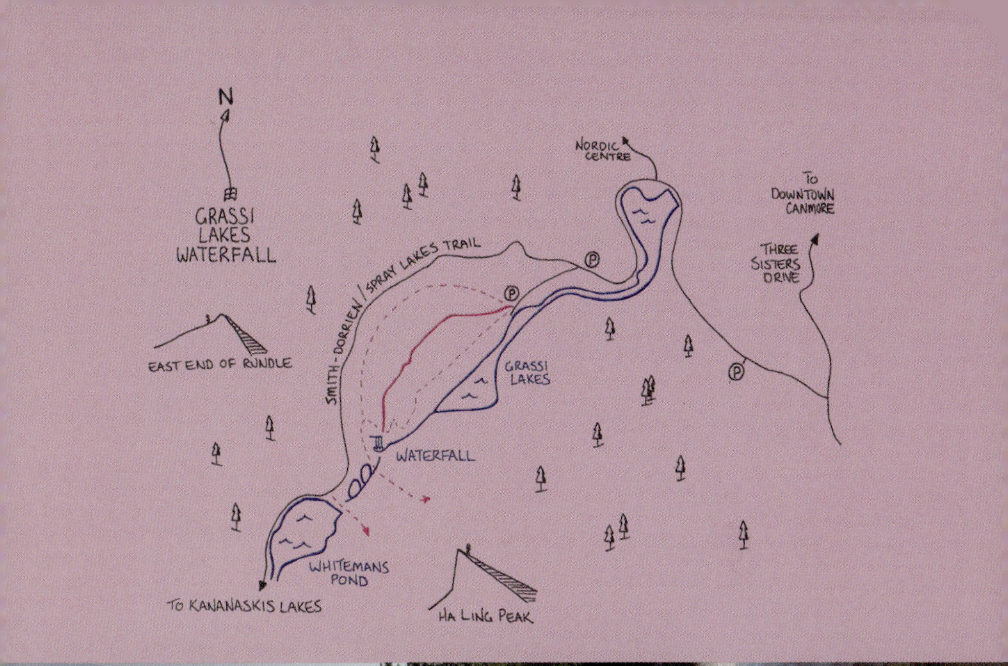

access the base of the falls. Return the way you came or complete the loop via the Upper Grassi Lakes trail.

More to explore: Grassi Lakes and beyond

There is a lot to choose from, and all the options are good. From the waterfall viewpoint you can continue ascending the trail to Upper Grassi Lakes or extend the hike even higher to Whiteman's Pond, which sits at the foot of Ha Ling Peak. Other popular hikes include the scrambles of Ha Ling Peak itself or EEOR (East End of Rundle) right across the street. The Grassi Lakes area is also a popular sport-climbing venue. There's a large network of mixed-use and mountain-biking trails in around Grassi and Quarry lakes as well as cross-country skiing in the winter. One could keep busy up here for days!

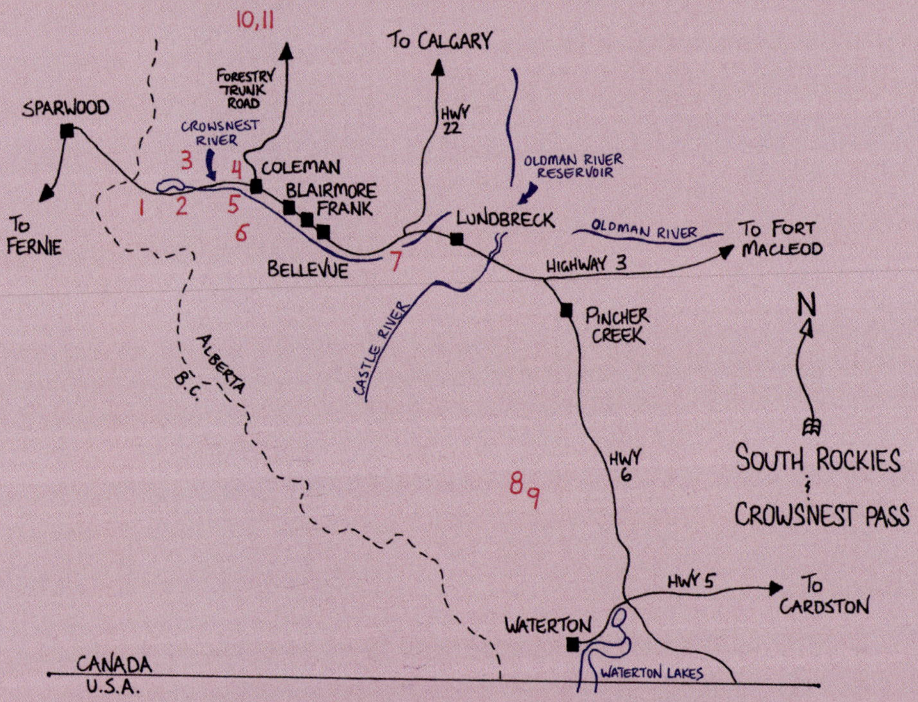
10,11
To CALGARY
FORESTRY TRUNK ROAD
SPARWOOD
CROWSNEST RIVER
HWY 22
3
4
COLEMAN
OLDMAN RIVER RESERVOIR
BLAIRMORE
FRANK
1
2
5
LUNDBRECK
To FERNIE
6
OLDMAN RIVER
To FORT MACLEOD
7
BELLEVUE
HIGHWAY 3
PINCHER CREEK
N
CASTLE RIVER
ALBERTA
B.C.
HWY 6
SOUTH ROCKIES
&
CROWSNEST PASS
8
9
HWY 5
To CARDSTON
WATERTON
CANADA
U.S.A.
WATERTON LAKES

CHAPTER 3

Southern Rockies and Crowsnest Pass

As you approach the Crowsnest Pass, sprawling prairies give rise to foothills and foothills to the Rocky Mountains. The setting sun is warm on your face, kissed by a gentle breeze. Except that this is not a gentle breeze. It's a 100 km/h gust of wind capable of knocking over a loaded semi-trailer as well as whipping skyscraper-sized windmill propellers into a frenzy to generate electricity. So take refuge with these waterfall hikes hidden throughout Alberta's southern Rockies.

This chapter covers the Crowsnest Highway (Highway 3) corridor and the surrounding area as it enters the southern Rocky Mountains, through to the BC–Alberta boundary. The region is steeped in a long mining history and is a service hub for industry and trucking. Today, it is slowly regenerating itself as a playground for outdoor enthusiasts, including fishing, hiking, biking, hunting and off-highway vehicle activities.

Highway 3 bisects this portion of southern Alberta, with the Crowsnest Pass municipalities (Bellevue, Hillcrest, Coleman and Blairmore) providing all necessary services. The town of Pincher Creek is just to the east and boasts all the amenities. The region is accessed by Highways 2 and 22 from the east and the north (about 230 km south of Calgary and 150 km west of Lethbridge), and by Highway 3 via Sparwood if entering from BC.

1. Crowsnest Creek Falls

LOCATION: Crowsnest Pass, AB
DRIVING DIFFICULTY: MODERATE
HIKING DIFFICULTY: EASY
HIKING DISTANCE: Zero
HIKING TIME: Also zero

Crowsnest Creek Falls is best saved as a picnic spot with the kids or a short stop to stretch your legs if passing through the area. While there's no hiking to be had, this small waterfall offers peaceful relief from your driver's seat with a fairy-tale-like ambience juxtaposed with its location next to a forestry road.

Driving directions

From the Crowsnest Lake rest area, drive west on Highway 3 for 1.5 km. Cross Crowsnest Creek and turn left onto a gravel road signed for Ptolemy Trailhead. Follow the gravel road for 3.0 km and park in a small widening on the left-hand side of the road.

Hiking directions

This small waterfall is on Crowsnest Creek and just off the side of the gravel road. A fire ring and makeshift log benches next to the creek make for a nice lunch stop.

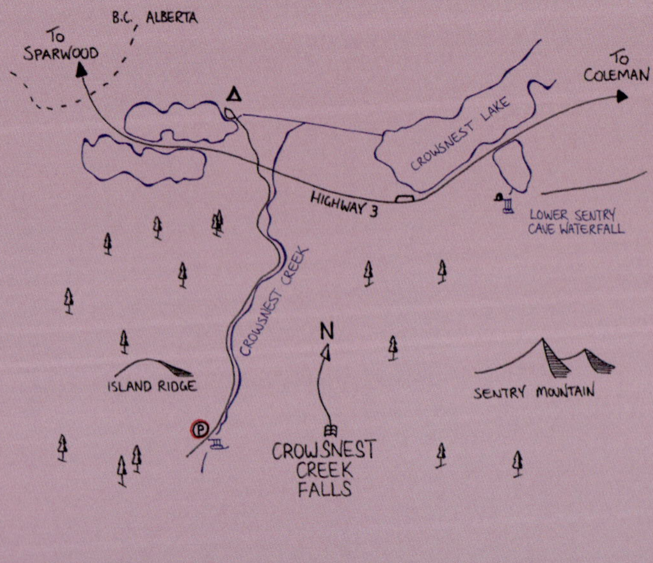

2. Low Sentry Cave Waterfall (unofficial)

LOCATION: Crowsnest Pass, AB
DRIVING DIFFICULTY: EASY
HIKING DIFFICULTY: EASY
HIKING DISTANCE: 100 m
HIKING TIME: minimum 9.58 seconds (current world record for 100 m dash)

This waterfall earned inclusion not for being a quality hike or even a waterfall visible year-round, but rather for the fact that during a brief period each spring it satisfies the definition of a waterfall. Despite its easy access and incredibly short walk, this fall may be the most elusive in the book. At certain times in late spring, when the snow is melting and ice thaws deep within Sentry Mountain, the meltwater looks for an exit to the outside world. Here, at Low Sentry Cave, that water pours out of a small hole in the steep limestone walls and into Emerald Lake below.

Driving directions

From the Crowsnest Lake Rest Area, drive east on Highway 3 for 3.0 km to an unsigned intersection on the right (the former site of a visitor centre, now closed). Turn right off the highway then stay immediately to the right. The unmarked road briefly turns to gravel for a couple hundred metres before regaining the pavement. Follow for 2 km to a gate at its end.

Hiking directions

From the parking area, the falls may or may not be visible straight ahead on the decommissioned roadway. But you'll know the minute you arrive if the waterfall is active or not, as it pours down right to the road. From below it is difficult to see the hole in the wall where the water flows out of the mountain, although it is possible to scramble up to get a closer look. The best time to see it, all things being equal, is from mid- to late June.

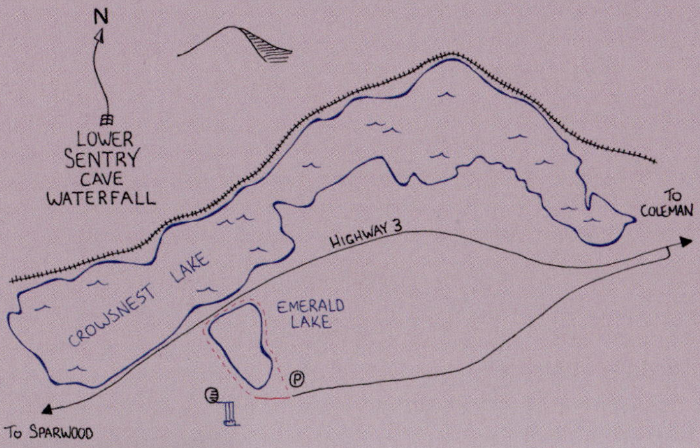

Caving in the Crowsnest Pass

Caving used to be a fringe activity, something that (literally) happened under cover of darkness. Maybe you had a friend of a friend of a friend that had done a bit of it. Like many outdoor activities once undertaken by only the craziest of outdoor masochists, caving and canyoneering have almost reached the threshold of mainstream. The limestone mountains of the Crowsnest Pass are home to many sizes of cave systems within their peaks. Names like Gargantua, Cleft Cave and Yorkshire Pot are now widely recognizable among the outdoor community, no longer just whispers from a small sect of aging speleologists from years gone by. Speleology is the study and exploration of caves and should only be undertaken with proper gear and training.

For more about caving in the Rockies, check out *Caves of the Canadian Rockies and Columbia Mountains*, by Jon Rollins (Rocky Mountain Books, 2004).

3. Allison Creek Falls

LOCATION: Crowsnest Pass, AB
DRIVING DIFFICULTY: MODERATE
HIKING DIFFICULTY: EASY (depending on water level)
HIKING DISTANCE: 1.8 km
HIKING TIME: 40 min.

Located beneath the silhouette of the Crowsnest's namesake peak, Crowsnest Mountain, Allison Creek Falls is an enjoyable hike that is becoming increasingly popular. With close proximity to Coleman, Chinook Lake, camping and other recreation opportunities as well as stunning views of nearby peaks, a quick visit can easily become a day well spent here.

Driving directions

From the town of Coleman, drive west on Highway 3 to the Allison Creek Road junction (signed for Atlas Staging Area). Turn right onto the paved Allison Creek Road and follow it for 2.7 km to a junction. Turn left and follow the now gravel road for 3.2 km to the Chinook Lake day-use parking area.

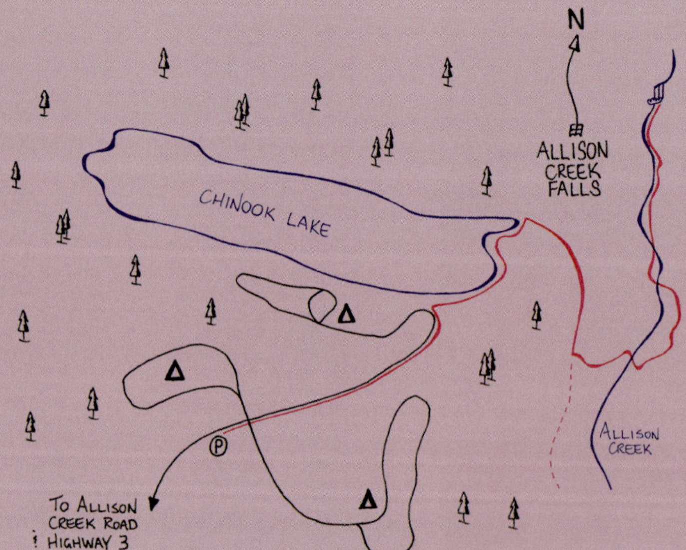

Hiking directions:

From the day-use parking, walk down the road (signed for a picnic area) for 400 m to the shore of Chinook Lake. Follow the lakeshore trail counter-clockwise for about 200 m to a crossing over a small flume. Turn right and walk along a wide gravel pathway for another 200 m to where a boot-beaten trail leads into the trees on the left, marked by a snowshoe trail sign. Shortly after entering the trees, the trail meets up with Allison Creek. Head to the left and follow along its left-hand side for nearly a kilometre before reaching the multi-tiered Allison Creek Falls.

While the trail follows alongside the creek all the way to the falls, there are a couple of steep and slippery sections of the bank that may be difficult, especially if the trail is wet. Smaller children will definitely need a hand navigating these. It is important to note that, depending on water level in the creek, it may be simpler and safer to cross the creek and follow a faint trail on the right-hand side. A sturdy pair of sandals is recommended for the creek crossings, which are generally mid-shin in depth in the calm or shallow portions of the creek. This may not be possible during runoff or periods of high stream flow.

4. Rainbow (Nez Percé) Falls

LOCATION: Coleman, AB
DRIVING DIFFICULTY: EASY
HIKING DIFFICULTY: EASY
HIKING DISTANCE: 1 km
HIKING TIME: 20 min.

While I don't generally promote the use of blindfolds or even pure deceit as a parenting method, I made a concerted effort to distract my kids as we pulled into the parking lot for this short hike. Had they seen the spray park on the way in, we might never have made it to the trail. As it happened, though, they had an equally enjoyable time playing in the pool at the base of the waterfall. So, from one parent to another, don't let them see the spray park.

Driving directions

From the Esso gas station in Coleman, drive west on Highway 3 for 500 m to 77th Street. Turn right, onto 77th Street (signed for Miner's Path Trail). After turning off the highway, take another immediate right and drive down into the parking area for Flumerfelt Park. Drive past the spray park and tennis courts. Park in the gravelled area where the road ends.

Hiking directions

From the parking area signed trailhead for Miner's Path Trail, follow a well-used and well-groomed pathway along Nez Percé Creek for about 1 km where a tiny waterfall drops into a bowl rimmed with small cliffs. On a hot day, the pool and creek below the waterfall can't be beat!

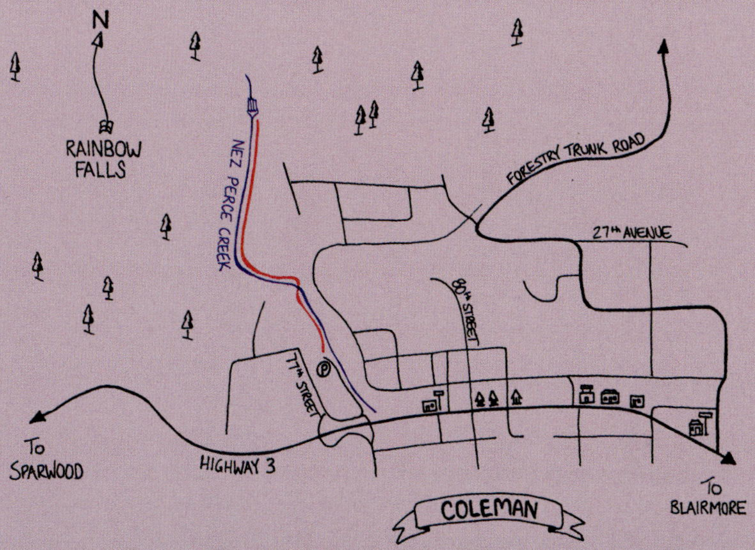
N
RAINBOW FALLS
NEZ PERCE CREEK
FORESTRY TRUNK ROAD
27TH AVENUE
80TH STREET
77TH STREET
To SPARWOOD
HIGHWAY 3
COLEMAN
To BLAIRMORE

5. Star Creek Falls

LOCATION: Coleman, AB
DRIVING DIFFICULTY: EASY
HIKING DIFFICULTY: EASY (upper loop)
or MODERATE (lower trail to base of falls, due to creek crossing)
HIKING DISTANCE: 2.0 km for Upper Loop or 500 m for Lower Trail
HIKING TIME: 45 min. for Upper Loop or 20 min. for Lower Trail

Driving directions

From the Esso gas station in Coleman, drive west on Highway 3 for 500 m to 77th Street and turn left. Follow 77th Street into downtown Coleman and turn right onto 18th Avenue. Follow 18th Avenue as it rounds a corner past residences, then turn left onto 17th Avenue. Follow 17th Avenue as it bends hard to the left and crosses the railway tracks, then turn right onto 16th Avenue. Follow 16th Avenue for 1.7 km, then turn left onto 54th Street (signed for Star Creek). Park off to either side of the road somewhere before the gravel road steepens and becomes rocky and loose, or, with a 4×4 vehicle, continue along the road to a clearing near the creek.

Hiking directions

Upper Loop: The upper loop trail is best followed in a clockwise direction so as not to get lost wandering around the mishmash of ATV trails. From the parking area, ascend the gravel road briefly before descending to a clearing near the creek. Follow the creek upstream along its right-hand side and cross a wooden bridge. The trail then ascends steeply to a plateau looking down into a narrow canyon and Star Creek Falls.

To complete the loop, the trail descends steeply from the viewpoints of the falls to a second wooden bridge above the falls. After crossing the creek, the trail climbs again briefly before joining up with a gravel ATV trail. Descend back to the clearing via ATV trails and return to the parking area.

Lower Trail: From the first clearing near the creek, follow the trail on the right-hand side of the creek. Continue past the lower bridge

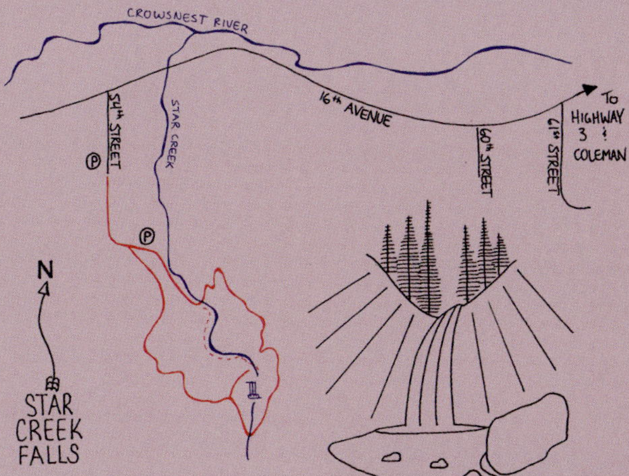

until a steep slope forces you to cross to the left side of the creek on logs and rocks. After a short time, the canyon walls narrow. The only way through the canyon is via a fixed rope to climb a slick limestone slab. Once through the constriction in the canyon, scramble over rocks and then back to the right-hand side of the creek to the base of the waterfall. **Note:** Accessing the base of the falls may not be safe or even possible during runoff or periods of high stream flow.

Winter wonderland

Star Creek Falls is a popular short ice climb in the winter. Walking up the frozen canyon requires crampons and careful footwork, but to see the canyon transformed into a fantasy land of ice, snow and rock is a unique experience.

6. North York Creek Falls

LOCATION: Coleman, AB
DRIVING DIFFICULTY: MODERATE
to DIFFICULT (due to distance and elevation gain)
HIKING DIFFICULTY: MODERATE
HIKING DISTANCE: 9.8 km
HIKING TIME: 3–4 h

It's not every day you go out in search of a waterfall and happen upon wreckage from a plane crash. In fact, for most people venturing up York Creek near Blairmore, the waterfall is not the main attraction. It is important to note that this is a shared-use trail network and it is very common to have ATVs and dirt bikes move past. Keep your eyes and ears open and move off to the side of the trail to let motorized users go by. Better yet, get your hands on an ATV yourself and dispatch this hike with even more ease!

Just kidding. This is a hiking guidebook. So pull up your socks and start walking.

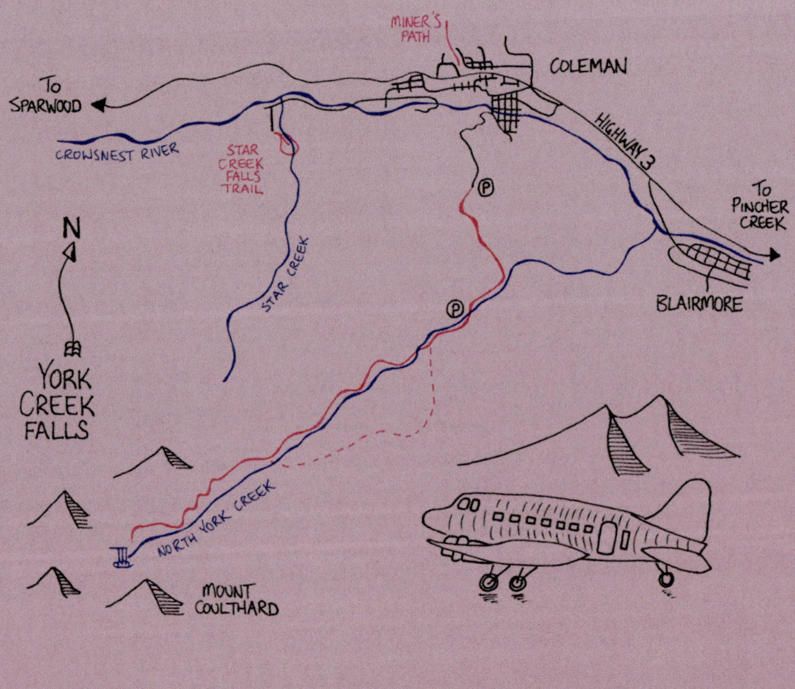

Driving directions

In the town of Coleman, turn south off Highway 3 onto 86th Street (traffic lights at the intersection near the Subway restaurant). From there, directions are as follows:

- Follow 86th Street to 16th Avenue, staying right.
- Follow 16th Avenue to 81st Street, turn left and cross tracks.
- Turn left onto 15th Avenue.
- Turn right onto 83rd Street.
- Cross the river and turn right onto 13th Avenue; reset your trip odometer.
- 13th Avenue turns into a gravel road shortly; stay right at 1.7 km.
- York staging and parking area at 2.1km.

It is possible to drive an additional 2.5 km on an increasingly rough road to a second small parking area. Just before a bridge over York Creek, turn right and park in a small clearing beside the creek.

Hiking directions

Note that directions are given from the York staging area. The hike is considered DIFFICULT from this point due to the nearly 10 km one-way distance and 500 vertical metres of elevation gain.

Hike the gravel road for 2.5 km. Then turn right off the main road onto a short spur that leads to the upper parking area (the hiking is MODERATE from this upper parking). From the upper parking area, pick up an ATV trail that crosses to the left side of the creek. From here, directions are as follows:

- 3.5 km from staging area / 1.0 km from upper parking: stay right at a fork.
- 3.7 km from staging area / 1.2 km from upper parking: cross bridge to right-hand side of creek.
- 4.0 km from staging area / 1.5 km from upper parking: junction; stay right (sign for Trans Canada Trail).
- 6.8 km from staging area / 4.3 km from upper parking: junction; stay right.
- 9.8 km from staging area / 7.3 km from upper parking: plane crash site and waterfall.

RCAF DC-3 Dakota crash site

Note: Please do not disturb any of the wreckage or memorials at the crash site.

On January 19, 1946, the seven crew members aboard this Royal Canadian Air Force plane lost their lives when their aircraft struck Mt. Ptolemy and then crashed into the North York Creek drainage. Foul weather had plagued their journey from Comox, BC, en route to their destination of Greenwood, Nova Scotia, with the plane last sighted near Cranbrook, BC. Remnants of the aircraft remain scattered around the valley to this day, and a memorial stands in their honour.[5]

7. Lundbreck Falls

LOCATION: Lundbreck Falls Provincial Recreation Area, AB
DRIVING DIFFICULTY: EASY
HIKING DIFFICULTY: EASY
HIKING DISTANCE: <100 m
HIKING TIME: 1-ish min.

Lundbreck Falls is one of the most recognizable cascades in southern Alberta and a popular landmark for photographers and travellers alike. This 12-metre-high waterfall is close to the road, close to a campground and pretty close to a perfect stop on the Crowsnest Highway.

Driving directions

From the A&W and Fas Gas at the east end of Blairmore, drive east on Highway 3 for 16.5 km. Turn right onto Range Road 24B/Township Road 73A (signed for Lundbreck Falls Provincial Recreation Area). Follow this road for an additional 1–1.5 km. There are multiple places to park and view the falls from platforms on both the north and south sides of the river as well as from the bridge.

Hiking directions

Another great option to view the falls is to access the large, flat rocks that line the river bed below the bridge. It can be accessed via the Lundbreck Falls Provincial Recreation Area campground. Park in the day-use area, walk down into the campground and then through the walk-in tenting sites at the bottom of the hill. Continue alongside the Crowsnest River under the bridge until the falls are in view.

I'd rather be fishing

The Crowsnest River is renowned for its world-class fly fishing. The river is home to an abundance of rainbow, cutthroat and brown trout that feed on a healthy population of hatching insects. Your best source of information and supplies is the Crowsnest Angler Fly Shop located in Bellevue in the Crowsnest Pass. They have been guiding these rivers for nearly 40 years, so when in doubt... ask a local!

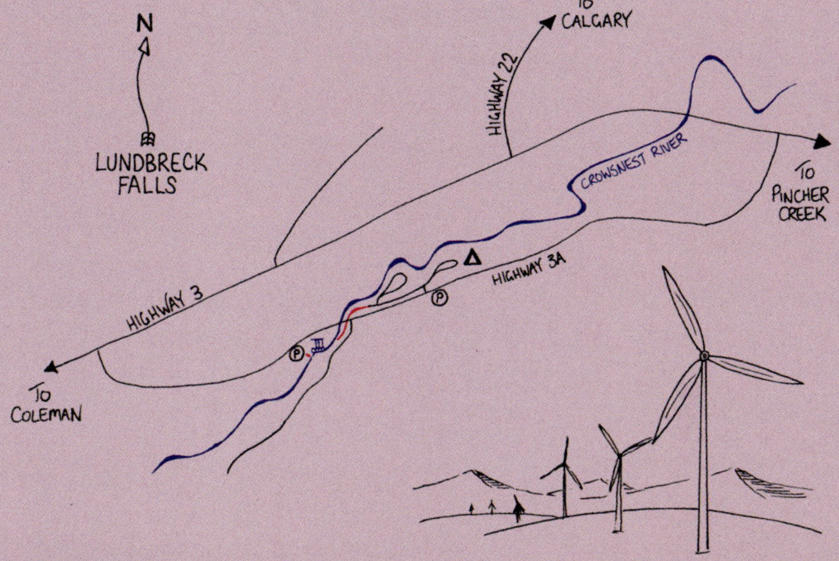
N
LUNDBRECK
FALLS
TO
CALGARY
HIGHWAY 22
CROWSNEST RIVER
TO
PINCHER
CREEK
HIGHWAY 3A
HIGHWAY 3
TO
COLEMAN

8. North Drywood Falls

LOCATION: Castle Wildland Provincial Park, AB
DRIVING DIFFICULTY: MODERATE
HIKING DIFFICULTY: EASY
HIKING DISTANCE: 4.1 km
HIKING TIME: 1.5 h

The hike up North Drywood Creek is a great stroll through a broad valley with wide open views the whole way. An old resource road provides excellent access nearly all the way to the waterfall, making it a very family-friendly hike.

Driving directions

From Pincher Creek, drive south on Highway 6 for 20 km and turn right, onto Township Rd 43 (signed for Shell Waterton Complex). The road transitions from pavement to well-maintained gravel at the Shell plant. Continue for 13.2 km to Butcher Lake. Turn left (blind intersection) just before Butcher Lake and follow for an additional 2.0 km to the trailhead, ignoring two branch roads on the right and continuing straight where the road bends significantly to the left.

Hiking directions

From the trailhead, walk through the gate on a gravel resource road that follows alongside North Drywood Creek in the valley bottom. Shortly past the trailhead, stay right at a Y-intersection. Continue for 3.5 km to the road's end, where the waterfall becomes visible. A well-used hiking trail continues the last 500 m to the base of North Drywood Falls, a great spot to take in the views. The trail continues to a rocky outcropping above the waterfall for a bird's eye view of the cascade.

The Castle Wildland: Alberta's newest provincial park

In 2015 the Government of Alberta formally recognized Castle Provincial Park and Castle Wildland Provincial Park, and finalized the parks' boundaries in 2017. After a long history of uninhibited off-road vehicle use, industrial activity, declining wildlife populations and impacts to watersheds, demands to protect the area by ecologists,

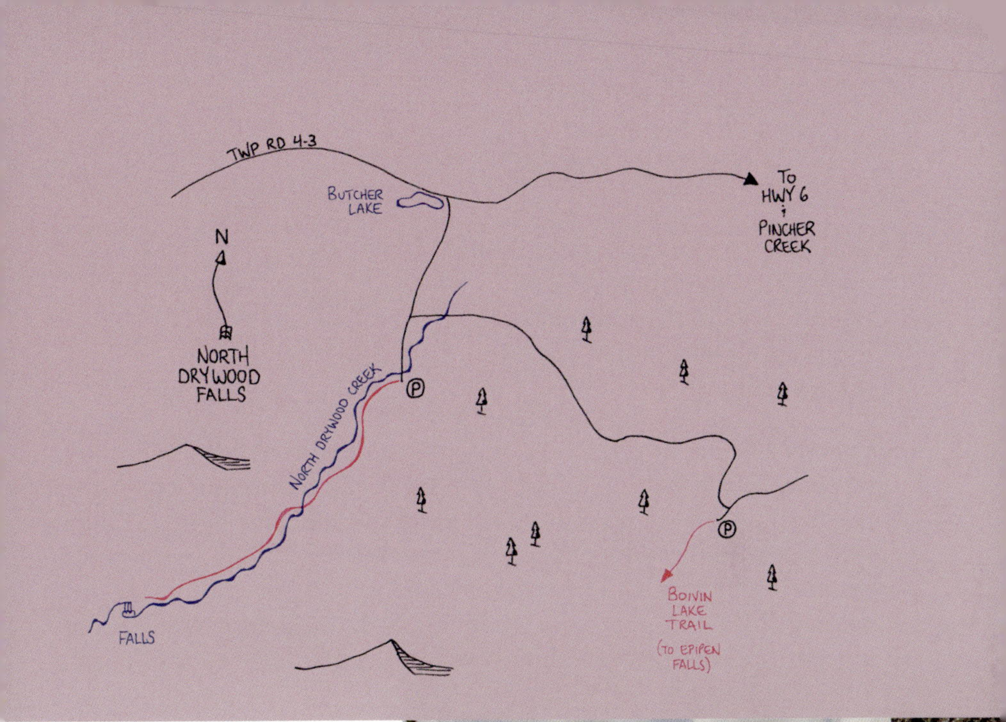

environmentalists, businesses and various organizations had gained enough traction with government to protect the area. A movement that had started nearly 50 years earlier resulted in close to 1700 square kilometres of protected wilderness area.[6]

9. Epipen Falls

LOCATION: Castle Wildland Provincial Park, AB
DRIVING DIFFICULTY: MODERATE
HIKING DIFFICULTY: MODERATE
HIKING DISTANCE: 3.9 km
HIKING TIME: 1.5 h

Contrary to my introduction, this is one of the few waterfall hikes where you can expect to get your legs a bit scratched up. While the first 3.5 km are no more than a casual stroll or a bike ride on a well-manicured gravel road, the last few hundred metres to the falls will no doubt have you (the reader) cursing me (the author) for promoting this spot; pants are recommended. This short hike ends at a beautiful waterfall carving through the red argillite rock of South Drywood Creek.

Driving directions

From Pincher Creek, drive 20 km south on Highway 6 and turn right, onto Township Road 43 (signed for Shell Waterton Complex). Reset your trip odometer. Directions from here are as follows:

9.2 km – Stay left at Shell facility.
13.2 km – Turn left at Butcher Lake.
14.7 km – Turn left onto Township Road 4-2.
19.8 km – Stay right.
20.0 km – Parking area for Boivin Lake.

Hiking directions

From the parking area, pass by the gate and walk along a lovely gravel road. After 500 m, stay left. At 2.7 km pass by a flare stack and some utility buildings. Note that these are active worksites; please remain on the road. At 3.5 km, just before an orange cattle guard, leave the road by turning onto a gravel trail and locate a barbed-wire fence to the left. A faint and overgrown trail follows along the right-hand side of the barbed wire fence nearly all the way to the creek (350 m). Once there, you will be above the waterfall. Cross the creek on rocks, then head left to where you can view the falls from above, or scramble down slabby rocks to near the base of the falls.

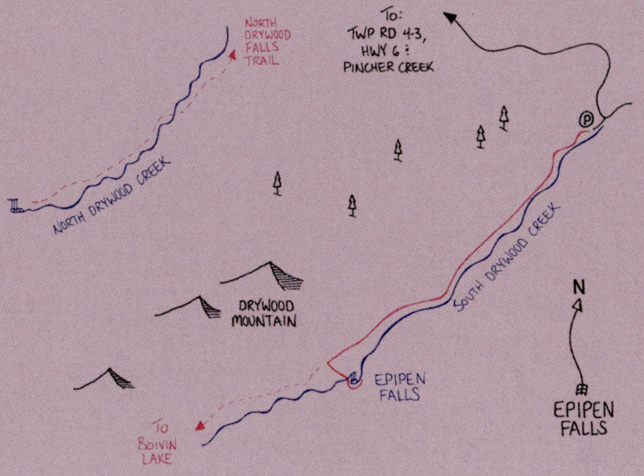

More to explore: Boivin (Blue) Lake

Boivin Lake has been one of the most popular hiking destinations near Pincher Creek for ages, long before Castle Wildland Provincial Park was established. It is a moderate 10 km hike to the lake, gaining 600 metres of elevation, which makes it a substantial day hike as a round trip. There are numerous small cascades along the creek between Epipen Falls and Boivin Lake to discover as well. Alternatively, there are a handful of primitive backcountry campsites at the lake which would make for a fairly casual overnight trip. Further exploration from Boivin Lake includes Loaf Mountain and Spionkop Ridge.

10. *Gap Falls*

LOCATION: Forestry Trunk Road, AB
DRIVING DIFFICULTY: EASY
HIKING DIFFICULTY: EASY
HIKING DISTANCE: 450 m
HIKING TIME: 10 min.

Gap Falls is a short, wide step across the width of the Oldman River. Here at *Waterfall Hikes of the Canadian Rockies*, we tend to focus less on the minutiae such as style of waterfall, height, rankings ... or even whether or not a waterfall actually qualifies as a waterfall. With our relaxed objectivity in the matter, we've managed to maintain a focus simply on having a good time. By many definitions, Gap Falls would not fit the criteria, but we don't actually care. Gap Falls is beautiful spot with incredible scenery and therefore ticks the box for "good time" even if it doesn't tick the one for "waterfall."

Driving directions

From the intersection of Highways 3 and 22, drive north on Highway 22 for 24 km. Turn left before crossing a bridge over the Oldman River (signed for Maycroft, Twp Rd 101A). Follow Township Road 101A for 17.5 km and turn right to enter an unsigned parking and day-use area.

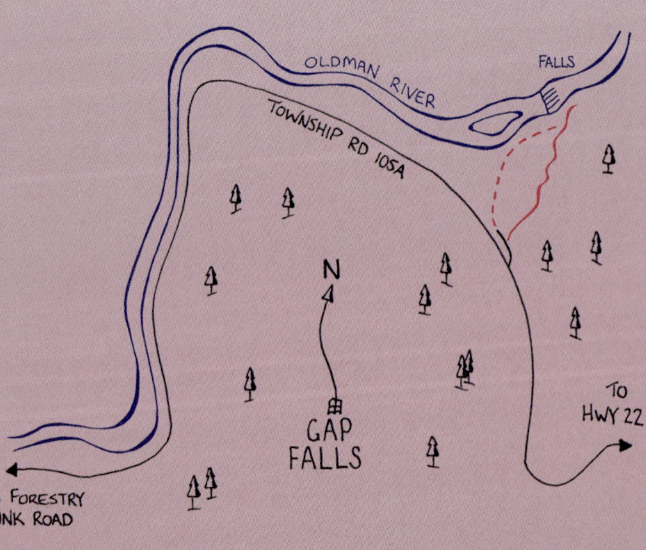

Hiking directions

From the parking lot, two trails descend through the trees to the banks of the Oldman: a larger, well-used horse trail and a less obvious hiking trail. Once at the river, stay to your right, continuing downstream. A large, slabby rock slope appears to bar the way, but there are some faint trails that zigzag up the slabs and lead to a viewpoint high above Gap Falls.

Hey Google, how tall does a waterfall have to be to be a waterfall?

According to US guidebook publisher Milestone Press, "To qualify as a waterfall, one segment of the falls must be at least five feet high. Most generally accepted true waterfalls must be located on a river, creek or stream that provides a source of water at least annually. Most falls have a significant amount of water flowing over boulders or plunging down a cliff." —Based on an actual conversation with Google.[7]

11. Oldman River Falls

LOCATION: Forestry Trunk Road, AB
DRIVING DIFFICULTY: MODERATE
HIKING DIFFICULTY: EASY
HIKING DISTANCE: 100 m
HIKING TIME: 2 min.

Oldman River Falls is the most remote waterfall described in this book. It's a pretty long way from anywhere. Dr. Seuss would describe it as being somewhere between hither and yon. Yet, as far away as these falls are, both from hither and from yon, you'll be surprised how many folks find themselves poking around this waterfall. A trip to explore the Forestry Trunk Road is something everyone should do. There are plenty of scenic spots along the way, including a detour here.

Driving directions

From the intersection of Highways 3 and 22, drive north on Highway 22 for 24 km. Turn left before crossing a bridge over the Oldman River (signed for Maycroft, Twp Rd 101, Highway 517) and drive 22 km to Forestry Trunk Road (Highway 40). Turn right and drive north on this wide and well-maintained gravel road for 11.3 km to Oldman North Road. Turn left and follow for 19.5 km to a parking lot on the left with a trailhead kiosk.

Hiking directions

From the parking area, follow wide pathways to a rocky outcropping overlooking the Oldman River. The descent to the base of the falls and the bank of the river is easily managed via a short, steep trail below the outcrop.

More to explore: Livingstone Falls

Another worthwhile stop along Forestry Trunk Road is Livingstone Falls. This provincial recreation site is found 60 km north of Highway 3 just off the roadway and is a well-known spot for fishing and camping. The "falls" themselves are more like a tilted creek slipping over a slab of rock than an actual waterfall, but they are quite unique and very picturesque nonetheless.

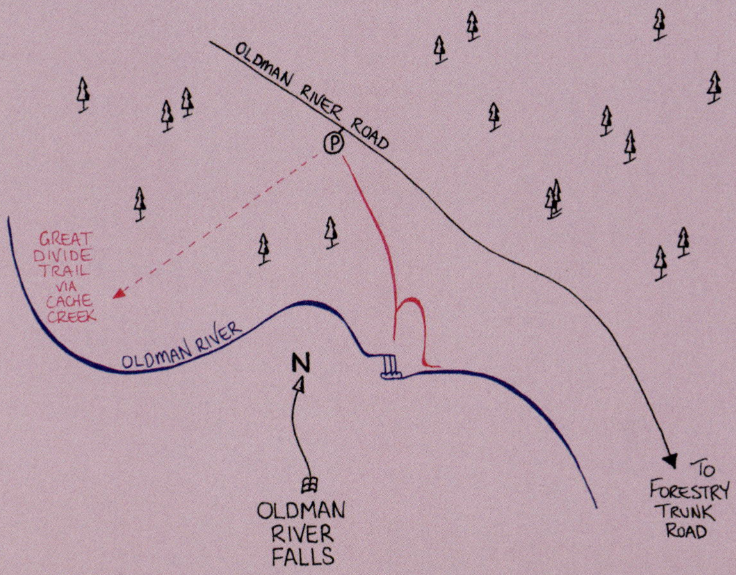
OLDMAN RIVER ROAD
GREAT DIVIDE TRAIL VIA CACHE CREEK
OLDMAN RIVER
N
OLDMAN RIVER FALLS
TO FORESTRY TRUNK ROAD

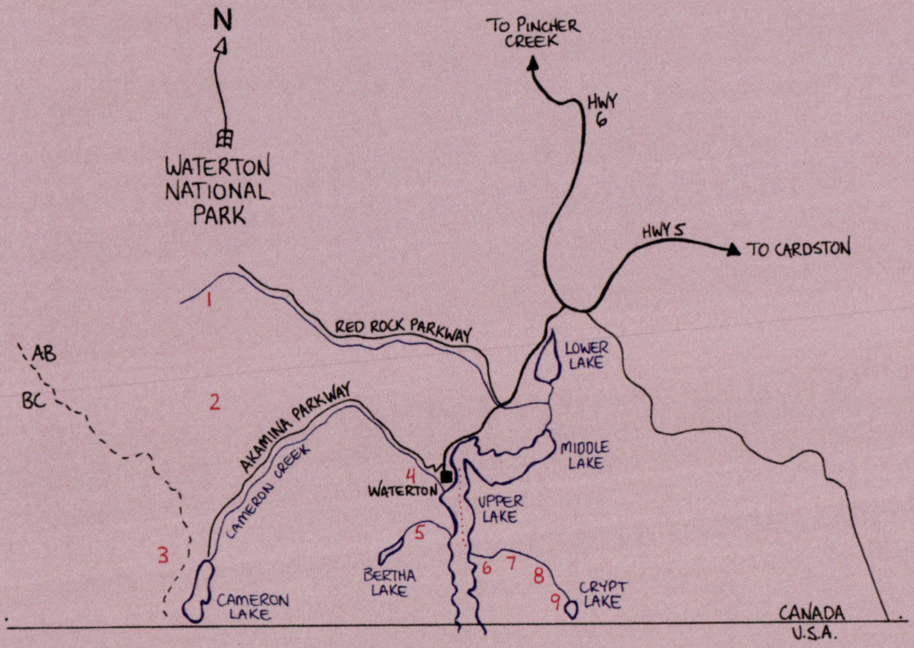
N
WATERTON
NATIONAL
PARK
TO PINCHER
CREEK
HWY
6
HWY 5
TO CARDSTON
1
RED ROCK PARKWAY
AB
BC
2
AKAMINA PARKWAY
CAMERON CREEK
LOWER
LAKE
MIDDLE
LAKE
4
WATERTON
UPPER
LAKE
3
5
BERTHA
LAKE
6
7
8
9
CRYPT
LAKE
CAMERON
LAKE
CANADA
U.S.A.

CHAPTER 4

Waterton Lakes National Park

Ahh, Waterton! A place where natural beauty is rivalled only by wind speed. Many a tent camper has been thwarted by constant gales, forced to seek refuge and sleep in their vehicle instead. All joking aside, while the wind tends to batter the valley bottom and frustrate people engaged in their water activities or tent-pitching, it quickly dissipates as you leave the lakeshore and head for the trails.

Waterton Lakes National Park is not large, so the modest numbers of visitors it receives are generally funnelled into just a handful of sites, giving the illusion that the park is busier than it actually is. Once your boots hit the trail, you'll be free to explore this beautiful place in relative solitude. The views along these trails have opened up in recent years courtesy of an immense wildfire that scorched a good swath of the park, with the forest now working to re-establish itself.

Access to the park is by way of either Highway 6 through Pincher Creek (56 km to the north) or Highway 5 via Cardston (54 km to the east). Both routes travel across Alberta prairie, with the southern Rockies rising prominently above the grasslands. The highways merge at the junction with Highway 5 before veering south into the park, with the entrance gates just beyond. From here it is 8 km to the village of Waterton.

A few logistical items of note:

First, a Parks Canada pass is required. Day-use or annual passes can be purchased at the park gate. Camping and backcountry reservations can be made through the Waterton Park visitor centre in person, by phone at 403-859-5133 or through the Parks Canada website.

Second, and this goes for all national or provincial parks, always check for closures and restrictions. The Kenow fire destroyed a great deal of Waterton Park infrastructure, including trailheads, buildings and campsites. At the time of writing, some parts of the park had not yet reopened.

Lastly, the Crypt Lake trail is generally accessed by taking a shuttle boat across Waterton Lake. Seats are first-come, first served. Departure and pickup times may vary, so check the schedule in advance. For more information visit watertoncruise.com or call 403-859-2362.

1. Blakiston Falls

LOCATION: Waterton Lakes National Park
DRIVING DIFFICULTY: EASY
HIKING DIFFICULTY: EASY
HIKING DISTANCE: 1 km
HIKING TIME: 20 min.

Red Rock Canyon and nearby Blakiston Falls are two of the most accessible attractions in Waterton Park with paved roads and short, casual walks. It will be tough to escape the masses here, although an early morning or evening trip up the Red Rock Parkway will weed out a large chunk of the day users.

Driving directions

From Waterton village, drive north on Highway 5 for 4 km to Red Rock Parkway (signed). Turn left and follow the paved road for 13 km to its end. Please note that this road is windy and undulating and has no shoulders, in addition to being heavily travelled. Numerous cyclists also use the roadway. Obey posted speed limits, pay careful attention and be respectful of other users.

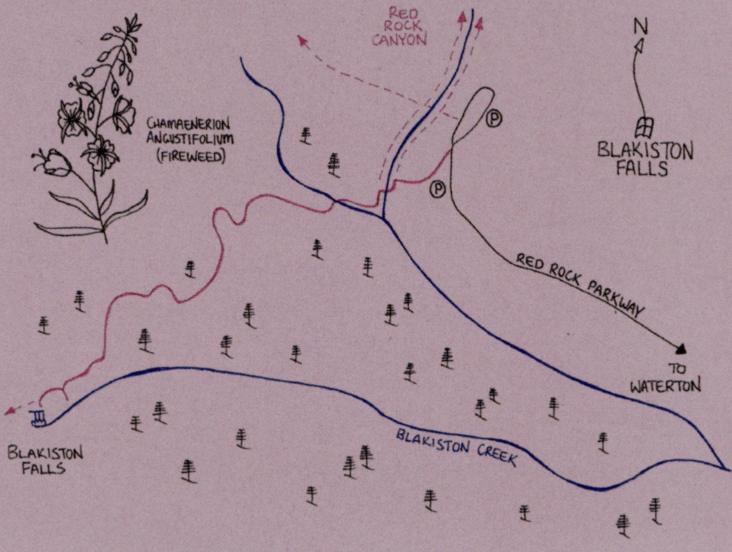

Hiking directions

From either the lower or the upper parking lot, follow trailhead signage for Blakiston Falls. Leave the flocks of people frolicking in Red Rock Canyon behind, cross Bauerman Creek and march in line with the numerous other hikers. A well-maintained pathway leads to the falls. Two large and excellent viewing platforms have been recently constructed above the waterfall.

The 2017 Kenow wildfire

The Bauerman Creek valley was stripped of vegetation during a massive wildfire in August and September of 2017. The blaze was triggered by a thunderstorm during one of the driest summers on record. It resulted in an evacuation of the town of Waterton, significant damage to infrastructure in the park and numerous closures in the years that followed. Nearly 40 per cent of the land within the park boundary had burned.[8]

2. Lineham Falls

LOCATION: Waterton Lakes National Park
DRIVING DIFFICULTY: EASY
HIKING DIFFICULTY: EASY
HIKING DISTANCE: 4.6 km
HIKING TIME: 2–2.5 h

Lineham Falls is one big cataract and definitely not to be missed if you're exploring Waterton Park. At 125 m tall it is one of the largest in southern Alberta and looks similar to other behemoths in the Rockies such as Takakkaw and Helmet Falls.

Driving directions

From Waterton village, drive north on the Akamina Parkway for 9 km to a parking lot on the right signed for Lineham.

Hiking directions

From the parking area, follow a well-used and well-maintained trail which starts by gaining elevation gently but steadily through scorched forest and grassy slopes. After 2.0 km, the trail levels off and enters a part of the forest that was spared from the wildfire. At 4.0 km Lineham Falls becomes visible through the trees from a small viewpoint. But don't stop here! The trail descends slightly and meets Lineham Creek before another short ascent takes you to a meadow with a wide-open view of the massive waterfall. The end of the trail is signed at this point, 4.6 km from the trailhead.

Lineham Discovery Well No. 1

Just down the road from the Lineham Creek trail is a national historic site celebrating the discovery of oil in the Waterton area and the home of the first oil well in western Canada. On September 21, 1902, John Lineham was able to drill through bedrock and struck oil alongside what is now Cameron Creek. The hole subsequently caved in, cutting off the supply of oil. The well was decommissioned, but the remains of its casing still stand at the site today.[9]

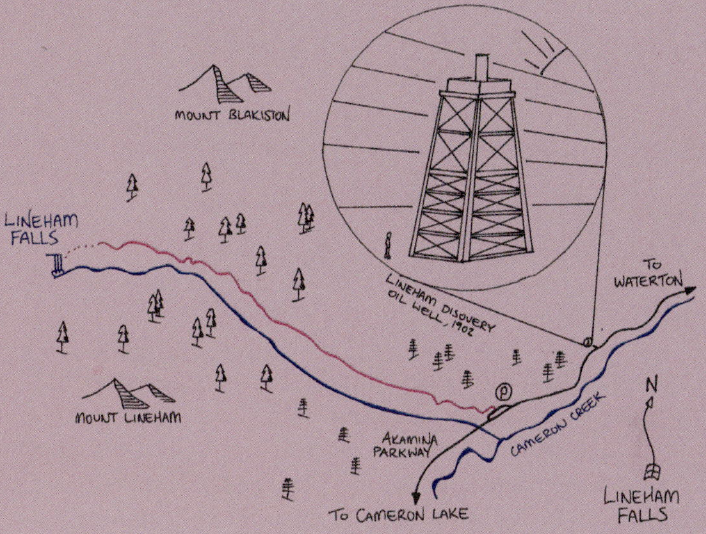
MOUNT BLAKISTON
LINEHAM FALLS
LINEHAM DISCOVERY OIL WELL, 1902
TO WATERTON
MOUNT LINEHAM
AKAMINA PARKWAY
CAMERON CREEK
N
TO CAMERON LAKE
LINEHAM FALLS

3. Forum Falls

LOCATION: Waterton Lakes National Park, AB / Akamina–Kishinena Provincial Park, BC
DRIVING DIFFICULTY: EASY
HIKING DIFFICULTY: EASY
HIKING DISTANCE: 2.5 km
HIKING TIME: 45–60 min.

Forum Falls has typically been a quick stop along the trail for hikers doing the better-known Akamina Ridge circuit, an alpine route high on the ridges above Cameron, Forum and Wall lakes. Until the 2017 wildfire stripped the vegetation along the trail and Forum Creek, the waterfall was tucked in a dark corner of the woods and out of sight from many would-be visitors. The falls now stand amid an otherworldly backdrop of scorched timber and the bright greens of a forest on the mend.

Driving directions

From Waterton village, drive north on the Akamina Parkway for 14.1 km to a parking area on the left signed for Akamina.

Hiking directions

From the parking area, cross the road and follow a wide gravel pathway for 2.2 km to a junction. Go left here, following signs for Forum Falls and Forum Lake. Shortly after, the trail approaches a BC Parks warden cabin: stay left here. At 2.4 km, stay right at another fork; Forum Falls is just a hundred metres farther.

More to explore: Akamina Ridge

While the steep trail to Akamina Ridge will leave your legs scorched (although not to the extent of the forest below), the reward for the effort may be the greatest bang for your buck around. Beyond Forum Falls, the trail climbs above Forum Lake and then rises to a high ridge straddling the Canada/US border. The route can be completed as a loop or as an out-and-back trail. This is a strenuous and advanced route requiring a high degree of fitness.

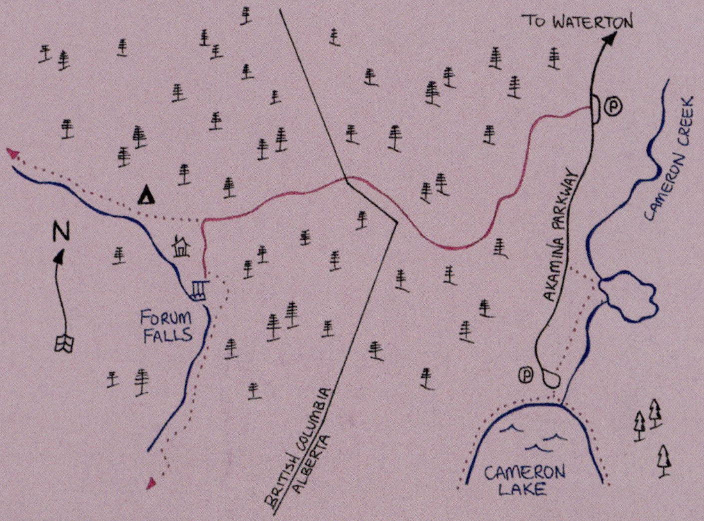
TO WATERTON
CAMERON CREEK
AKAMINA PARKWAY
N
FORUM FALLS
BRITISH COLUMBIA
ALBERTA
CAMERON LAKE

4. Cameron Falls

LOCATION: Waterton Lakes National Park, AB
DRIVING DIFFICULTY: EASY
HIKING DIFFICULTY: EASY
HIKING DISTANCE: 100 m
HIKING TIME: a shade less than a minute

The roadside view of Cameron Falls is the most familiar in Waterton National Park. Here, Cameron Creek slips over a series of tilted bedrock shelves before carrying on towards its final destination in nearby Waterton Lake. Be sure to visit early in the morning or later in the evening, as this will avoid the busy midday period when visitors congregate around the viewpoint.

Driving directions

The Cameron Falls viewpoint is located at the south end of the village of Waterton, along Evergreen Avenue. It is conveniently located adjacent to the campground, the day-use area near the lake and the Bertha Lake trailhead.

Hiking directions

While the best view of the falls, and the main vantage point for most visitors, is from the bridge over Cameron Creek, you can catch a good look from beside and above the falls by a quick stroll up the walkway to the right of the creek. The trail to the left of the falls climbs to another viewpoint but is generally used by hikers descending from the Carthew–Alderson route from Cameron Lake to Cameron Falls.

Why is the rock red?

The red rock that is abundant throughout Waterton National Park, the most obvious example being Red Rock Canyon, is thick layers of red argillite. Argillite is a sedimentary rock composed of fine particles of silt and clay that have been compressed over the course of 1.5 billion years. The red colour comes from oxidized iron within the rock formation.

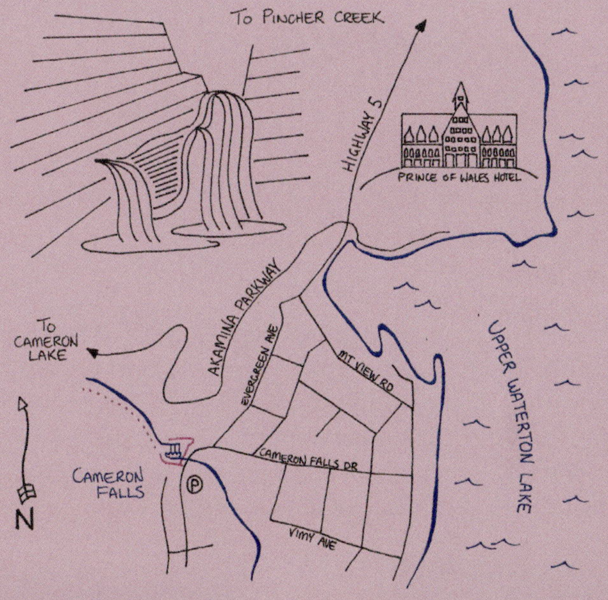

TO PINCHER CREEK
HIGHWAY 5
PRINCE OF WALES HOTEL
AKAMINA PARKWAY
TO CAMERON LAKE
EVERGREEN AVE
MT VIEW RD
UPPER WATERTON LAKE
CAMERON FALLS DR
CAMERON FALLS
P
N
VIMY AVE

5. Bertha Falls

LOCATION: Waterton Lakes National Park
DRIVING DIFFICULTY: EASY
HIKING DIFFICULTY: EASY
HIKING DISTANCE: 2.8 km
HIKING TIME: 1 h

With its trail starting right in the village of Waterton and in close proximity to the main attraction of Cameron Falls, don't be surprised to see the parking area for Bertha Lake also bulging at the seams. It is one of the most popular hikes in the park and makes for a great day hike or short backpacking trip to the alpine lake. For those hiking only to the falls, the reward to effort ratio is great!

Driving directions

The Bertha Lake trailhead is at the south end of the village of Waterton, adjacent to the campground, the Cameron Falls viewpoint and the day-use area near the lake, all of which can be reached via Evergreen Avenue through town.

Hiking directions

From the parking area, trailhead signage for Bertha Lake starts hikers on a well-used and well-maintained trail which ascends gently

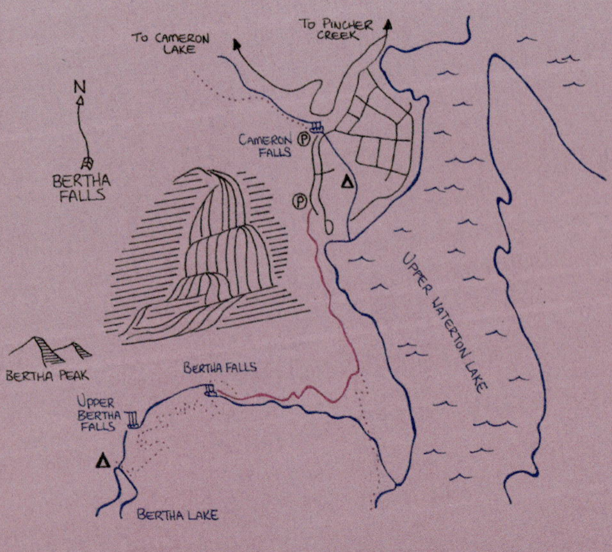

above Waterton Lake. After 1.5 km, approach a viewpoint overlooking the lake while the trail veers to the right. Here, a signed junction provides directions for Bertha Bay and Bertha Lake. Stay to the right for Bertha Lake and continue the gentle ascent high above the creek through a charred section of forest. At 2.8 km, stay left to reach the base of the falls; the trail to the right continues to Bertha Lake. Bertha Falls is just a couple hundred metres farther from this point.

More to explore: Upper Bertha Falls and Bertha Lake

For those carrying on to Bertha Lake, the trail begins to climb sharply once above Bertha Falls. As you switchback up the slopes, another large cascade is occasionally visible through the trees. Upper Bertha Falls cartwheels down the steep mountainside to the valley below. From the trailhead it is 5.6 km to Bertha Lake, with most of the elevation gain occurring above Bertha Falls. Once at the lake, stay right for the campground and pit toilets, or hike a 4 km loop around the lakeshore.

Bertha Falls is generally accessible by the end of May or early June, while Bertha Lake may be snowbound until mid-June or even later in some years.

6. Hellroaring Falls

LOCATION: Waterton Lakes National Park
DRIVING DIFFICULTY: EASY
HIKING DIFFICULTY: EASY
HIKING DISTANCE: 1.4 km
HIKING TIME: 30 min.

Nowhere along Crypt Creek is its chaotic journey more evident than Hellroaring Canyon. The creek crashes, plunges and dives toward Waterton Lake with its culmination at Hellroaring Falls. This is the first of four impressive waterfalls along the renowned Crypt Lake trail and is accessed via a short detour from the main trail. These cascades are often overlooked, as most hikers head out with Crypt Lake as their prime directive.

Driving directions

The Crypt Lake trail is across the lake from the village of Waterton and generally accessed via a boat shuttle offered by the Waterton Shoreline Cruise Company. Parking is at the Shoreline Cruise departure docks located at 101 Waterton Avenue in town. As you come into town, turn left onto Mount View Road and follow it to its end at the Bayshore Inn. Turn left onto Waterton Avenue and enter the marina parking lot. At the time of writing, the Crypt Lake shuttle was $31/person. Departure times may vary.

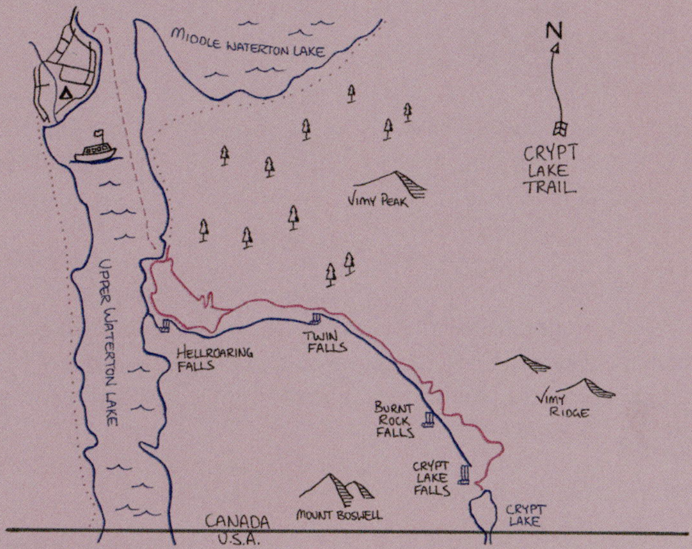

Hiking directions

From Crypt Landing on the east shore of the lake, follow signage for Crypt Lake Trail. Some 400 m from the trailhead is a junction signed for Hellroaring Canyon. If hiking directly to the falls, stay right at this junction. The canyon and falls come into view another kilometre farther.

It is recommended to stop by Hellroaring Falls on the return trip from Crypt Lake, for a couple reasons. The first is to ensure you leave yourself enough time to return to Crypt Landing to catch the boat for its return trip to town. The second reason is that the trail above the falls becomes quite steep and is much rougher than the main trail – best enjoyed on the descent.

7. Twin Falls

LOCATION: Waterton Lakes National Park
DRIVING DIFFICULTY: EASY
HIKING DIFFICULTY: EASY
HIKING DISTANCE: 3.5 km
HIKING TIME: 1.5 h

This Twin Falls is not to be mistaken for the other one in this guidebook but it's every bit as picturesque. A short descent off the Crypt Lake trail takes you to the base of a stunning multi-tiered waterfall tucked in the forest.

Driving directions

The Crypt Lake trail is across the lake from the village of Waterton and generally accessed via a boat shuttle offered by the Waterton Shoreline Cruise Company. Parking is at the Shoreline Cruise departure docks located at 101 Waterton Avenue in town. As you come into town, turn left onto Mount View Road and follow it to its end at the Bayshore Inn. Turn left onto Waterton Avenue and enter the marina parking lot. At the time of writing, the Crypt Lake shuttle was $31/person. Departure times may vary.

Hiking directions

From Crypt Landing on the east shore of the lake, follow signage for the Crypt Lake trail. Stay left at junctions for Hellroaring Canyon at 0.4 km and 2.4 km. At 3.5 km, Twin Falls can be observed from the main pathway, and the base of the falls is easily accessed via a short but steep spur off the main trail.

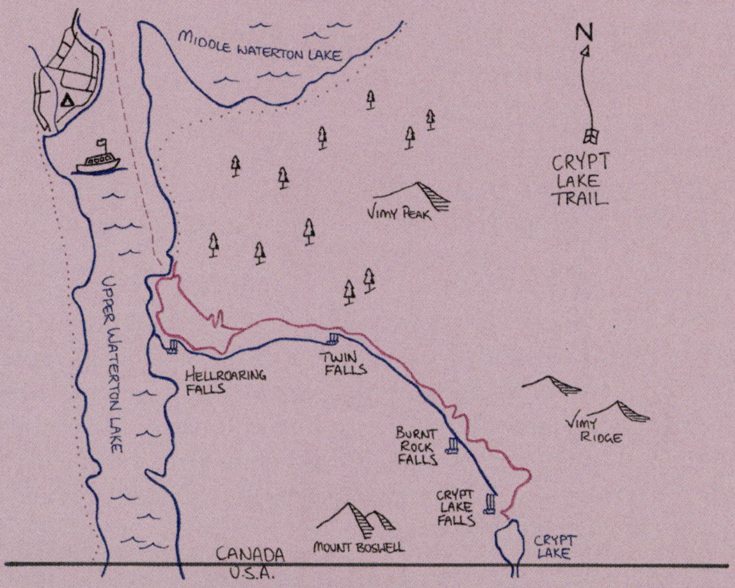
MIDDLE WATERTON LAKE
N
CRYPT
LAKE
TRAIL
VIMY PEAK
UPPER WATERTON LAKE
HELLROARING
FALLS
TWIN
FALLS
BURNT
ROCK
FALLS
VIMY
RIDGE
CRYPT
LAKE
FALLS
MOUNT BOSWELL
CRYPT
LAKE
CANADA
U.S.A.

8. Burnt Rock Falls

LOCATION: Waterton Lakes National Park
DRIVING DIFFICULTY: EASY
HIKING DIFFICULTY: MODERATE
HIKING DISTANCE: 5.5 km
HIKING TIME: 2.5 h

Burnt Rock Falls is a spectacular cascade plunging into a cliff-rimmed bowl. It is also referred to as Swirling Mist Falls, an accurate name given the frequent strong winds in the park. When the breezes whip up, water from the falls reaches the ground only as a fine spray. The rock in the vicinity of the waterfall is much darker than much of the other rock surrounding it and appears charred. Call it what you will, both names are incredibly accurate and suitable.

Driving directions

The Crypt Lake trail is across the lake from the village of Waterton and generally accessed via a boat shuttle offered by the Waterton Shoreline Cruise Company. Parking is at the Shoreline Cruise departure docks located at 101 Waterton Avenue in town. As you come into town, turn left onto Mount View Road and follow it to its end at the Bayshore Inn. Turn left onto Waterton Avenue and enter the marina parking lot. At the time of writing, the Crypt Lake shuttle was $31/person. Departure times may vary.

Hiking directions

From Crypt Landing on the east shore of the lake, follow signage for the Crypt Lake trail. Stay left at junctions for Hellroaring Canyon at 0.4 km and 2.4 km. Pass Twin Falls at 3.5 km and continue through thinning forest as you ascend the valley. At 5.2 km the trail steepens and switches back on itself a few times before reaching an amazing viewpoint of Burnt Rock Falls at 5.5 km. There are a couple more great vantage points from higher up along the trail as well.

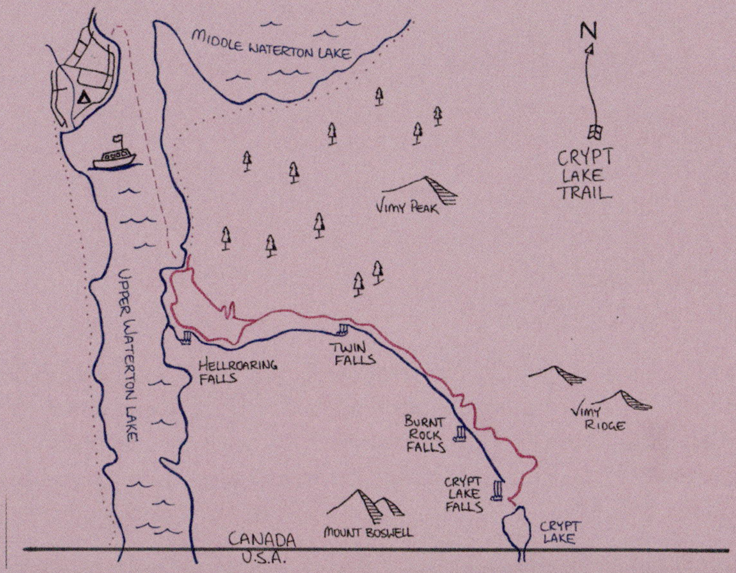
MIDDLE WATERTON LAKE
N
CRYPT
LAKE
TRAIL
VIMY PEAK
UPPER WATERTON LAKE
HELLROARING
FALLS
TWIN
FALLS
BURNT
ROCK
FALLS
VIMY
RIDGE
CRYPT
LAKE
FALLS
MOUNT BOSWELL
CRYPT
LAKE
CANADA
U.S.A.

9. Crypt Falls

LOCATION: Waterton Lakes National Park
DRIVING DIFFICULTY: EASY
HIKING DIFFICULTY: DIFFICULT (to Crypt Lake, due to distance, elevation gain and exposure)
HIKING DISTANCE: 6.3 km (to view of falls); 8.0 km to Crypt Lake
HIKING TIME: 2.5–3.5 h

Crypt Falls is a large cascade slithering down the headwall below Crypt Lake. As waterfalls go, Twin Falls and Burnt Rock Falls are certainly the rock stars, but this mammoth cataract is just as captivating. The main attraction on this trail remains Crypt Lake, a deep, blue alpine lake entombed by the towering walls of surrounding peaks.

Driving directions

The Crypt Lake trail is across the lake from the village of Waterton and generally accessed via a boat shuttle offered by the Waterton Shoreline Cruise Company. Parking is at the Shoreline Cruise departure docks located at 101 Waterton Avenue in town. As you come into town, turn left onto Mount View Road and follow it to its end at the Bayshore Inn. Turn left onto Waterton Avenue and enter the marina parking lot. At the time of writing, the Crypt Lake shuttle was $31/person. Departure times may vary.

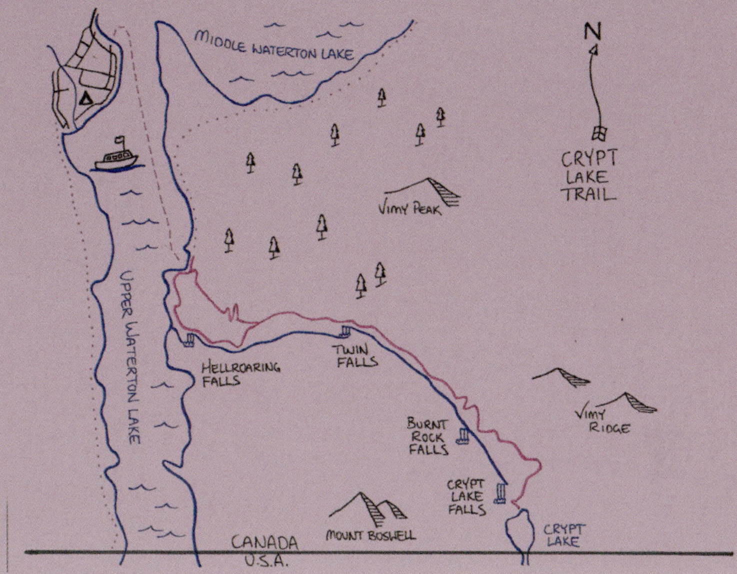

Hiking directions

From Crypt Landing on the east shore of the lake, follow signage for the Crypt Lake trail. Trail waypoints are as follows:

0.0 km – Crypt Landing
0.4 km – Junction signed for Hellroaring Canyon, stay left
2.4 km – Junction signed for Hellroaring Canyon, stay left
3.5 km – Twin Falls: short, steep descent off main trail to base of falls
3.7 km – Creek crossing, small waterfall in canyon above trail
5.2 km – Trail steepens, switchbacks
5.5 km – Burnt Rock Falls
6.3 km – Crypt Falls comes into view
7.5 km – Trail levels off, outhouse
7.7 km – Tunnel
8.0 km – Crypt Lake

The Crypt Lake trail gains elevation steadily, more than 650 metres from start to finish. It is important to know your abilities and limitations when hiking, and most importantly, leaving enough time to return to the landing for the boat ride back to the village. To miss the final departure of the day would result in a very long and unpleasant trip back to the highway via the Wishbone trail.

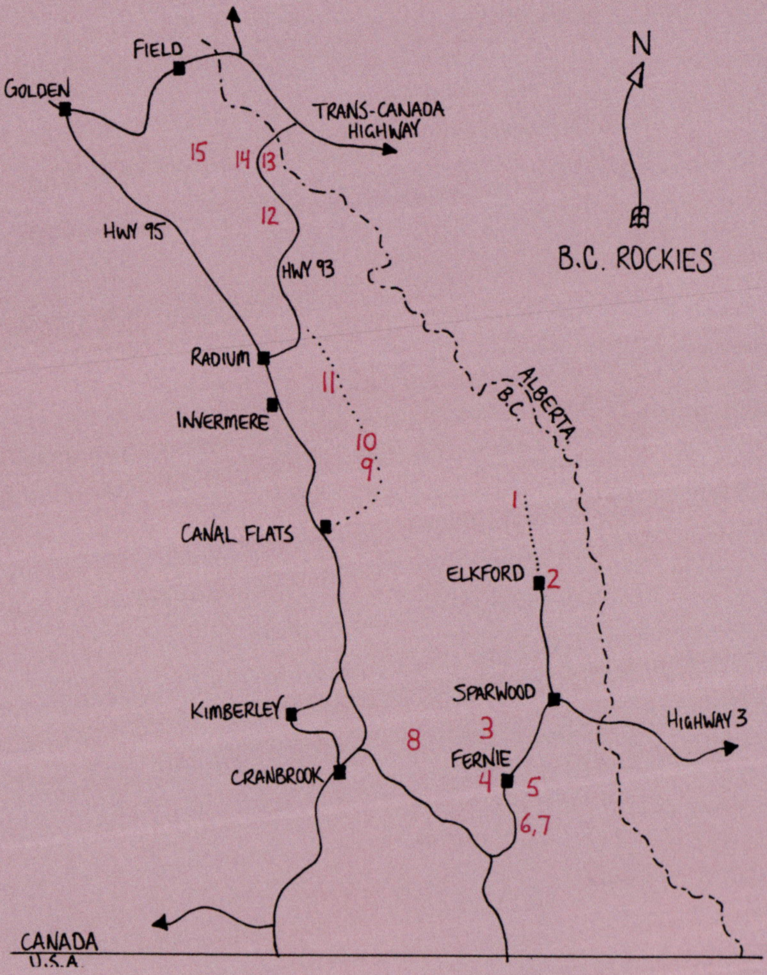
N
B.C. ROCKIES
FIELD
GOLDEN
TRANS-CANADA HIGHWAY
15
14
13
12
HWY 95
HWY 93
RADIUM
11
INVERMERE
10
9
ALBERTA
B.C.
1
CANAL FLATS
ELKFORD
2
SPARWOOD
HIGHWAY 3
KIMBERLEY
3
8
FERNIE
4
5
CRANBROOK
6,7
CANADA
U.S.A.

CHAPTER 5

British Columbia Rockies

The East Kootenay region of southeast British Columbia is highlighted by a long north–south valley and is home to the Columbia and Kootenay rivers. The region is bounded by the Great Divide to the east, the Trans-Canada Highway to the north, the Purcell Mountains to the west and the United States border to the south. Within this area are numerous provincial parks as well as the gem that is Kootenay National Park.

Highway 3 traverses the southern portion of the region, providing travellers both an east–west route near the US border and access to southern Alberta via the Crowsnest Pass. Highway 93/95 runs north–south and facilitates connection with the Trans-Canada Highway as well as providing access to Alberta and Banff National Park.

Cranbrook is the largest city and economic hub in the region, offering plenty of amenities for travellers. With that being said, most communities in the region also have extensive services, including fuel, groceries and accommodations. Additional towns along Highway 3 providing full amenities include Elkford, Sparwood and Fernie. Towns along the Highway 93/95 corridor that offer full services include Kimberley, Canal Flats, Fairmont, Invermere and Radium.

1. *Pétain Falls**

LOCATION: Elk Lakes Provincial Park, Elkford, BC
DRIVING DIFFICULTY: MODERATE
HIKING DIFFICULTY: MODERATE
HIKING DISTANCE: 7.2 km
HIKING TIME: 2.5–3.5 h

Why Elk Lakes Provincial Park is not busier is beyond my comprehension. This place has it all and most people don't even know it exists. Sure, it's a long drive down a forestry road just to get within sniffing distance of the park, but it is worth every tire-jarring bump to get there. While the drive may feel like an expedition in itself, the real journey finally begins. Tucked away amongst limestone giants, alpine streams and mountain lakes is the spectacular Pétain Falls!

Driving directions

From the town of Elkford, head north on the Elk River FSR, following BC Parks signage for Elk Lakes Provincial Park. Just north of town the road transitions to gravel but is well maintained for the first 40 km. The last 30 km of road to the trailhead narrows and becomes fairly rough. Allow a minimum of 90 minutes from Elkford to the parking area and signed trailhead.

Hiking directions

From the trailhead, follow a well-maintained and well-marked trail signed for Upper Elk Lake and Pétain Falls. You will pass the Elk Lakes cabin (operated by the Alpine Club of Canada), followed by Lower Elk Lake and the main campground. After reaching the Upper Lake, the trail becomes a little more rugged along the lakeshore. As you leave the shoreline and enter the outwash area at the end of the lake, flagging and cairns mark the route through the gravel flats before the trail re-enters the forest. Continue following trail markers signed for Pétain Falls.

The route to Pétain is a long day out, especially if you aren't staying overnight at the cabin or the main campground. However, it is a beautiful hike which gains very little elevation along the way and is well worth the effort.

Know before you go

The flood event of 2013 washed out parts of the trail past the Upper Lake as well as the original Pétain Creek campground. Wilderness camping is still permitted at the site, where a couple of tent pads were cleared of rocks and debris left over from the flood. There is a cooking area, bear locker and outhouse. The campground is not marked on the trail anymore nor is it referenced on the current provincial park map, but it is a beautiful and quiet spot only 1.5 km from the end of the Upper Lake and 1.5 km from Pétain Falls. The trail sits across from the outhouse and descends into a rocky flat.

*Renaming Pétain

At the time of writing, the name Pétain Falls in Elk Lakes Provincial Park, as well as other features with the same name (Pétain Creek, Pétain Glacier, Mount Pétain) have been identified by many opponents as being candidates to have their names rescinded. Pétain Mountain was named in 1918 after Marshal Henri Philippe Pétain, a French hero from the First World War. During the Second World War the French president resigned and Pétain was declared his successor. During that time, he collaborated with the Nazis, resulting in policies that included the deportation of Jewish people to concentration camps. After the war he was convicted of treason and ultimately found to be responsible in part for the deaths of tens of thousands of Jewish civilians.

This is only one example of a push to change the names of mountains, ecological features, even climbing routes to help reconcile historic wrongs.[10]

2. Josephine Falls

LOCATION: Elkford, BC
DRIVING DIFFICULTY: EASY
HIKING DIFFICULTY: EASY
HIKING DISTANCE: 2.5 km
HIKING TIME: 45 min.

Known more for coal mining than for hiking, the village of Elkford will surprise you with its easy access to many trails and wilderness opportunities. While Josephine Falls isn't exactly wilderness, it is a good opportunity to break yourself in slowly while exploring the trails around this small mining town.

Driving directions

From the main intersection (four-way stop) in Elkford, turn east onto the Fording River Road. Reset your trip odometer. Follow the paved Fording River Road for 4.8 km to an unmarked parking area on the right for Josephine Falls and for Lily and Lost lakes.

Hiking directions

From the trailhead the path forks immediately. Stay left, following signs for Josephine Falls. The trail is well used and well maintained

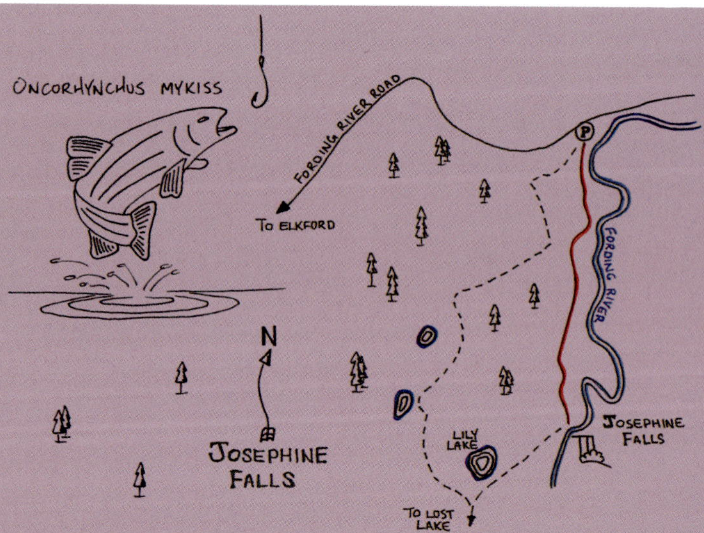

but with lots of roots, so watch your step. At 2.5 km you will come to a fenced viewpoint and picnic area overlooking the falls.

Return the way you came or continue on to Lost Lake and Lily Lake to complete the loop. The trail is accessible by early May and generally snow free until late October, or bring your snowshoes and tackle it in the winter months. The falls can be viewed year-round but are most impressive in May and June during runoff. Although it's located alongside one of the most popular trails around Elkford, Josephine Falls is secluded and quiet.

Silly fact

Josephine Falls was reportedly discovered by Professor Henry Fairfield Osborn, who named it in honour of his daughter, Josephine Osborn. She had caught a trout there that was the largest ever recorded up to that time.

3. Jumping Waters

LOCATION: Fernie, BC
DRIVING DIFFICULTY: MODERATE / DIFFICULT
HIKING DIFFICULTY: EASY
HIKING DISTANCE: 3.5 km
HIKING TIME: 1.5 h

Although Bisaro Cave is certainly the main attraction along this trail, Jumping Waters is a unique feature that makes for an interesting outing itself (but you should still go see the cave). This trail was formerly referred to as the Alpine Lakes trail and was recently renamed Heiko's Trail in honour of the late Heiko Socher, whose vision for developing the trail was critical in establishing this local favourite.

Driving directions

From Fernie, drive east on Highway 3 for 5 km to Dicken Road. Turn left on Dicken Road. After 500 m, turn right onto an obscure road that is partially obstructed from view, signed shortly after as the Hartley Creek FSR. Reset your trip odometer. Drive this road for 11.3 km and turn left into a grassy parking area. This is the recommended starting point for your hike.

For those with little regard for their vehicle's suspension or tires, it is possible to drive the first 2.5 km of the trail, a very rough mountain

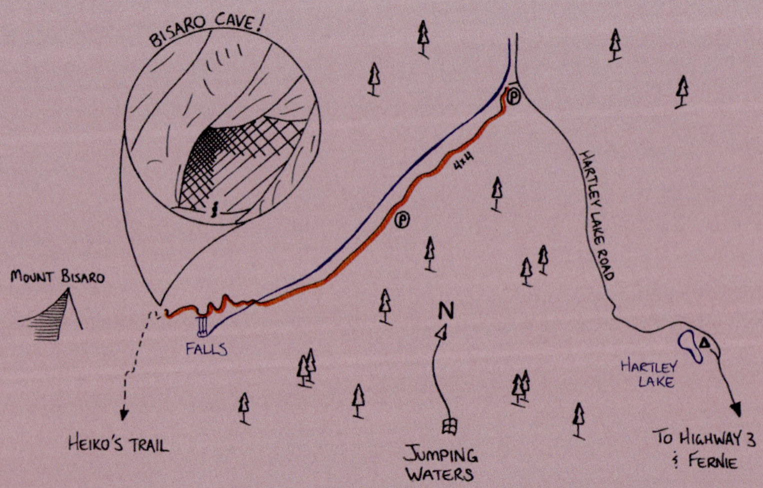

road, to the original parking area. High clearance and four-wheel drive are essential.

Hiking directions

From the lower parking area, hike the rough road for 2.5 km. As you walk along, imagine your hands choking the life out of your steering wheel as you negotiate the deep ruts, loose rock, mud and pools of water.

The road ends at the upper parking area and is replaced by a well-used and well-maintained trail. A couple hundred metres farther, the trail starts to gain elevation using wooden ladders and steps crafted by the trail builders. At 3.5 km, find yourself at the base of Jumping Waters, a series of cascades tumbling down a steep, mossy staircase. Continue along the trail a short distance farther, bringing you alongside the largest drop in the waterfall. But don't stop here! One more switchback in the trail brings you to the "Watergate," the source of the fall where the water gushes from the earth.

Since you've come this far and done nearly all of the elevation gain, you might as well tack on the additional 700 m to the spectacular Bisaro Cave, an otherworldly hole in the side of this mountain that is sure to leave your eyes wide and jaw dropped.

The hiking season is short up here. The trail may not be accessible until mid-June in some years and may be snowbound by mid- to late-October. Consider bringing extra layers, even if it's warm in the valley.

4. Fairy Creek Falls

LOCATION: Fernie, BC
DRIVING DIFFICULTY: EASY
HIKING DIFFICULTY: EASY
HIKING DISTANCE: 2.0 km
HIKING TIME: 40 min.

Fairy Creek Falls is one of the most popular trails near Fernie and it won't take long to figure out why. This is a classic local hike in any season and a great way to stretch your legs if you are simply passing through town. It's also a great destination in itself. The falls are accessible year-round, although snowshoes might be required in the winter months or after a heavy snowfall.

Driving directions

From downtown Fernie, head east on Highway 3. Cross the Elk River and turn left into the parking area for the Fernie visitor centre, highlighted by a large wooden oil derrick. Park here. Trailhead information and signage are beside the visitor centre.

Hiking directions

From the trailhead, follow a well-used trail to the falls. Green trail markers lead the way alongside Fairy Creek to the base of the

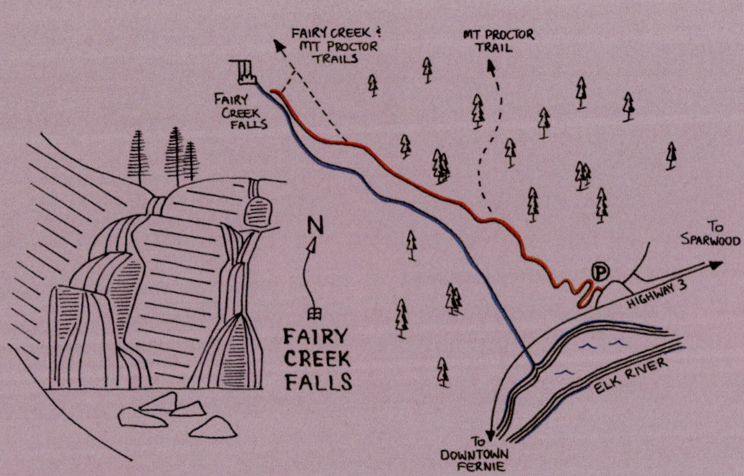

waterfall. Numerous other trails and roads intersect the main trail and are used heavily by mountain bikers. Be aware of other users, as this is a mixed-use trail and one of the most popular recreation areas in Fernie in the summer.

What's with the wooden tower?

The wooden oil derrick at the trailhead is a reconstruction of the Akamina No. 2 derrick which operated near Fernie in the Flathead River valley prior to the First World War. The original, Akamina No. 1, was the first oil well drilled in British Columbia, in 1907. The project was abandoned after tools were lost down the hole. Components of that first well were transferred to Akamina No. 2, but it too ended with a similar fate. Small petroleum discoveries in the late 1800s had spurred exploration, and a number of drilling operations near Fernie were worked between 1907 and 1930. Petroleum extraction never took hold in the region, however, and with coal mining and forestry booming, oil was quickly forgotten. Today the Elk Valley remains a hub for the coal industry, although Fernie itself is more recognizable as a ski destination.[11]

5. Matheson Falls

LOCATION: Fernie, BC
DRIVING DIFFICULTY: MODERATE
HIKING DIFFICULTY: MODERATE (due only to creek crossing)
HIKING DISTANCE: 1.5 km
HIKING TIME: 25 min.

If Fairy Creek Falls is one of the best-known hikes around Fernie, Matheson Falls would be the opposite. There is no trailhead kiosk here and the creek crossing might prevent you from seeing the falls altogether, but the reward for a little extra work is one of Fernie's hidden gems. Although Matheson Falls is only modest in height, what it lacks in stature it makes up for in ambience. The moss-rimmed bowl that encircles the waterfall will have you feeling much more secluded than just a 10-minute drive from town would have you believe.

Driving directions

Drive into downtown Fernie via 4th Street. At the four-way stop, continue straight through and cross the railway tracks. Turn right onto Pine Avenue. Pass the aquatic centre and turn left onto Coal Creek Road, which passes alongside homes before becoming a well-used gravel road. Reset your trip odometer. At 5.3 km stay right and cross a bridge. At 9.1 km cross a second bridge and park on the left-hand side of the road in a wide, unmarked pullout.

Hiking directions

Walk back across to the right side of the road and pick up a trail that drops away from the roadside. The trail works its way along the left-hand side of the creek. After a few hundred metres the trail meets the creek and bends to the left. You can shimmy across on a downed log or find a calm, low-water spot to ford. Note that this may not be safe or even possible during runoff or periods of high stream flow. Pick up the trail again on the right-hand side of the creek and follow it to the base of the waterfall. Occasionally the trail drops down out of the forest onto rocks in the creekbed. These are generally slick, so use caution. Best time to view is midsummer to early October when the water levels are lower.

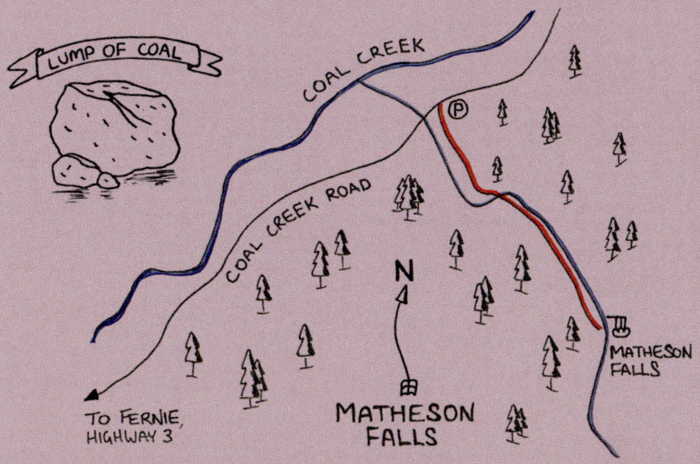
LUMP OF COAL
COAL CREEK
COAL CREEK ROAD
N
MATHESON FALLS
TO FERNIE,
HIGHWAY 3
MATHESON
FALLS

6. Morrissey Falls (Upper)

LOCATION: Fernie, BC
DRIVING DIFFICULTY: MODERATE
HIKING DIFFICULTY: MODERATE (due only to steepness of trail)
HIKING DISTANCE: <100 m
HIKING TIME: 5 min.

Morrissey Falls may be one of the least-known waterfalls in the Kootenays. Many people driving Morrissey Road probably have no idea of the spectacle on display beyond their driver's side window. The creek is just enough out of sight that not one but two good-sized cascades, the Upper and Lower Morrissey falls, are concealed from view yet only spitting distance away.

Driving directions

From Fernie, drive west on Highway 3 to Morrissey Road (signed). Turn left (south) onto Morrissey Road. Reset your trip odometer. Cross the bridge over the Elk River and stay right. At 3.7 km the road splits in three directions; stay straight. Stay left at 5.6 km. Stay left again at 7.4 km. Follow Morrissey Road to 12.2 km. The road widens slightly with a small pullout on the left. Turn around and park here.

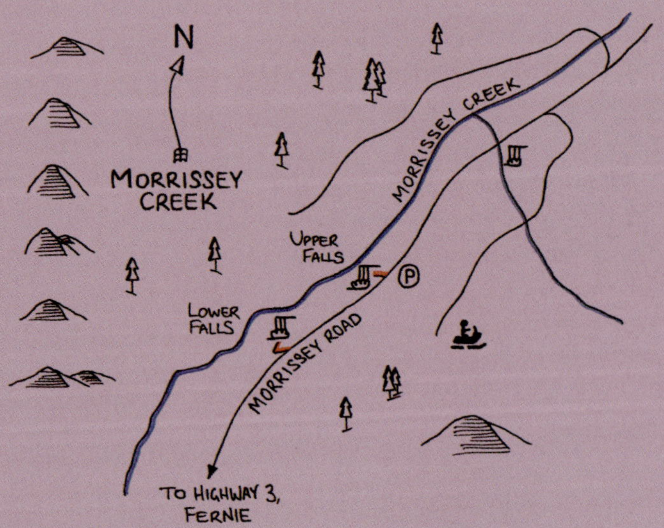

Hiking directions

From your car Morrissey Falls can be heard below. A faint trail drops sharply off the side of the road directly to the base of the falls. The trail is very steep and slippery, especially if wet, so tread carefully. Morrissey Creek falls into a small bowl ringed by cliffs.

Some obscure history

At the turn of the 1900s, the Crowsnest Pass Coal Company was so adamant about Morrissey's coal-mining prospects that the Canadian Pacific Railway had completed a Crowsnest branch line by 1898. The operation turned up poor-quality coal, however, and was plagued by accidents, eventually leading to its premature closure in 1909. The site was used as an internment camp during the First World War and finally shut down in 1918. Today Morrissey is better known for its snowmobiling than its coal production.[12]

7. Morrissey Falls (Lower)

LOCATION: Fernie, BC
DRIVING DIFFICULTY: MODERATE
HIKING DIFFICULTY: MODERATE (due only to steepness of trail)
HIKING DISTANCE: 300 m
HIKING TIME: 10 min.

Everyone likes free stuff. Two-for-one deals are basically free things. So, when you venture up Morrissey Road to see one waterfall, don't leave without cashing in on its equally impressive twin just below.

Driving directions

As per Morrissey Falls (Upper), drive west on Highway 3 to Morrissey Road (signed). Turn left (south) onto Morrissey Road. Reset your trip odometer. Cross the bridge over the Elk River and stay right. At 3.7 km, where the road splits in three directions, stay straight. Stay left at 5.6 km. Stay left again at 7.4 km. Continue on Morrissey Road to 12.2 km, where the road widens slightly with a small pullout on the left. Turn around and park here.

Hiking directions

From the pullout, walk back down the road about 200 m. Keep your eye on the creek and you will just see the lower waterfall from the road. Similar to the upper falls, a faint, boot-beaten trail drops steeply away from the road to the base of the falls. Also similar to the upper falls, use extra caution as you descend. It is very steep and will be extremely slippery if wet.

Bonus waterfall

Since you've come this far, why stop at just two waterfalls? Another 200 m past the pullout/parking area for the Upper Falls, there is a third cataract on the right as you cross a bridge. This small stream feeds Morrissey Creek below the bridge and is worth the extra minute of driving to check out this small cascade.

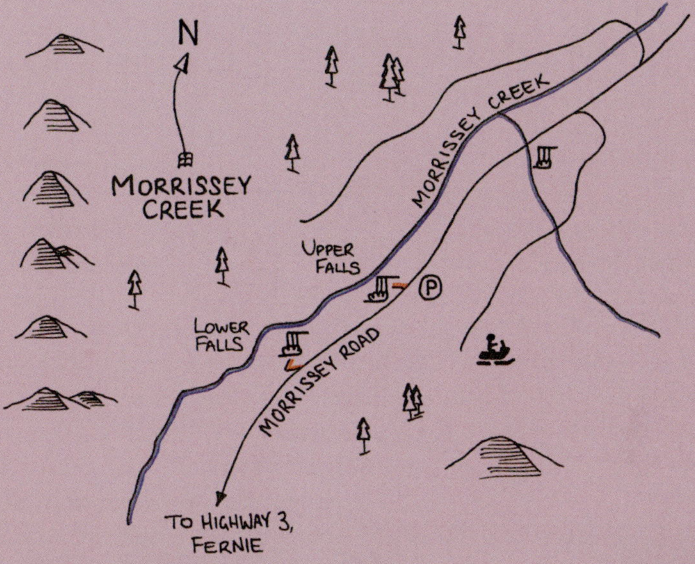
N
MORRISSEY CREEK
MORRISSEY CREEK
UPPER FALLS
LOWER FALLS
P
MORRISSEY ROAD
TO HIGHWAY 3, FERNIE

8. Cliff Lake Falls

LOCATION: Cranbrook, BC
DRIVING DIFFICULTY: DIFFICULT (4WD required)
HIKING DIFFICULTY: EASY (to view of falls), MODERATE (to Cliff Lake)
HIKING DISTANCE: 1.5 km
HIKING TIME: 40 min.

Do you hate your car? You can prove it by forcing it up the Van Creek forestry service road to the Cliff Lake trail. Or, better yet, grab a buddy's truck to check out Cliff Lake Falls. The waterfall itself is a vertical stream cartwheeling down the headwall below Cliff Lake with a total elevation drop that is quite impressive. If you have made the effort to get a view of the falls, don't stop there. While the route to Cliff Lake is a bit of a grunt, the view up top is worth every step.

Driving directions

From Cranbrook, drive south on Highway 3/93. Cross the Kootenay River bridge at Wardner and turn left onto the Wardner–Ft. Steele road. Turn right onto the Bull River road and reset your trip odometer. At 8.1 km cross the bridge over the canyon (worth stopping for a look into the gorge from the bridge). At 8.3 km make a left-hand turn (note that you will still be on the Bull River road). Drive to 19.7 km and turn left onto the signed Van Creek Road. Cross a creek at 28.6 km and look for a pullout on the left with a signed trailhead for Cliff Lake Trail (at the 41 km sign).

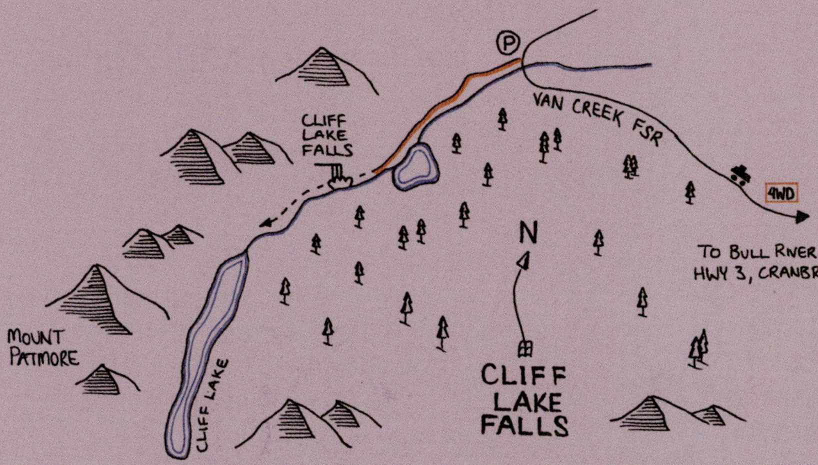

Note: The Van Creek road deteriorates rapidly, with rocky washouts at 20.2 km and 22.7 km. A high-clearance SUV or truck is required for negotiating these washouts.

Hiking directions

From the signed trailhead, follow a moderately used but well-maintained trail. There are numerous trails that break away from the main one, but they usually end quickly or reconnect with the main path. At around 1.5 km the trail meets the creek and a steep, slabby rock face. Scramble up the rock where the view of Cliff Lake Falls opens up shortly thereafter. Travel to Cliff Lake beyond this point is via a faint, boot-beaten trail marked by cairns which gains steep elevation up the headwall on the right side of the creek and waterfalls.

More to explore: Cliff Lake and beyond

Beyond Cliff Lake Falls and Cliff Lake there is a paradise to explore. A series of high alpine passes moves you from basin to basin, tarn to tarn, and gets you within range of one of the most southerly glaciers in Canada. For trail descriptions, check out *Mountain Footsteps* by Cranbrook author Janice Strong.

9. Pedley Falls

LOCATION: Canal Flats, BC
DRIVING DIFFICULTY: MODERATE
HIKING DIFFICULTY: EASY
HIKING DISTANCE: 1.7 km
HIKING TIME: 40 min.

If you are searching for data on Pedley Falls, well, good luck. There is no trail, no trailhead and no information for accessing or viewing the falls. In fact, the vast majority of people who have actually seen the falls first-hand have done so while rafting or paddling the Kootenay River.

Driving directions

From downtown Canal Flats, turn onto the Kootenay River forest service road at the main intersection (a four-way stop) and reset your trip odometer. Follow the well-used, well-maintained gravel road. Stay to the right at 31.9 km. Cross the Kootenay River on a bridge at 32.5 km. Stay left at 33.2 km and drive to 42.2 km, where an unmaintained dirt road signed BR.A is on your left. Park here or drive down the dirt road to its end.

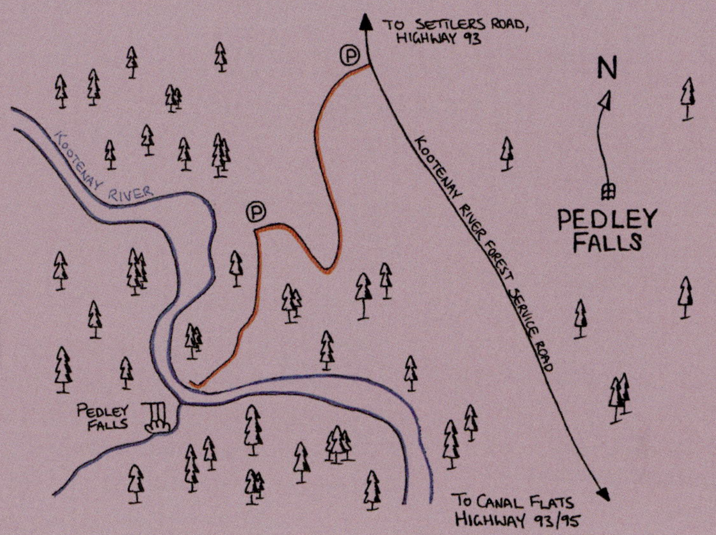

Hiking directions

Follow the dirt road down and around to the left, followed by a hard right-hand bend near the 1 km mark. The dirt road ends in a small clearing just beyond. From here, pick up a game trail trending south along a treed plateau above the Kootenay River. After a few hundred metres the game trail peters out in a small clearing. Bend to the right (west) back towards the river. The falls can be heard at this point, and within a couple hundred metres there is an excellent overlook where Pedley Falls tumbles into the Kootenay River.

Know before you go

Without an established trail to Pedley Falls, this could be one of the least-known cascades in the East Kootenay and is generally seen only from the Kootenay River itself. A hike to these falls is a great little test of navigational skills without the benefit of a signed or a marked trail. Refer to the map for the rough location of the game trail where you leave the dirt road. A more typical vantage point is from a raft such as those used by many local guiding companies offering trips on the Kootenay River.

10. Fenwick Creek Falls

LOCATION: Canal Flats, BC
DRIVING DIFFICULTY: MODERATE
HIKING DIFFICULTY: EASY
HIKING DISTANCE: 200 m
HIKING TIME: 5 min.

Hidden just out of view from the Kootenay River Road is a gorgeous waterfall that splits a bowl of cliffs. It is a long drive on a gravel road to get to Fenwick Falls but the rewards are plentiful, with free camping nearby and easy access to the creek and waterfall, as well as being close to the Kootenay River and its many paddling and fishing opportunities.

Driving directions

From Canal Flats, turn onto the Kootenay River forestry service road at the main intersection (a four-way stop at Burns Avenue and the Kootenay River FSR) and reset your trip odometer. Follow a well-used, well-maintained gravel road. Stay to the right at 31.9 km. Cross the Kootenay River on a bridge at 32.5 km. Stay left at 33.2 km. Drive to 43.4 km, where a bridge crosses Fenwick Creek. You can park in a pull-out on the left-hand side of the road before the bridge or cross the bridge and pull into the recreation site on the right side of the road.

Hiking directions

Downstream of the bridge there are trails on both sides of the creek, each being only a couple

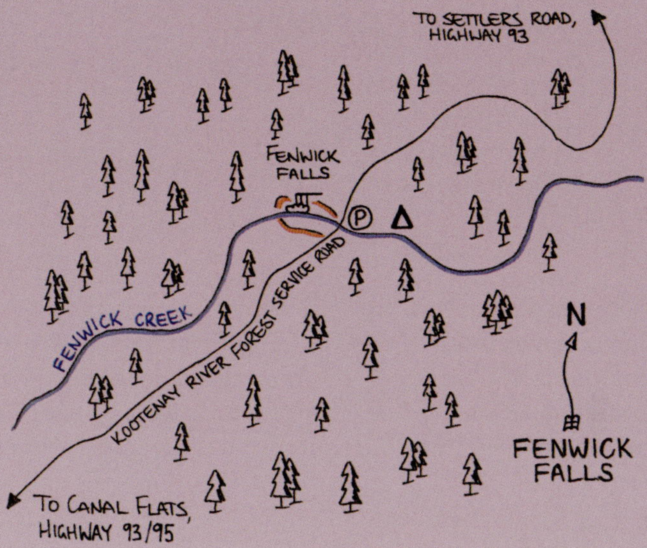

hundred metres in length. The first is a well-worn track that leaves the pullout before the bridge and leads to a large, flat rock right on top of the waterfall, as well as a viewing area with a wooden guard-rail just beyond.

The second trail starts on the other side of the creek, across from the entry to the recreation site. It is boot beaten and cuts across steeper, slippery slopes before reaching a couple of great vantage points for the waterfall. The falls are accessible from late May to late October, but the best time is in June during runoff.

Know before you go

The Fenwick Creek recreation site offers remote, quiet, free camping and is maintained by Recreation Sites and Trails BC. There are four campsites, available on a first come, first served basis, which are popular in the fall with hunters. Forestry recreation sites are a privilege in British Columbia and there are many similar to Fenwick Creek. Most are user-maintained, so please do your part to keep these areas clean for the enjoyment of others. Pack out all your garbage and leave the area better than you found it!

11. Cross River Falls

LOCATION: Nipika Resort, BC
DRIVING DIFFICULTY: MODERATE
HIKING DIFFICULTY: EASY
HIKING DISTANCE: 3.4 km
HIKING TIME: 1.5 h

The brilliant blue Cross River tumbles down a series of small steps as they make their way towards the Kootenay River from high up in the Rocky Mountains. Nipika Resort has capitalized on the abundance of natural beauty near the confluence of the two rivers to create an outdoor recreation playground. The trail to Cross River Falls is only one of many to explore!

Driving directions

From Radium, drive east on Highway 93 into Kootenay National Park. Turn right onto Settlers Road (signed). Follow a good gravel road for 14.5 km to Nipika Resort. Turn left into Nipika and the hikers parking area.

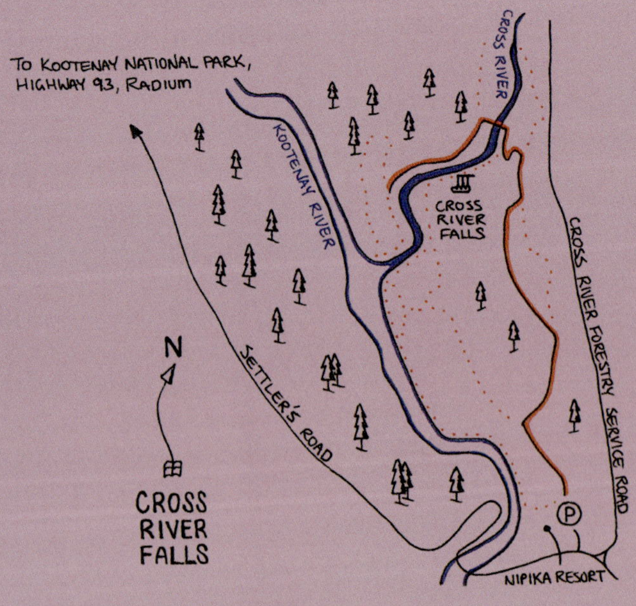

Hiking directions

Note: In the summer of 2021, excessive damage to the Canyon Bridge over the Cross River forced its removal. A temporary bridge was installed closer to the confluence of the Cross and Kootenay rivers. The description below is updated from *Waterfall Hikes in Southern BC* for the temporary bridge.

From the parking area there are numerous combinations of trails that lead to Cross River Falls. The most direct route is to cross the field and follow "Main Street," the utility road, for 2.3 km all the way to the bank of the Cross River. Take the temporary bridge over the river, then stay to the right, continuing along a gravel road (a sign reads "Trail: No Left/Right Turns"). At 2.8 km stay to your right at marker #11 (another sign: "Waterfall Trail"). Pass by a warming hut just before reaching a viewpoint of the falls from high up above at 3.4 km.

Trail information is available at the trailhead kiosk and through Nipika Resort. A map of the Nipika trail network is also available on Trailforks.com.

More to explore: Nipika Resort

Nipika Resort maintains over 50 km of trails in the area. Summer sees them used for hiking, biking or trail running, while in the winter they are groomed for Nordic skiing, fat biking and snowshoeing. Winter users will pay a small fee to access the trails, while admission is by donation in the summer months. Another must-see on the Nipika trail network is the Natural Bridge. For more information visit nipika.com.

12. Numa Falls

LOCATION: Kootenay National Park
DRIVING DIFFICULTY: EASY
HIKING DIFFICULTY: EASY
HIKING DISTANCE: 100 m
HIKING TIME: 5 min.

Numa Falls is a popular rest stop and picnic area in Kootenay National Park along Highway 93. It also serves as a trailhead and access point to the renowned Rockwall Trail high above the roadway. Here the bright blue waters of the Vermilion River constrict and fall through a short, narrow canyon.

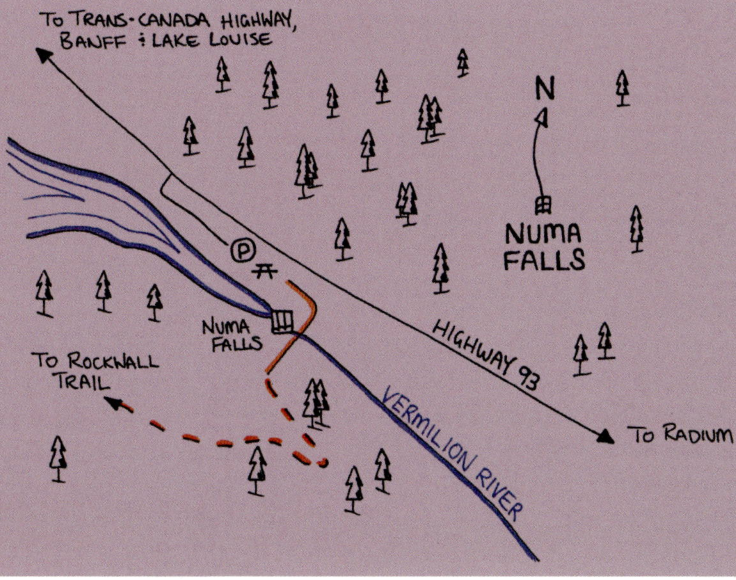

Driving directions

From the four-way stop in Radium, at the junction of Highways 93 and 95, drive east on Highway 93 into Kootenay National Park. Follow the highway for 80 km and look for a signed parking area for Numa Falls on the left (west) side of the road.

Hiking directions

From the parking area follow trailhead signage to a bridge over the Vermilion River at Numa Falls, just a hundred metres away. The bridge was replaced in 2020 and the falls were cleared of logs and debris, restoring this classic Rockies postcard to its recognizable glory.

More to explore: the Rockwall trail

With the bridge over the Vermilion River replaced, access to the Rockwall trail via Numa Creek has been re-established. While hiking the famous trail is most often done from the Paint Pots to Flue Lake or vice versa, the cut-off trail up Numa Creek enables people to shorten the trip to meet their schedules and provides an option for hikers to bail if the weather has let them down.

13. Haffner Canyon (Ice)

LOCATION: Kootenay National Park
DRIVING DIFFICULTY: EASY
HIKING DIFFICULTY: EASY (winter only)
HIKING DISTANCE: 1 km
HIKING TIME: 25 min.

Haffner is one of the more popular training grounds for ice and mixed (rock and ice) climbing, partly because it is safe in the winter, with virtually no avalanche hazard. Ice climbs typically form from water seeping through and over the rock and then freezing in layers. The canyon is relatively inaccessible in the summertime, but in winter it is transformed into a wonderland of snow and ice. The Canadian Rockies' steep limestone walls that rise up from the valley floors are home to an abundance of world-class ice climbing.

Driving directions

From Radium, drive east on Highway 93 into Kootenay National Park. It is about 87 km from the four-way stop in Radium to the parking area. Just after you cross Haffner Creek there is an unmarked pullout on the right-hand side that ice climbers use for parking. The signed

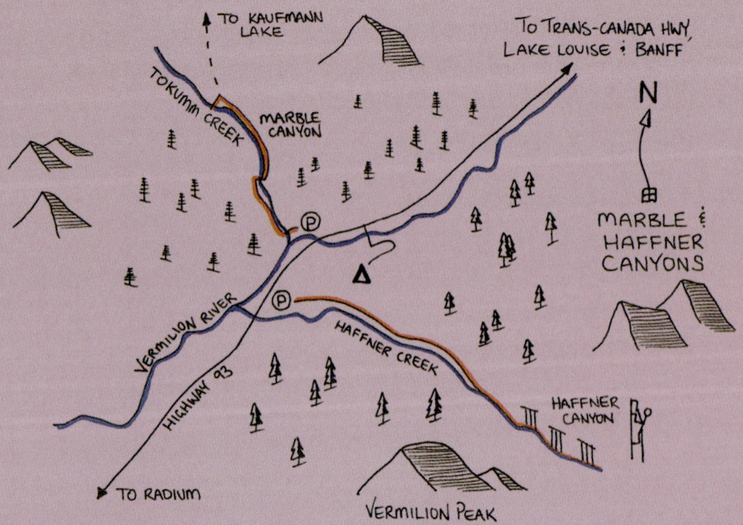

parking for Marble Canyon is a couple hundred metres farther on the left, so if you end up there, you've gone just a bit too far.

Hiking directions

From the car park, follow an unmarked trail that rises into the trees on the left side of Haffner Creek. It is generally well worn and well used in the winter by people venturing into the canyon to climb frozen pillars of ice. The narrow canyon is inaccessible in the spring, summer and autumn because the snow and ice that cover Haffner Creek are required just to access the area. Haffner is best explored from late December to mid-March.

The ice climbers trail starts in the trees and follows the left bank of the creek. After just a few minutes the trail drops down into the rocky creekbed. After about 15 minutes the trail approaches the mouth of the canyon and crosses to the right-hand side of the creek. The first few ice formations start to come into sight between the canyon walls.

Once in the canyon you can watch climbers test their skill on more than two dozen routes. If people are climbing, be sure to stay well back from the walls, as ice and rock can become dislodged. The ice formations are different every year depending on autumn and winter precipitation and temperatures. Take care crossing the creek, especially early in the season or as spring approaches.

14. Marble Canyon

LOCATION: Kootenay National Park
DRIVING DIFFICULTY: EASY
HIKING DIFFICULTY: EASY
HIKING DISTANCE: 800 m
HIKING TIME: 20 min.

Marble Canyon is one of the highlights of Kootenay National Park, if not of the entire Canadian Rockies. It is a popular stop along Highway 93 at any time of the year and deservedly so. The blue waters of Tokumm Creek are squeezed through a deep, dark, narrow canyon before joining the Vermilion River near the highway. If you are stopping in a national park, you are required to hold a valid park pass, which can be purchased at the visitor centre in Radium or at the park gate just east of town.

Driving directions

From the four-way stop in Radium at the junction of Highways 93 and 95, drive east on Highway 93 to Kootenay National Park. Follow the highway for 87 km and look for a signed parking lot for Marble Canyon on the left.

Hiking directions

From the parking area, follow the signed trail for Marble Canyon. The trail loses elevation briefly and crosses Tokumm Creek, then climbs to the top of the canyon walls. The trail crosses the creek once again and you can walk on either side of the canyon en route to where the creek initially plunges into the chasm, creating the waterfall. Numerous bridges span the canyon, offering glimpses into the dark abyss below.

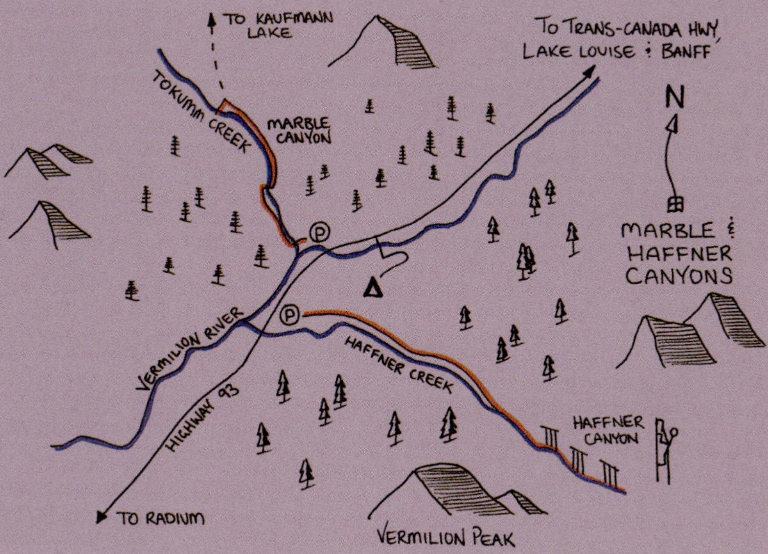

More to explore: Prospector's Valley

The Tokumm Creek / Prospector's Valley trail beyond Marble Canyon is no longer maintained by Parks Canada. After the Fay Hut was lost in a fire, the route fell out of favour with backcountry enthusiasts, although it is still possible to reach Kaufmann Lake. The trail is now littered with deadfall, although with the forest now more or less scorched, the views are a little more open.

15. Helmet Falls

LOCATION: Kootenay National Park
DRIVING DIFFICULTY: EASY
HIKING DIFFICULTY: DIFFICULT (due to distance; overnighting recommended)
HIKING DISTANCE: 15 km
HIKING TIME: 5–6 h

At a staggering 352 vertical metres, Helmet Falls is one of the highest cataracts in the country, plummeting over the headwall and draining West Washmawapta Glacier. The nearby Helmet Falls campground is typically used by those hiking the Rockwall trail, one of the premier backpacking trips in Canada. Most parties will take a relaxed five days to complete the 55-km trip while taking in the high alpine passes, meadows, lakes and 360-degree views of the lofty peaks of Kootenay National Park.

Driving directions

From Radium, drive east on Highway 93 to Kootenay National Park. Look for the signed parking area for the Paint Pots, 84 km from the four-way stop In Radium. National park and trail information, as well as outhouse facilities, are located at the busy trailhead.

Hiking directions

From the car park, follow the signed trail, which crosses the Vermilion River shortly after departing. The trail is initially busy and well used by tourists scoping out the Paint Pots. After you've left the hordes behind, the trail narrows and gently gains elevation as it winds along Helmet Creek through fir, pine and spruce forests. There isn't much in terms of views along the way, but your efforts are rewarded with an incredible scene upon reaching the Helmet Creek warden's cabin 14 km later.

From the cabin, cross the creek and pass through the campground. It is recommended to spend a night here before either returning the way you came or continuing along the spectacular Rockwall trail. A few hundred metres past the campground, the main trail bends to the left and a lesser used trail continues straight ahead to the base of the waterfall. The extra kilometre is well worth the effort to stand under one of the country's tallest cataracts. The hike is recommended for mid-July to the end of September and would be considered inaccessible in the winter months.

Know before you go

Reservations are required for the Helmet Falls campground and can be made online through Parks Canada at reservation.pc.gc.ca or by calling 1-877-RESERVE (1-877-737-3783).

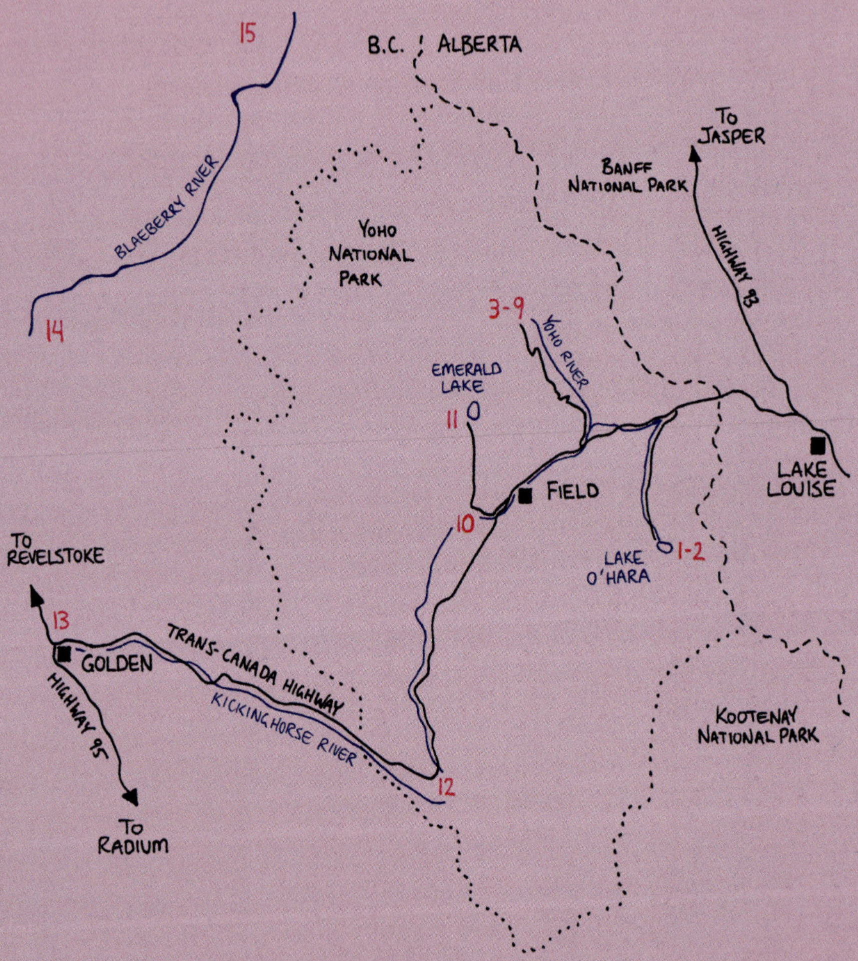

15
B.C.
ALBERTA
TO JASPER
BANFF NATIONAL PARK
BLAEBERRY RIVER
YOHO NATIONAL PARK
HIGHWAY 93
14
3-9
YOHO RIVER
EMERALD LAKE
11
FIELD
LAKE LOUISE
10
1-2
LAKE O'HARA
TO REVELSTOKE
13
GOLDEN
TRANS-CANADA HIGHWAY
KICKINGHORSE RIVER
HIGHWAY 95
KOOTENAY NATIONAL PARK
12
TO RADIUM

CHAPTER 6

Yoho National Park to Golden

Amid the chaos of the Formula One racetrack that the Trans-Canada Highway has become, there are many hidden escapes tucked just out of sight from the snaking motorway. Waterfalls are plentiful along the country's busiest highway as it winds through the Rocky Mountains. The high glaciers that cling to these landmarks fuel the creeks, rivers and waterfalls year-round.

The region detailed in this section extends from the BC/Alberta boundary in Yoho National Park down to the town of Golden as well as a few treasures tucked into the western slopes of the Rockies. Access to the area is provided by the Trans-Canada Highway, which travels westward from the BC/Alberta line, through Yoho National Park, and descends along the Kickinghorse River to the town of Golden. From Revelstoke, continue east along the Trans-Canada through Glacier National Park and Rogers Pass to reach Golden. The highway is well signed and well maintained but not without its challenges.

In the wintertime, check road conditions often. Highways can be closed with a moment's notice due to avalanches or avalanche control. The Kickinghorse Canyon segment has been in a perpetual state of construction and reconstruction since the dawn of time and continues to this day. Many of the access roads are closed seasonally, such as the Yoho Valley road. In addition, all vehicles stopping in Yoho National Park must display a valid park pass.

Lake Louise and Golden have all the services and amenities needed for travel and longer stays, including gas, groceries, accommodations and restaurants. Options in Field are somewhat more limited, with only the essentials being offered to travellers. The Yoho National Park visitor centre is located just off the highway in Field.

For more information or camping reservations, contact pc.gc.ca/en/pn-np/bc/yoho; 250-343-6783.

1. Seven Veils Falls

LOCATION: Yoho National Park
DRIVING DIFFICULTY: EASY
HIKING DIFFICULTY: EASY
HIKING DISTANCE: 1.5 km (to falls via Lake O'Hara Shoreline Trail)
HIKING TIME: 30 min.

Seven Veils Falls is a gorgeous waterfall but will undoubtedly be overshadowed by the many iconic vistas in the Lake O'Hara region of Yoho National Park. While it would be easy to overlook these cascades as you explore the area, a stop along the Lake O'Hara shoreline to admire this waterfall is a must!

Driving directions

From Field, drive east on the Trans-Canada Highway towards the BC/Alberta boundary. Turn right, into the parking area signed for Lake O'Hara. If you are one of the lucky few to secure a seat on the bus, a campsite at the lake or a spot in the Alpine Club of Canada's Elizabeth Parker Hut, you'd best be counting your blessings. Lake O'Hara has become one of the most sought-after outdoor destinations in Canada, much to the dismay of local backcountry enthusiasts.

Hiking directions

If you aren't so fortunate as to get a spot on the bus, don't worry! You can still hike the 11 km road in. Once you reach the lake, whether on foot or by way of Parks Canada's luxurious chauffeur service, locate the trailhead kiosk near the bus stop. Cross Cataract Brook and wind around the lake in a clockwise direction, following signs for Lake Oesa. At a junction at the far end of the lake, stay low and right; Seven Veils Falls is a short distance beyond. The Lake O'Hara shoreline trail is a 2.8 km circuit from the trailhead, where the bus stops. Seven Veils Falls is roughly at the halfway point where a short detour off the main trail takes you to the base of the falls.

Alternatively, from the Le Relais day-use area, walk south past the Lake O'Hara Lodge and continue counter-clockwise on the trail around the lake. The falls are visible from many points as you follow the shoreline.

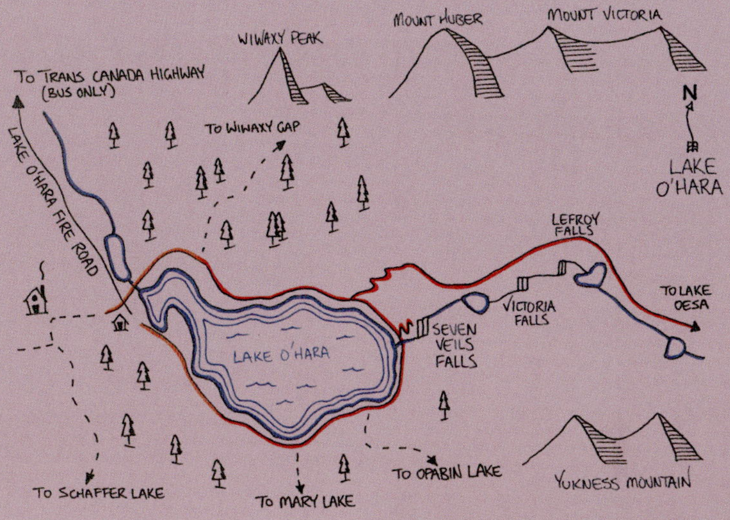

More to explore

Let's face it, you didn't come here for a waterfall. You came to Lake O'Hara to experience one of the natural wonders of this country. The trail network around this lake can take you high into the alpine, where deep, blue lakes sit peacefully at the base of some of the tallest and most majestic mountains in the Rockies. Expertly crafted pathways meander around alpine tarns and meadows. Climb stone staircases and cling to butt-puckering ledges as you tour the alpine high above the bustling base camp near the lakeshore. This may be the closest thing to heaven an earthbound person could envision.

2. Victoria Falls and Lefroy Falls (unofficial)

LOCATION: Yoho National Park
DRIVING DIFFICULTY: EASY
HIKING DIFFICULTY: EASY
HIKING DISTANCE: 2.5 km (to falls via Lake O'Hara Shoreline and Lake Oesa trails)
HIKING TIME: 45 min.

Small fish in a big pond, these two waterfalls link a series of colourful, serene tarns between Lake O'Hara and Lake Oesa, two of the much larger fish in the area.

Driving directions

From Field, drive east on the Trans-Canada Highway towards the BC/ Alberta boundary. Turn right, into the parking area signed for Lake O'Hara. If you are one of the lucky few to secure a seat on the bus, count your blessings. The Lake O'Hara shuttle makes short work of the 11 km gravel road and drops off guests at the Le Relais day-use area.

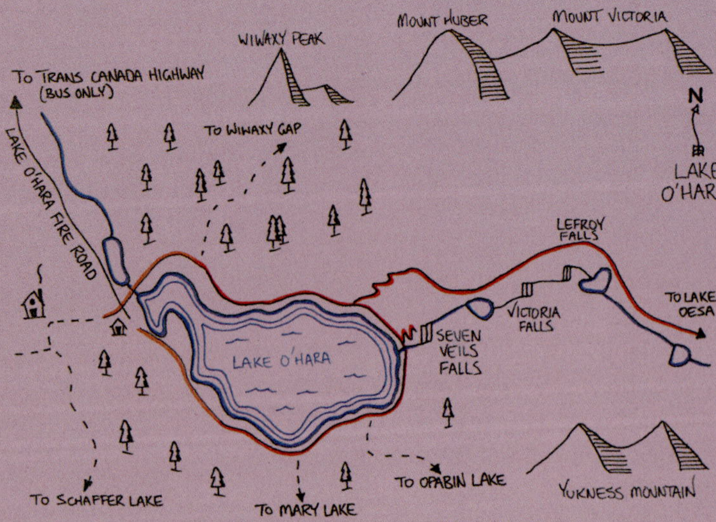

Hiking directions

As with Seven Veils Falls, take the bus or hike the 11 km Lake O'Hara fire road to Le Relais day-use area. Cross Cataract Brook and wind around the lake in a clockwise direction, following signs for Lake Oesa. At a junction at the far end of the lake, stay left and begin ascending a series of wonderfully manicured switchbacks. As the trail levels near the top of the headwall, the lower of the two waterfalls (Victoria Falls) comes into view. It is 2 km from the trailhead to this point.

Five hundred metres farther, the trail begins to switchback again beside a second cascade (Lefroy Falls) which is just out of sight from the trail. As the trail approaches the creek and before it cuts back to the left, continue beyond the trail just a few steps to view this waterfall tucked into a very narrow slot in the rocky wall. Another great look at this waterfall is across from the Yukness Ledges alpine route, accessed from Lake Oesa.

Lawrence Grassi, trail builder extraordinaire

During his five-year tenure as assistant warden at Lake O'Hara, Lorenzo (Lawrence) Grassi constructed many of the incredible trails around Lake O'Hara. His vision, skill and craftsmanship are obvious as you climb above Lake O'Hara toward Lake Oesa. Many of the switchbacks are impressive stone staircases built with incredible precision and comfort given the crude nature of his building materials. Much has been written about Grassi's life as an immigrant, a miner, a climber, a mountain guide and a park warden. Many landmarks in the Rockies now bear his name, including Mount Lawrence Grassi, Grassi Lakes and Lawrence Grassi Middle School in Canmore, as well as a classic alpine climb above Lake O'Hara: Grassi Ridge on Wiwaxy Peak.

3. Whiskey Jack Falls

LOCATION: Yoho National Park
DRIVING DIFFICULTY: EASY
HIKING DIFFICULTY: EASY
HIKING DISTANCE: n/a
HIKING TIME: n/a

Whiskey Jack Falls is only a sample of the sights and sounds of the Yoho Valley, as if you had arrived at Disneyland only to find Donald Duck holding the welcome sign instead of Mickey. Fear not, for in no time at all you'll be surrounded by all your favourite characters, or in this case, the classic Canadian Rockies hikes and vistas, including the renowned Iceline Trail, the historic Yoho Valley Trail to Twin Falls, and the Disneyland castle itself: Takakkaw Falls.

Driving directions

From Field, drive east on the Trans-Canada Highway for 3.5 km and turn onto the signed Yoho Valley road. Follow this for 13.0 km to just before the Takakkaw Falls parking area. Note that the parking on the left is only for people staying at the Whiskey Jack hostel. The falls are visible from the roadway.

Hiking directions

You don't have to get out of your car to see Whiskey Jack Falls unless human congestion requires you to park on the road at this point. Snap a photo from here and keep going to the main parking area. You won't be able to get too much closer to the falls anyway, even if starting one of the many day hikes in the area at this trailhead.

Know before you go

A park pass is required to stop on the Yoho Valley road. Passes can be purchased at the visitor centres in Field, Radium, Lake Louise or Banff and at the highway kiosks for Kootenay and Banff national parks. If visiting the Takakkaw Falls and Yoho Valley area, be sure to arrive early to get parking. This is one of the most popular day-use and backpacking areas in the Rockies once the Yoho Valley road opens in late June.

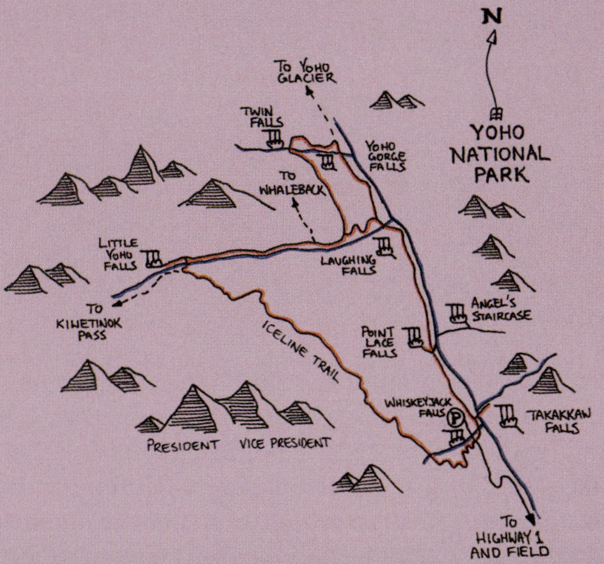
N
YOHO NATIONAL PARK
TO YOHO GLACIER
TWIN FALLS
YOHO GORGE FALLS
TO WHALEBACK
LITTLE YOHO FALLS
LAUGHING FALLS
TO KIWETINOK PASS
ANGEL'S STAIRCASE
ICELINE TRAIL
POINT LACE FALLS
WHISKEYJACK FALLS
TAKAKKAW FALLS
PRESIDENT
VICE PRESIDENT
TO HIGHWAY 1 AND FIELD

4. Takakkaw Falls

LOCATION: Yoho National Park
DRIVING DIFFICULTY: EASY
HIKING DIFFICULTY: EASY
HIKING DISTANCE: 600 m
HIKING TIME: 15 min.

As you round the final curves of the Yoho Valley Road your gaze is likely to shift up and right. Your eyes will go wide and your jaw will slowly assume the "dropped" position. That, my friends, is Takakkaw Falls, one of the most impressive cataracts in this country, if not in all of North America. The iconic rooster tail of the upper portion launches glacial meltwater nearly 400 vertical metres to the valley floor below. This is one of the truly spectacular scenes you will experience in your lifetime and one that you will not soon forget!

Driving directions

From Field, drive east on the Trans-Canada Highway for 3.5 km and turn onto the signed Yoho Valley road. Continue for 13.5 km to the Takakkaw Falls parking area. Signed trailhead kiosks mark the Takakkaw Falls hike as well as the Yoho Valley trails. There are washroom facilities and picnic areas around the parking lot.

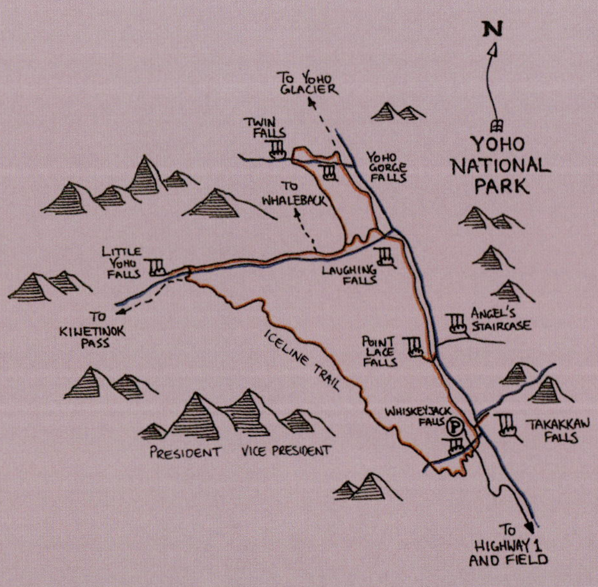

Hiking directions

From the signed trailhead, follow the large gravel pathway along the Yoho River with the falls towering above you. After about 200 m take the bridge across the river and follow the trail towards the base of the one of the most awe-inspiring waterfalls in the country.

Another viewing option is to hike the steep trail to the Yoho Iceline. The trailhead for this is near the Whiskey Jack hostel and the route is unrelenting before breaking treeline at a rocky alpine area. This option would be considered difficult due to the elevation gain, but the views across the valley to Takakkaw Falls are breathtaking.

Know before you go

According to Parks Canada, Takakkaw Falls drops a total of 384 m, making it the second highest waterfall in the country after Della Falls on Vancouver Island. Takakkaw is a Cree word that expresses awe and wonder.

5. Point Lace Falls

LOCATION: Yoho National Park
DRIVING DIFFICULTY: EASY
HIKING DIFFICULTY: EASY
HIKING DISTANCE: 2.7 km
HIKING TIME: 45–60 min.

Point Lace Falls is often overlooked intentionally or missed entirely by hikers hell-bent on reaching Twin Falls or the Little Yoho valley. Oh well, their loss. This is an elegant cascade tucked just out of sight from the Yoho Valley "super highway," and chances are you will enjoy it in some measure of solitude.

Driving directions

From Field, drive east on the Trans-Canada Highway for 3.5 km and turn onto the signed Yoho Valley road. Continue for 13.5 km to the Takakkaw Falls parking area. Signed trailhead kiosks mark the Takakkaw Falls hike as well as the Yoho Valley trails. There are washroom facilities and picnic areas around the parking lot.

Hiking directions

Point Lace Falls is a beautiful cascade situated along the Yoho Valley trail and is often overlooked in favour of the more recognizable waterfalls. From the signed trailhead, follow directions for Laughing Falls. You will hike through the walk-in campground along a large gravel trail. At 2.5 km there is a signed junction for Point Lace Falls to your left, Laughing Falls farther ahead and Angels Staircase to the right. Leave the main trail and follow a short spur for 200 m to the base of the falls.

More to ~~explore~~ see – The Angels Staircase

Near the junction of the main Yoho Valley trail and Point Lace Falls is a second short detour to a viewpoint of the Angels Staircase. From a distance, this stream can be seen cartwheeling down the entire mountainside in a series of steps before its eventual confluence with the Yoho River. The Staircase is best viewed with binoculars or with a telephoto lens on your camera.

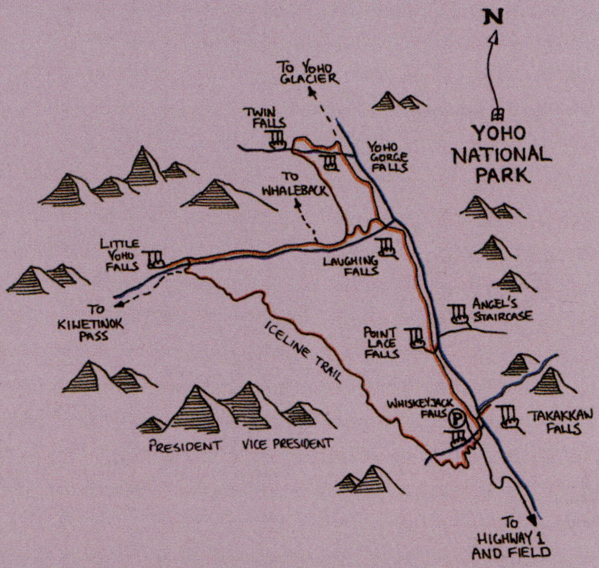
N
TO YOHO GLACIER
TWIN FALLS
YOHO GORGE FALLS
YOHO NATIONAL PARK
TO WHALEBACK
LITTLE YOHO FALLS
LAUGHING FALLS
TO KIWETINOK PASS
ANGEL'S STAIRCASE
ICELINE TRAIL
POINT LACE FALLS
WHISKEYJACK FALLS
P
TAKAKKAW FALLS
PRESIDENT
VICE PRESIDENT
TO HIGHWAY 1 AND FIELD

6. Laughing Falls

LOCATION: Yoho National Park
DRIVING DIFFICULTY: EASY
HIKING DIFFICULTY: EASY
HIKING DISTANCE: 4.6 km
HIKING TIME: 1.5 h

Laughing Falls is occasionally overshadowed by other attractions in the Yoho Valley, including Takakkaw Falls, Twin Falls and the Iceline Trail. Yet, if this waterfall were anywhere else, it would have massive appeal all on its own with its easy access and a backcountry campground within a stone's throw. The cascade stands more than 30 m tall and relentlessly propels the waters of Little Yoho Creek year-round. It is visible from the main Yoho Valley trail, making it a great lunch spot for backpackers heading to the Twin Falls or Little Yoho campgrounds. It can be a great objective in itself or simply a spot to lay over.

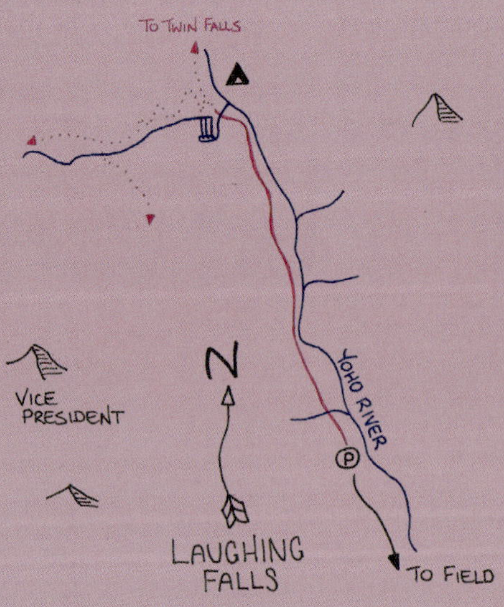

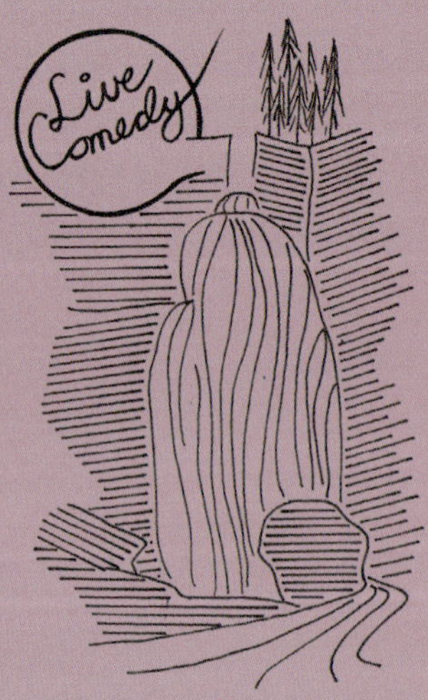

Driving directions

From Field, drive east on the Trans-Canada Highway for 3.5 km and turn onto the signed Yoho Valley road. Continue for 13.5 km to the Takakkaw Falls parking area. Signed trailhead kiosks mark the Takakkaw Falls hike as well as the Yoho Valley trails. There are washroom facilities and picnic areas around the parking lot.

Hiking directions

From the Takakkaw Falls parking area, follow the well-used and well-marked trail to Laughing Falls. The route gains very little elevation over the first 2.5 km to the junction of Angels Staircase and Point Lace Falls. After the junction the trail narrows slightly and gains modest elevation for the next 2 km before crossing a bridge over the Little Yoho River. The impressive falls are visible on your left; the Laughing Falls campground is on the right.

7. Yoho Gorge / Marpole Falls (unofficial)

LOCATION: Yoho National Park
DRIVING DIFFICULTY: EASY
HIKING DIFFICULTY: MODERATE
HIKING DISTANCE: 7.3 km
HIKING TIME: 2.5–3.0 h

It seems Twin Falls has effectively stolen the show from this little-known feature along the Yoho Valley trail. Available resources have referenced this narrow gorge as both Yoho Gorge Falls and Marpole Falls, although it is not reflected in any Parks Canada mapping or trail descriptions. But don't let that stop you from dropping your pack and pulling out the camera once you arrive.

Driving directions

From Field, drive east on the Trans-Canada Highway for 3.5 km and turn onto the signed Yoho Valley Road. Continue for 13.5 km to the Takakkaw Falls parking area. Signed trailhead kiosks mark the Takakkaw Falls hike as well as the Yoho Valley trails. There are washroom facilities and picnic grounds around the parking lot.

Hiking directions

Hike the well-signed and well-maintained Yoho Valley Trail for 7 km to the Twin Falls campground. Along the way you will pass the Angels Staircase viewpoint, Point Lace Falls, Laughing Falls and the junction for the Little Yoho Valley. Once through the Twin Falls campground, the trail starts to gain elevation moderately to Twin Falls and the site of the historic Twin Falls Chalet. Along the trail on the left, the mouth of the gorge is just visible near a picnic bench. You can wiggle through the trees for a better look of the creek as it slips down and out of the narrow canyon.

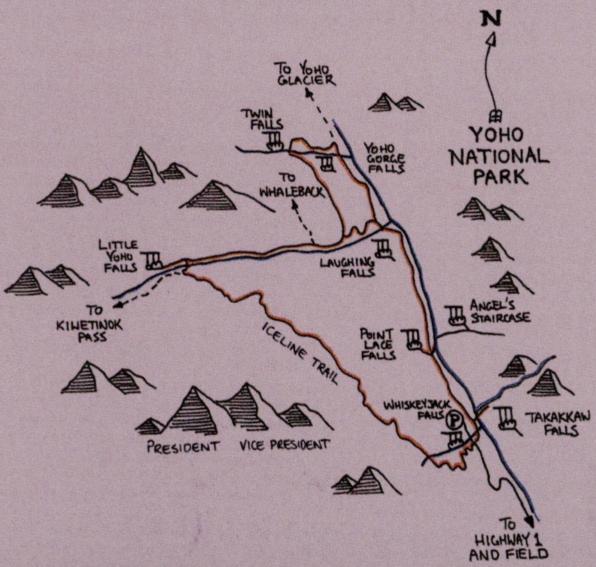
N
TO YOHO GLACIER
TWIN FALLS
YOHO GORGE FALLS
YOHO NATIONAL PARK
TO WHALEBACK
LITTLE YOHO FALLS
LAUGHING FALLS
TO KIWETINOK PASS
ANGEL'S STAIRCASE
POINT LACE FALLS
ICELINE TRAIL
WHISKEYJACK FALLS
TAKAKKAW FALLS
PRESIDENT
VICE PRESIDENT
TO HIGHWAY 1 AND FIELD

8. Twin Falls

LOCATION: Yoho National Park
DRIVING DIFFICULTY: EASY
HIKING DIFFICULTY: MODERATE
HIKING DISTANCE: 8.4 km
HIKING TIME: 3–4 h

Decision time: what do you explore first? The site of the historic Twin Falls Chalet? Or the trails around this postcard-worthy waterfall? If that deliberation is the hardest thing you have to do upon reaching the falls, you're probably having a fantastic day.

Driving directions

From Field, drive east on the Trans-Canada Highway for 3.5 km and turn onto the signed Yoho Valley Road. Continue for 13.5 km to the Takakkaw Falls parking area. Signed trailhead kiosks mark the Takakkaw Falls hike as well as the Yoho Valley trails. There are washroom facilities and picnic spots around the parking lot.

Hiking directions

A well-used and well-marked trail for Twin Falls follows alongside the Yoho River and initially gains minimal elevation. After passing through the Laughing Falls campsite at 4.6 km, cross the Yoho River and continue to the Twin Falls campsite at 7.0 km. The trail then gains moderate elevation to the site of the Twin Falls Chalet. A small loop from the building takes you to a series of viewpoints of the iconic falls. Another trail gains elevation steeply to the top of the waterfall.

It does make for a long day hike, especially with the addition of travel to and from the trailhead.

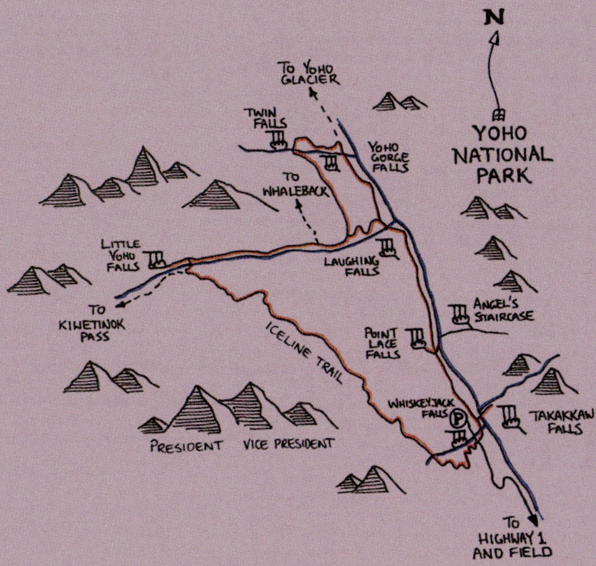

However, with multiple campgrounds in the valley, the Alpine Club of Canada's Stanley Mitchell Hut and the chalet itself, there are many ways to slow the pace and extend the trip over several days.

The Twin Falls chalet

Construction of the iconic structure by the Canadian Pacific Railway began in 1908. The main lodge was completed in 1923 and opened the following year. The CPR operated it as a tea house through the 1950s until rail-based tourism dropped off. The facility reopened in 1959 for backcountry accommodation and operated from 1962 to 2019 under the watchful eye of Fran Drummond.[13]

9. Little Yoho Falls (unofficial)

LOCATION: Yoho National Park
DRIVING DIFFICULTY: EASY
HIKING DIFFICULTY: DIFFICULT (overnight recommended)
HIKING DISTANCE: 10.2 km
HIKING TIME: 3.5–4.5 h

It shouldn't be a shock to find out there is yet another waterfall to explore in the Yoho Valley. What might be a surprise is that it's tucked away just out the back door of the Little Yoho campground. How many people have enjoyed this campsite – cooking meals, filtering water from the creek or just good old-fashioned freezing in their sleeping bags – and all the while a pretty little waterfall was right around the corner?

Driving directions

From Field, drive east on the Trans-Canada Highway for 3.5 km and turn onto the signed Yoho Valley Road. Continue for 13.5 km to the Takakkaw Falls parking area. Signed trailhead kiosks mark the falls hike as well as the Yoho Valley trails. There are washrooms and picnic areas around the parking lot.

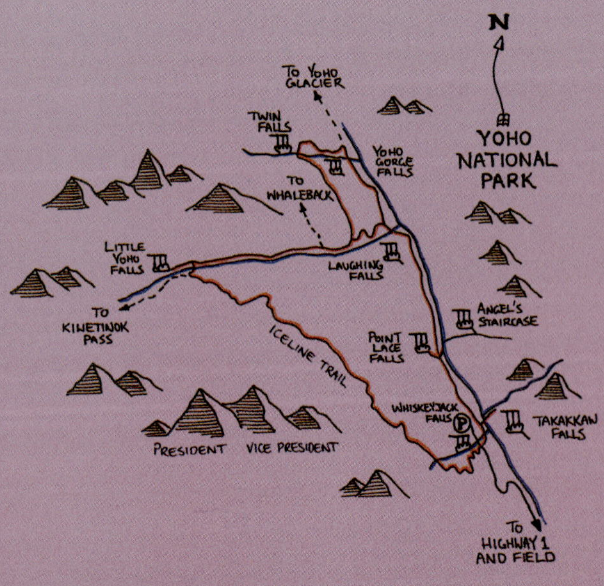

Hiking directions

From the signed trailhead, follow the Yoho Valley trail to Laughing Falls at 4.6 km. Cross the bridge over the Little Yoho River, pass the Laughing Falls campground and take a left at the junction signed for Little Yoho and Stanley Mitchell Hut. The trail gains moderate elevation over the next 5.0 km to the hut. Follow the trail for an additional 200 m to the Little Yoho campground. Walk through the campground past the food poles and pick up a boot-beaten trail down to the river. A small waterfall is tucked away just out of sight past the far end of the campground.

A second fall is another 200 m beyond this point. Follow the faint trail up and past the lower falls. Step with care, as the trail briefly sideslopes across a steep, loose shoulder before delivering you to a larger upper cascade. The waterfall is not noted on any Parks Canada maps or resources, making it a beautiful and quiet spot to hide out. Take the extra five minutes and go explore!

It is possible to catch partial glimpses and obscured views of these waterfalls from the trail to Kiwetinok Pass, although the best look at them is through the campground from alongside the creek.

More to explore

The Little Yoho campground and Stanley Mitchell Hut make great basecamps for exploring the world-famous Iceline Trail as well as take side trips to Kiwetinok Pass, Kiwetinok Lake and the Whaleback. For the more adventurous there are numerous scrambling and mountaineering opportunities afoot.

Reservations for the Little Yoho campground can be made through Parks Canada, while a spot at Stanley Mitchell Hut can be booked through the Alpine Club of Canada. If you are fortunate enough to secure a reservation, you will be well rewarded with the chance to enjoy one of the most stunning areas in the Canadian Rockies.

10. Natural Bridge

LOCATION: Yoho National Park
DRIVING DIFFICULTY: EASY
HIKING DIFFICULTY: EASY
HIKING DISTANCE: <100 m
HIKING TIME: < 5 min.

One of the most recognizable photos from the Canadian national parks is the raging Kickinghorse River being squeezed through the eye of a needle under the Natural Bridge. Its close proximity to the Trans-Canada Highway, accessible pathways and unique setting make it one of the busiest pit stops in all of western Canada. This landmark is spectacular in any season!

Driving directions

From Field, drive west on the Trans-Canada Highway for 1.5 km and turn right, onto the signed Emerald Lake Road. Follow Emerald Lake Road for 2.5 km to a busy parking area on the left signed for the Natural Bridge.

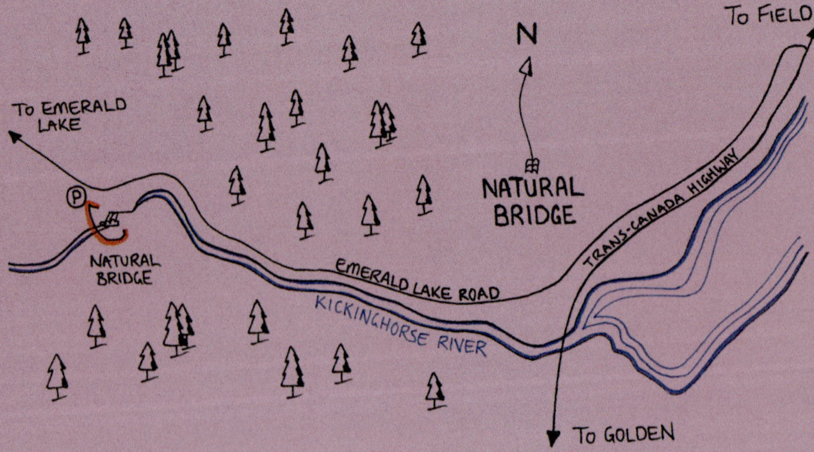

Hiking directions

Walk to a lookout atop a small chasm where you can view the Kickinghorse River just before it is forced through a narrow slot in the rocks. Alternatively, you can take the bridge across the river for a view of the water leaving the narrow opening. The Natural Bridge is a very unique formation that has withstood the relentless power of running water for thousands of years. While the falls can be viewed year-round, they are most impressive in late June and early July during runoff, when the Kickinghorse is at its peak.

11. Hamilton Falls

LOCATION: Yoho National Park
DRIVING DIFFICULTY: EASY
HIKING DIFFICULTY: EASY
HIKING DISTANCE: 700 m
HIKING TIME: 15 min.

It is easy to get sucked into elbowing your way around the shoreline at Emerald Lake and firing off a thousand photos of the picturesque Emerald Lake Lodge. But your blood pressure would benefit more by taking the less used Hamilton Lake trail just a few hundred metres away from the throngs of people, and seeking out the pretty Hamilton Falls instead.

Driving directions

From Field, drive west on the Trans-Canada for 1.5 km to the signed Emerald Lake Road. Continue for 9.0 km to the Emerald Lake parking area at the end of the road. Park where you can. It is best to get there early in the day, especially on weekends, as this place fills up fast and furiously. If you arrive later in the morning or in the afternoon, you might end up parking up to 2 km down the road from the main lot.

Hiking directions

Hamilton Falls is a welcome refuge from the madding crowds milling around Emerald Lake. Note that the trail does not leave from the main kiosk at the lakeshore and so

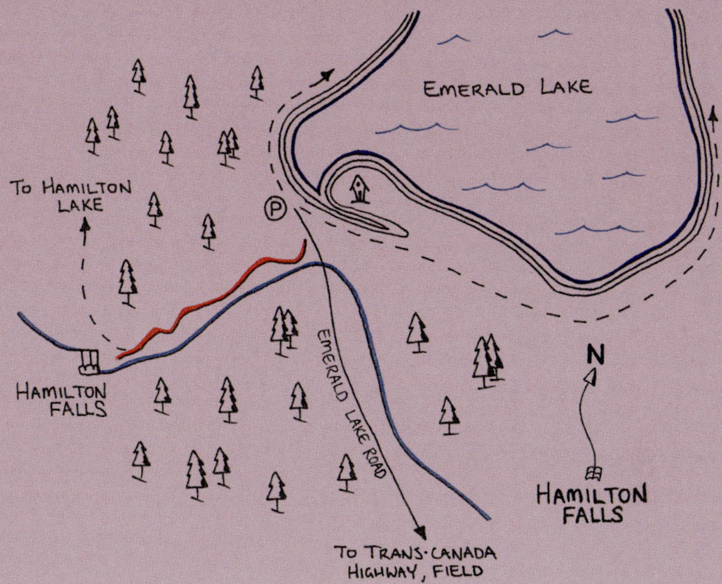

goes undetected by most visitors. At the south end of the main parking area, a brown Parks Canada sign marks the trail for Hamilton Falls and Hamilton Lake. Follow this for 700 m to a small waterfall that is just visible from the trail. Much of the cascade is obscured from sight but comes into view if you drop down from the trail to the edge of the creek.

More to explore

While Emerald Lake and the lodge itself are the obvious attractions for most people, the hike past the falls to Hamilton Lake is a far quieter outing and worth the effort if you have the time. It is 6 km one way, and the trail gains a strenuous 840 m to this secluded alpine lake. On the other hand, Emerald Lake remains one of the Canadian Rockies' classic views, if you're okay taking it in shoulder to shoulder with others around the busy lakeshore trail.

12. Wapta Falls

LOCATION: Yoho National Park
DRIVING DIFFICULTY: MODERATE
HIKING DIFFICULTY: EASY
HIKING DISTANCE: 2.4 km
HIKING TIME: 45–60 min.

Wapta Falls is HUGE! Here you will witness the full force of the Kickinghorse River as its entire volume vaults over a wall 30 m high and 150 m wide. This cataract is one of the largest in the country by volume, a fact that will become obvious from the moment you first see it. While you can expect your clothing to be drenched by the spray from it, the views are well worth the soaking at any time of the year!

Driving directions

From Field, drive west on the Trans-Canada Highway for 25 km. There is no signed trailhead for westbound traffic, as there is no turning lane. Continue for a couple more kilometres to the Yoho National Park boundary, turn around and drive back east to the signed turnoff on your right. Follow the rough gravel road for 1.8 km to a signed

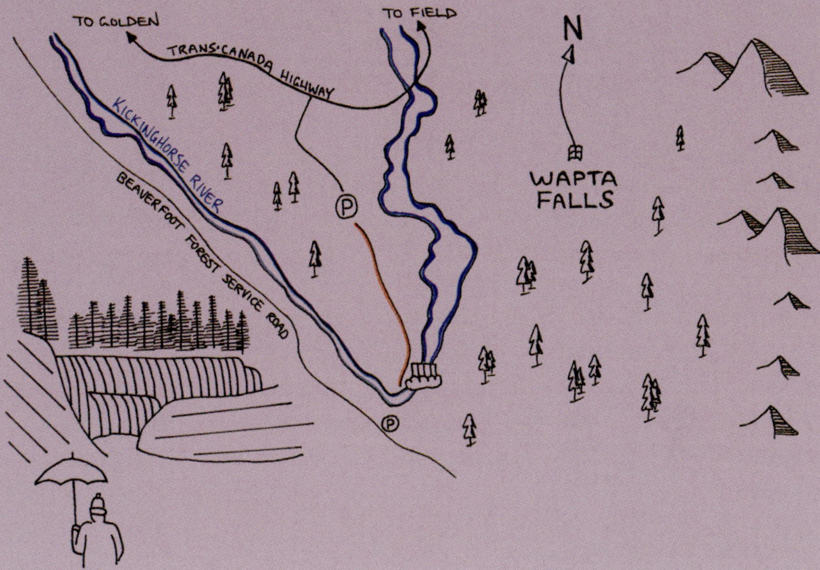

trailhead with biffies. This is one of the most popular and easily accessible trails off the Trans-Canada. It is recommended to get there by mid-morning or early evening, especially during the summer.

Alternatively, a viewpoint of the falls from the other side of the river can be accessed via the Beaverfoot forestry service road and the Wapta Falls recreation site, which is located at the 7 km mark of the FSR.

Hiking directions

Follow the wide, well-used trail through forest to a fenced overlook above the Kickinghorse River. The falls won't be visible just yet, but you'll hear the roar from below. From the first viewpoint, the trail begins to descend, with various forks that all end down at the riverbank. From here you can scramble up a rocky mound for a front-row seat to the 30-metre-high waterfall. Expect to get wet, as the spray from Wapta Falls is unbelievable, even late in the summer. The falls are accessible year-round, except maybe after a large snowfall.

13. Hospital Creek Falls

LOCATION: Golden, BC
DRIVING DIFFICULTY: EASY
HIKING DIFFICULTY: EASY (depending on creek depth)
HIKING DISTANCE: 800 m
HIKING TIME: 30 min.

While the short hike to Hospital Creek Falls is certainly not stroller friendly, you just might find one along the way. Need a short hike to stretch your legs or maybe some parts for your car? You've come to the right place. If you can ignore all the trash along the creek, the trail to the falls actually is quite nice. The waterfall itself is a true hidden gem!

Driving directions

From the intersection of the Trans-Canada and Highway 95 in Golden, drive west a few hundred metres on the Trans-Canada through the town's service strip. At the Ramada Hotel, turn right, onto 12th Street North. Drive into the mobile-home park. Stay left at the fork and follow to the end of the road, which has a large turnaround and an unsigned gravel parking area.

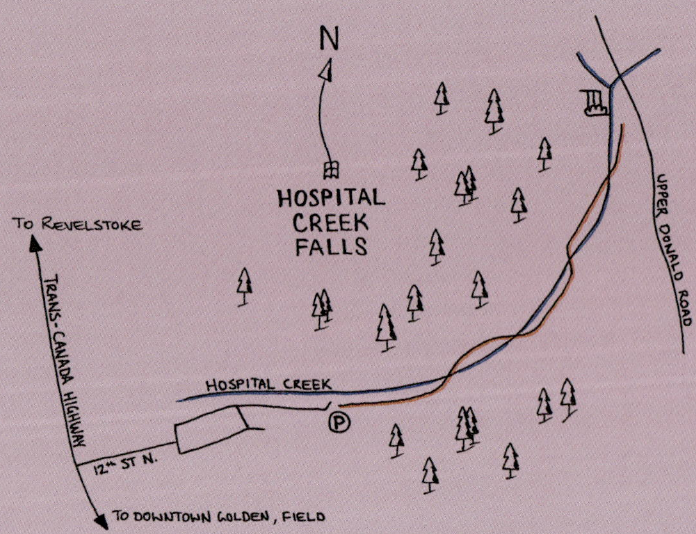

Hiking directions

From the parking area, the unmarked trail starts at concrete blocks and initially follows the right-hand side of the creek. After a couple hundred metres you'll be forced to cross the creek. At low water the crossing can be made on rocks or logs but it is best to bring a pair of good sandals and simply expect to get your feet wet on this one.

A short time later a rocky outcrop blocks your passage and you'll have to cross the creek again, and then again, and then one final time before reaching the base of the falls. Best to save this hike for later in the summer, as the creek will be very difficult and dangerous to cross during runoff or after a big rain. The secluded falls are tucked away at the back of the canyon along Hospital Creek.

14. Thompson Falls (Blaeberry Falls)

LOCATION: Golden, BC
DRIVING DIFFICULTY: MODERATE
HIKING DIFFICULTY: EASY
HIKING DISTANCE: 750 m
HIKING TIME: 10 min.

Thompson Falls is a sudden, narrow drop in the Blaeberry River. Consider the size and volume of the water just upstream of the falls and how narrow a slot it drops through. During runoff the river becomes so swollen that the falls are almost entirely submerged.

Driving directions

From Golden, drive west on the Trans-Canada Highway for about 10 km and turn right onto Moberly Branch Road. Go 2.0 km up the hill to a T-intersection and turn left onto Golden Donald Upper Road. After 1.0 km trend right onto Oberg Johnson Road and continue for 1.8 km to another T. A large Recreation Sites and Trails BC sign will be visible across the intersection. Turn left here and reset your trip odometer.

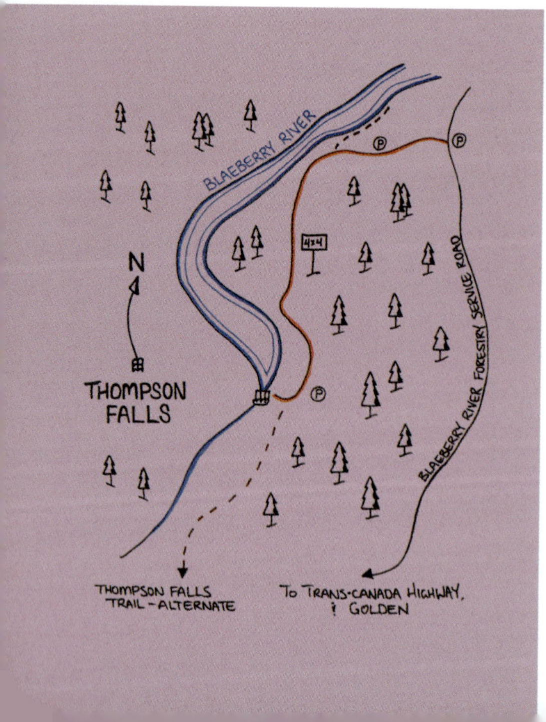

At 0.5 km stay right as the road becomes Blaeberry Road. At 7.2 km stay right again. At 12.5 km there is an unmarked spur road that drops off to the left. It is recommended that you park on the shoulder of the main road and walk the 200 m down to the lower parking area. With complete disregard for your vehicle, or with an ATV, it is possible to drive all the way to the river near the falls.

Hiking directions

From the Blaeberry road, walk down the spur road for 700 m to its end. From here the falls are just a short descent through the trees and are visible from a rocky outcrop above the small, narrow gorge. Alternatively, Thompson Falls can be reached by hiking from the camping area you passed previously on Blaeberry Road. From here the 6 km trail follows alongside the brilliant blue waters of the river, ending at the falls. It is about 2–2½ hours each way if you choose this option.

More to explore

Near the first parking area, a trail drops down onto the slabby riverbed where the Blaeberry squeezes through a narrow channel, in some places no more than a metre wide. Take care here, as the rocks are very polished and slippery as seen in the photo.

15. Mummery Glacier Falls

LOCATION: Golden, BC
DRIVING DIFFICULTY: MODERATE
HIKING DIFFICULTY: EASY (to viewpoint)
HIKING DISTANCE: 2.5 km
HIKING TIME: 1.0 h

Some things are worth a little extra effort, like chewing your food. Mummery Glacier is a hike that gets better and better the more you chew. Sure, you can hike to the viewpoint at the gravel flats, but what if you decide to finish your meal there? Why not chew your way up the moraine and watch these waterfalls go down nice and easy?

Driving directions

From Golden, drive west on the Trans-Canada for about 11 km and turn right onto Moberly Branch Road. Go 2.0 km up the hill to a T-intersection and turn left onto Golden Donald Upper Road. After 1.0 km trend right, onto Oberg Johnson Road and continue for 1.8 km to another T. A large Recreation Sites and Trails BC sign will be visible across the intersection. Turn left here and reset your trip odometer.

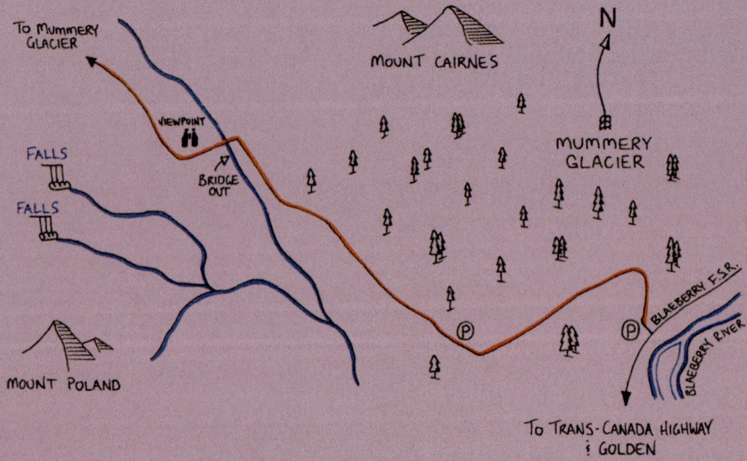

At 0.5 km stay right as the road becomes Blaeberry Road. At 7.2 km and 17.3 km stay right again. At 22.4 km cross the bridge over the Blaeberry River. At 38.8 km cross a bridge over Mummery Creek. At 40.0 km there is an old logging road on the left, typically marked with plenty of flagging tape. Park out of the way, off to the side of either the spur road or the main forestry road. With a high-clearance vehicle it is possible to drive up the old logging road for an additional kilometre, but it is quite steep and occasionally rough with loose rock.

Hiking directions

From the junction of the main forestry road and the old logging road, hike up the old logging road for 1 km to the second parking area. A brown pole marks the trail where it enters the forest and weaves up, down and around large trees for about 1.5 km. The trail exits the trees as it approaches a creek full of large boulders where remnants of a small suspension bridge atop the rocks can be seen. With the bridge out, crossing here is no longer possible. It is best to continue upstream from this point and pick a spot to cross using logs or rocks. Take note of the location where you crossed. Once past the creek, enter onto a rocky gravel flat with views of numerous waterfalls pouring over a massive headwall below Mummery Glacier. Most folks will take in the views from this point, as the trail becomes indistinct among the rocks and is marked with only intermittent cairns.

More to explore: Mummery Glacier

From the viewpoint, pick up cairns on the far side of the rocky outwash where the trail can be found re-entering the trees. The route then ascends a moraine with close-up views of the waterfalls before delivering you to the top of the headwall and the toe of Mummery Glacier. It is a steep ascent, gaining about 700 metres over 2.5 km from the viewpoint on the rocky flats to the toe of the glacier. Allow for an additional two hours each way for this spectacular addition to the hike. It is well worth every effort!

JOHNSTON CANYON LOWER FALLS

CHAPTER 7

More To Explore

The waterfalls described in this guidebook are by no means an exhaustive list of all the cascades in the region. While this book was designed primarily with families in mind, there are so many more opportunities to venture into the countless drainages, valleys and watersheds in the Canadian Rockies. Have fun exploring!

A few additional waterfalls, recognizable to some, have been omitted due to overly lengthy approaches, excessive bushwhacking, or trail closures at the time of writing. Brief descriptions are included below.

1. EGYPT LAKE FALLS – BANFF NATIONAL PARK, AB

Egypt Lake is a long stroll via either Redearth Creek off the Trans-Canada Highway or a much more interesting approach via Healy Pass from the Sunshine Village parking area. Anticipate spending a night or two out at the Egypt Lake campground, where you'll find lots to explore, including Scarab, Mummy and Pharaoh lakes. Egypt Lake Falls is a tall cataract that slides down a large headwall above Egypt Lake, draining the lakes and basin from high above.

2. MEMORIAL LAKES WATERFALLS – SPRAY VALLEY PROVINCIAL PARK, KANANASKIS COUNTRY, AB

This is a series of waterfalls along North Ribbon Creek on the Memorial Lakes trail. Park as per the Ribbon Falls hike. At the trail junction at 3.5 km, stay right. There is a waterfall off the trail in a canyon at around 7.0 km, another one at about the 7.5 km mark and yet third tumbling down a headwall at around 8 km. All three are beautiful waterfalls and, combined with the lakes, make a very worthwhile outing.

3. STANLEY GLACIER FALLS – KOOTENAY NATIONAL PARK, BC

As you descend from the Continental Divide at the BC/AB boundary, you'll often notice a parking lot bursting at the seams, with vehicles parked precariously on the shoulder of Highway 93. This is the parking area for the Stanley Glacier trail. The 4.8 km hike takes you into a high alpine valley below a rapidly retreating glacier. As you break out of the trees and enter the basin, a large waterfall tumbles down a steep headwall under Stanley Peak. The unofficial name of this waterfall is Stanley Glacier Falls. In the wintertime it freezes and becomes its winter alter ego, the ice climb called Nemesis.

4. OTTERTAIL FALLS – YOHO NATIONAL PARK, FIELD, BC

If you fancy really long walks in the forest with no objective of significance, then Ottertail Falls is the hike for you. From Field, drive west for 8.2 km to a small parking area on the south side of the Trans-Canada Highway. The Ottertail Valley trail connects with Goodsir Pass and the Rockwall Trail. From the trailhead it is 14.9 km to the backcountry campground at McArthur Creek. Ottertail Falls is another 2.8 km beyond the campground. You can shorten the time frame by biking to the McArthur Creek campground.

Author's Picks

FAVOURITES

Junction Falls, Sheep River Provincial Park
Burnt Rock Falls, Waterton National Park
Twin Falls, Yoho National Park

BEST PICNIC AREAS

Sheep River Falls, Sheep River Provincial Park
Cascade Ponds, Cascade Falls, Banff National Park
Buller Mountain Day-Use Area, Peter Lougheed Provincial Park

BEST "STROLLER-ABLE" FALLS

Troll Falls, Spray Valley Provincial Park
Takakkaw Falls, Yoho National Park
Bow Falls, Banff, Banff National Park

BEST SWIMMING HOLES

Cat Creek Falls, Highwood Junction
Rainbow (Nez Percé) Falls, Coleman
Red Rock Canyon, Waterton National Park

BEST OTHER PLACES TO GET WET

Wapta Falls, Golden
Takakkaw Falls, Yoho National Park
Helmet Falls, Kootenay National Park

BEST DRIVE-UP WATERFALLS (ACCESSIBLE IN 5 MINUTES OR LESS)

Takakkaw Falls, Yoho National Park
Cameron Falls, Waterton National Park
Low Sentry Cave Waterfall, Crowsnest Pass

BEST PLACES TO SPEND A NIGHT

Little Yoho campground, Yoho National Park
Lake O'Hara campground, Yoho National Park
Elbow Lake campground, Peter Lougheed Provincial Park

SUNDANCE CANYON

ENDNOTES

1. Banff Springs Hotel," thecanadianencyclopedia.ca/en/article/banff-springs-hotel, accessed 2022-06-15.
2. "Cave and Basin National Historic Site of Canada," is.gd/KeOXGq, accessed 2022-06-15.
3. "In Castle Mountain's Shadow: The Story of Silver City," whytemuseum.blogspot.com/2019/05/in-castle-mountains-shadow-story-of.html, accessed 2022-06-15.
4. "The Sheep River: The Land and the People," onthisspot.ca/cities/okotoks/sheepriver, accessed 2022-06-15.
5. "North York Creek Plane Crash Trail," crowsnestheritage.ca/heritage-trails, accessed 2022-06-15.
6. "The Castle," albertawilderness.ca/issues/wildlands/areas-of-concern/castle, accessed 2022-06-15.
7. "Waterfalls: What Defines Them?" milestonepress.com/waterfalls-what-defines-them, accessed 2022-06-15.
8. "Waterton Lakes National Park: Kenow Wildfire," is.gd/iwJXZi, accessed 2022-06-15.
9. "First Oil Well in Western Canada National Historic Site," is.gd/8yJzhK, accessed 2022-06-15.
10. "Mount Pétain in the Rockies to have name rescinded," cranbrooktownsman.com/news/mount-ptain-in-the-rockies-to-have-name-rescinded, accessed 2022-06-15.
11. "Fernie Derrick," fernie.com/about-fernie/history/fernie-derrick, accessed 2022-06-15.
12. "Morrissey," ghosttownpix.com/bc/morrissey.html, accessed 2022-06-15.
13. "Backcountry lodge operator of 57 years gets one last season to run historic Yoho site," is.gd/1iR535, accessed 2022-06-15.

TWIN FALLS

REFERENCES

Alberta Wilderness Association. "The Castle." albertawilderness.ca/issues/wildlands/areas-of-concern/castle, accessed 2022-06-15.

Canadian Encyclopedia, The. "Banff Springs Hotel." thecanadianencyclopedia.ca/en/article/banff-springs-hotel, accessed 2022-06-15.

CBC News. "Backcountry lodge operator of 57 years gets one last season to run historic Yoho site." is.gd/1iR535, accessed 2022-06-15.

Cranbrook Daily Townsman. "Mount Pétain in the Rockies to have name rescinded." cranbrooktownsman.com/news/mount-ptain-in-the-rockies-to-have-name-rescinded, accessed 2022-06-15.

Crowsnest Heritage Initiative. "North York Creek Plane Crash Trail." crowsnestheritage.ca/heritage-trails, accessed 2022-06-15.

Fernie.com. "Fernie Derrick." fernie.com/about-fernie/history/fernie-derrick, accessed 2022-06-15.

Ghost Towns of British Columbia. "Morrissey." ghosttownpix.com/bc/morrissey.html, accessed 2022-06-15.

Milestone Press. "Waterfalls: What Defines Them?" milestonepress.com/waterfalls-what-defines-them, accessed 2022-06-15.

Okotoks & District Historical Society. "The Sheep River: The Land and the People." onthisspot.ca/cities/okotoks/sheepriver, accessed 2022-06-15.

Parks Canada. "Cave and Basin National Historic Site of Canada." is.gd/KeOXGq, accessed 2022-06-15.

________. "First Oil Well in Western Canada National Historic Site." is.gd/8yJzhK, accessed 2022-06-15.

________. "Waterton Lakes National Park: Kenow Wildfire," is.gd/iwJXZi, accessed 2022-06-15.

Whyte Museum of the Canadian Rockies. "In Castle Mountain's Shadow: The Story of Silver City." whytemuseum.blogspot.com/2019/05/in-castle-mountains-shadow-story-of.html, accessed 2022-06-15.

JUNCTION CREEK FALLS

ONLINE RESOURCES

Alberta Motor Association: Alberta Road Conditions
roadreports.ama.ab.ca

Alberta Parks: Trail Conditions and Backcountry Reservations
albertaparks.ca

Alpine Club of Canada: Backcountry Hut Bookings
alpineclubofcanada.ca/web

BC Provincial Parks: Trail Conditions and Backcountry Reservations
bcparks.ca

Drive BC: British Columbia Road Conditions
drivebc.ca

Parks Canada: Trail Conditions, Park Pass Information and Backcountry Reservations
pc.gc.ca/en/index

Recreation Sites and Trails BC: Interactive Map
is.gd/AIq3ij

WildsafeBC: Wildlife Safety, Bear Aware and Human/wildlife Conflict Awareness wildsafebc.com

PARK VISITOR CENTRES

Banff National Park
pc.gc.ca/en/pn-np/ab/banff
224 Banff Avenue, Banff, AB
403-762-1550
Camping reservations: 1-888-737-3783

Kananaskis Provincial Park
albertaparks.ca/parks/kananaskis/kananaskis-country
Highway 40, Kananaskis, AB
403-678-0760
Camping reservations: 1-877-537-2757

Waterton National Park
pc.gc.ca/en/pn-np/ab/waterton
404 Cameron Falls Drive, Waterton Park, AB
403-859-5133
Camping reservations: 403-859-5133

Yoho National Park
pc.gc.ca/en/pn-np/bc/yoho
Trans-Canada Highway, Field, BC
250-343-6783
Camping reservations: 1-888-737-3783

DYSON FALLS

Index of Waterfalls

Acephale Falls 108
Akamina–Kishinena Provincial Park, BC
  Forum Falls 152
Allison Creek Falls 126
Aster Lake Falls 76
Banff National Park
  Bow Falls 26
  Bridal Veil Falls 42
  Cascade Falls 24
  Egypt Lake Falls 241
  Giant Steps, The 38
  Johnston Canyon Lower Falls 30
  Johnston Canyon Upper Falls 32
  Silverton Falls 34
  Sundance Canyon 28
  Tessa Falls 22
  Wolverine Creek Waterfall (unofficial) 36
Baril Creek Falls 64
Bertha Falls 156
Blaeberry Falls. *See* Thompson Falls (Blaeberry Falls)
Blakiston Falls 148
Bow Falls 26
Bow Valley Provincial Park, AB
  Acephale Falls 108
  Jewell Falls 106
Bow Valley Wildland Provincial Park, AB
  Kananaskis Falls (unofficial) 102
Bridal Veil Falls 42
Buller Creek Falls 90
Burnt Rock Falls 162
Cameron Falls 154
Canal Flats, BC
  Fenwick Creek Falls 188
  Pedley Falls 186
Canmore, AB
  Canmore Creek Falls 116
  Grassi Lakes Waterfall 118
  Three Sisters Creek Waterfalls 114
Canmore Creek Falls 116
Cascade Falls 24
Castle Wildland Provincial Park, AB
  Epipen Falls 140
  North Drywood Falls 138
Cataract Creek Recreation Area, AB
  Hercules Falls 60
  Titan Falls 60
Cat Creek Falls 66
Cliff Lake Falls 184
Coleman, AB
  North York Creek Falls 132
  Rainbow (Nez Percé) Falls 128
  Star Creek Falls 130
Commonwealth Creek Falls 88
Cornwall Creek Falls 48
Cranbrook, BC
  Cliff Lake Falls 184
Cross River Falls 190
Crowsnest Creek Falls 122

Crowsnest Pass, AB
- Allison Creek Falls 126
- Crowsnest Creek Falls 122
- Low Sentry Cave Waterfall (unofficial) 124

Crypt Falls 164
Dead Man's Flats, AB
- Spray Falls 112

Dyson Falls 58
Edworthy Falls 70
Egypt Lake Falls 241
Elbow Falls Provincial Recreation Area, Bragg Creek, AB
- Elbow Falls 46

Elkford, BC
- Josephine Falls 172

Elk Lakes Provincial Park, BC
- Pétain Falls 168

Epipen Falls 140
Evan Thomas Provincial Recreation Area, AB
- Marmot Creek Waterfalls (unofficial) 100
- Marmot Falls 98
- Ribbon Falls 94
- Troll Falls 96
- Troll Falls, Upper 98

Exshaw, AB
- Grotto Falls 110

Fairy Creek Falls 176
Fenwick Creek Falls 188
Fernie, BC
- Fairy Creek Falls 176
- Jumping Waters 174
- Matheson Falls 178
- Morrissey Falls (Lower) 182
- Morrissey Falls (Upper) 180

Forestry Trunk Road, AB
- Gap Falls 142
- Oldman River Falls 144

Forum Falls 152
Fossil Falls 74
French Creek Falls 86
Gap Falls 142
Giant Steps, The 38
Golden, BC
- Hospital Creek Falls 230
- Mummery Glacier Falls 236
- Thompson Falls (Blaeberry Falls) 232

Grassi Lakes Waterfall 118
Grotto Falls 110
Haffner Canyon (ice) 194
Hamilton Falls 226
Hellroaring Falls 158
Helmet Falls 198
Hercules Falls 60
Highwood Junction, AB
- Baril Creek Falls 64
- Cat Creek Falls 66

Hospital Creek Falls 230
Jewell Falls 106
Johnston Canyon Lower Falls 30
Johnston Canyon Upper Falls 32
Josephine Falls 172
Jumping Waters 174
Junction Creek Falls 50
Kananaskis Country
- Baril Creek Falls 64

Cat Creek Falls 66
Cornwall Creek Falls 48
Dyson Falls 58
Edworthy Falls 70
Elbow Falls 46
Hercules Falls 60
Junction Creek Falls 50
Ptarmigan Cirque Waterfalls 68
Sheep River Falls 54
Tiger Jaw Falls 56
Titan Falls 60
Kananaskis Falls, Lower 78
Kananaskis Falls (unofficial) 102
Kananaskis Falls, Upper 80
Kootenay National Park
Haffner Canyon (ice) 194
Helmet Falls 198
Marble Canyon 196
Numa Falls 192
Kootenay National Park, BC
Stanley Glacier Falls 241
Laughing Falls 214
Lefroy Falls (unofficial) 204
Lineham Falls 150
Little Elbow Provincial Recreation Area, AB
Cornwall Creek Falls 48
Little Yoho Falls (unofficial) 220
Low Sentry Cave Waterfall (unofficial) 124
Lundbreck Falls 136
Lundbreck Falls Provincial Recreation Area, AB
Lundbreck Falls 136
Marble Canyon 196
Marmot Creek Waterfalls (unofficial) 100
Marmot Falls 98
Marpole Falls. *See* Yoho Gorge / Marpole Falls
Matheson Falls 178
Memorial Lakes Waterfalls 241
Morrissey Falls (Lower) 182
Morrissey Falls (Upper) 180
Mummery Glacier Falls 236
Natural Bridge 224
Nez Percé Falls. *See* Rainbow (Nez Percé) Falls
Nipika Resort, BC
Cross River Falls 190
North Drywood Falls 138
North York Creek Falls 132
Numa Falls 192
Old Goat Glacier Waterfall (unofficial) 92
Oldman River Falls 144
Ottertail Falls 242
Pedley Falls 186
Pétain Falls 168
Peter Lougheed Provincial Park
Aster Lake Falls 76
Buller Creek Falls 90
Commonwealth Creek Falls 88
Edworthy Falls 70
Fossil Falls 74
French Creek Falls 86
Kananaskis Falls, Lower 78
Kananaskis Falls, Upper 80
Old Goat Glacier Waterfall (unofficial) 92

Ptarmigan Cirque Waterfalls 68
Sarrail Falls 72
Three Isle Lake Falls 82
Warspite Cascades 84
Point Lace Falls 212
Ptarmigan Cirque Waterfalls 68
Rainbow (Nez Percé) Falls 128
Ribbon Falls 94
Sarrail Falls 72
Seven Veils Falls 202
Sheep River Falls 54
Sheep River Provincial Park, AB
Dyson Falls 58
Junction Creek Falls 50
Sheep River Falls 54
Tiger Jaw Falls 56
Silverton Falls 34
Spray Falls 112
Spray Valley Provincial Park, AB
Memorial Lakes Waterfalls 241
Stanley Glacier Falls 241
Star Creek Falls 130
Sundance Canyon 28
Takakkaw Falls 210
Tessa Falls 22
Thompson Falls (Blaeberry Falls) 232
Three Isle Lake Falls 82
Three Sisters Creek Waterfalls 114
Tiger Jaw Falls 56
Titan Falls 60
Troll Falls 96
Troll Falls, Upper 98
Twin Falls 160, 218
Victoria Falls (unofficial) 204
Wapta Falls 228
Warspite Cascades 84
Waterton Lakes National Park
Bertha Falls 156
Blakiston Falls 148
Burnt Rock Falls 162
Cameron Falls 154
Crypt Falls 164
Forum Falls 152
Hellroaring Falls 158
Lineham Falls 150
Twin Falls 160
Whiskey Jack Falls 208
Wolverine Creek Waterfall (unofficial) 36
Yoho Gorge/Marpole Falls (unofficial) 216
Yoho National Park
Hamilton Falls 226
Laughing Falls 214
Lefroy Falls (unofficial) 204
Little Yoho Falls (unofficial) 220
Natural Bridge 224
Ottertail Falls 242
Point Lace Falls 212
Seven Veils Falls 202
Takakkaw Falls 210
Twin Falls 218
Victoria Falls (unofficial) 204
Wapta Falls 228
Whiskey Jack Falls 208
Yoho Gorge/Marpole Falls (unofficial) 216